D0758546

Worlds of Sound

Worlds of Sound

The Story of Smithsonian Folkways

Richard Carlin

In association with

Smithsonian Folkways Recordings

Smithsonian Books

COLLINS

An Imprint of HarperCollins Publishers

WORLDS OF SOUND. Copyright © 2008 by Smithsonian Institution. All rights reserved. Printed in the United States of America. No part of this book may be used or reproduced in any manner whatsoever without written permission except in the case of brief quotations embodied in critical articles and reviews. For information, address HarperCollins Publishers, 10 East 53rd Street, New York, NY 10022.

Unless otherwise noted, all photographs and illustrations are courtesy of the Moses and Frances Asch Collection, Ralph Rinzler Folklife Archives and Collections, Smithsonian Institution.

Every attempt has been made to locate the copyright holders of the material in this book. Should we have inadvertently failed to give proper credit, please contact the publisher.

HarperCollins books may be purchased for educational, business, or sales promotional use. For information, please write: Special Markets Department, HarperCollins Publishers, 10 East 53rd Street, New York, NY 10022.

FIRST EDITION

Designed by Laura Lindgren

Library of Congress Cataloging-in-Publication Data is available upon request.

ISBN 978-0-06-156355-3

08 09 10 11 12 ov/qw 10 9 8 7 6 5 4 3 2 1

This book is dedicated to Moses Asch (1905–1986),
who taught me the importance of
dedication, tenacity, and vision
for achieving your dreams.

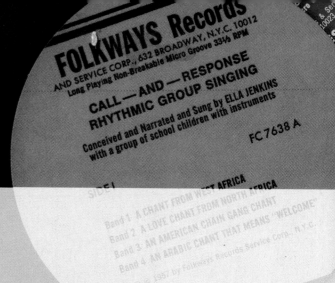

CONTENTS

ACKNOWLEDGMENTS

The author wishes to thank the following individuals for assisting in the publication of this work.

At the Smithsonian Institution's Center for Folklife and Cultural Heritage: Atesh Sonneborn, associate director of Smithsonian Folkways, served as the point person throughout this process, coordinating the many voices who contributed to the book. Atesh's intelligent critique of the text helped me sharpen my own thinking about Folkways. His perceptive and even-handed analysis of the many issues that arose during the research and writing of this text was invaluable. Richard James Burgess, Smithsonian Folkways' director of marketing and sales, had the original inspiration to create an illustrated book celebrating Smithsonian Folkways' unique collection, and shared his insights into the challenges facing specialty recording companies in the twenty-first century. Jeff Place and Stephanie Smith, archivists, opened the doors to the Ralph Rinzler Folklife Archives and Collections to me. Their advice and helpful direction made it possible for me to locate many important documents and images. Jeff also read the manuscript with an eagle eye, carefully correcting many details that otherwise would have gone unchecked. Mary Monseur, creative director, graciously helped me with issues surrounding photos and illustrations and gave a sympathetic reading to the manuscript. Dan Sheehy, director and curator of Smithsonian Folkways, shared his vision for the future of Smithsonian Folkways and also carefully read the manuscript as it was developed. Curator emeritus Anthony Seeger spoke to me at length about his vision for Smithsonian Folkways, and also provided a useful critique of the manuscript. Mark Gustafson and Pete Reigner provided invaluable assistance preparing the sampler CD for this book.

At Smithsonian Books, I wish to thank Caroline Newman, acquisition editor, for recognizing the potential of this project and for her enthusiasm from day one. I also wish to thank Bruce Nichols, Tom McNellis, Jean Marie Kelly, and Corinne Kalasky at HarperCollins Publishers.

Thanks also to Michael and Margaret Asch, who gave unique insights into Folkways and particularly Moses Asch's final years. Their willingness to open their hearts and memories for this project was invaluable. I am grateful to

Caricature of Moses Asch, 1953.

Ronald Cohen, "Mr. Folk Music," who carefully read and critiqued the manuscript. For sharing their memories of working with Moses Asch, I wish to thank Peter Bartók, Kenneth Bilby, Sam and Ann Charters, John Cohen, Eric H. Davidson, David Gahr, Donald Hill, David A. Jasen, Morton Marks, Bruno Nettl, Art Rosenbaum, Pete Seeger, and Ruth Stone.

I also drew on my own memories and many informal conversations with Moses Asch from 1975 to 1980, when I produced records for him at Folkways.

I was able to listen to many important interviews with Moe thanks to tapes deposited in the Smithsonian Folkways Archives. Interviewers included: Israel G. "Izzy" Young, who conducted a long and important interview with Moe in New York on June 13, 1970 (David Gahr was also in attendance; an edited transcript appeared in *Sing Out!* magazine, volume 26, numbers 1 and 2, which I referred to, but I also retranscribed portions of the tapes); David Dunaway, May 8, 1977; Gary Kenton, several interviews, 1980–83; Jon Appleton, November 7, 1982; Ashley Kahn, brief radio interview, January 1985; Elizabeth Perez Luna, NPR interview with Moe and Frederic Ramsey Jr., New York City, February 10, 1985 (transcript from Peter Goldsmith's papers, Smithsonian Folkways collection).

Special thanks to Gary Kenton for sharing his memories, archives, and taped interviews from his planned biography of Moses Asch. Among his materials that I consulted were interviews with John Asch, Harold Courlander, Frederic Ramsey Jr., George Mendelssohn, Pete Seeger, Irwin Silber, and Harry Smith.

The late Peter Goldsmith's biography of Moses Asch, published in 1998 by Smithsonian Institution Press, was a major source of information on Asch's life and career. I also consulted his taped interviews and notes at Smithsonian Folkways, including interviews with Frances Asch, John Asch, Michael Asch, Guy and Candie Carawan, Sam Charters, John Cohen, Sidney Cowell, Kenneth Goldstein, Ella Jenkins, Mel Kaiser, Harold Leventhal, Frederic Ramsey Jr., Ralph Rinzler, Tony Schwartz, and Irwin Silber.

For business aspects of the Folkways label, I am indebted to *Folkways Records: Moses Asch and His Encyclopedia of Sound* by Tony Olmsted published by Routledge in 2003. Olmsted's knowledgeable and thorough study of Folkways' business records was most helpful in furthering my understanding of the label.

For providing imagery for this text, I wish to thank John Cohen, whose music and photographs have long inspired me, and whose interview with Harry Smith conducted in 1968 was also an important source, as was the interview he gave to Peter Goldsmith in 1991; the Diana Davies Collection, a wonderful asset documenting folk music and its performers from the 1960s through the 1990s; Frank Driggs, whose knowledge and professionalism are without parallel; the late master photographer David Gahr, who also shared his memories and (often strong) opinions; Daniel Hammer, reference assistant, Williams Research Center, Historic New Orleans Collection, for making available images from Jim Chapelle from the Frederic Ramsey Jr. collection; David A. Jasen, Mr. Ragtime, for supplying sheet music imagery; the late, great Fred W. McDarrah, master documenter of Greenwich Village, and his wife, Gloria; Tony Martin, for graciously allowing us to reproduce the work of his father, David Stone Martin; Georgette Mayo, reference archivist at the Avery Research Center for African American History and Culture, College of Charleston, South Carolina, for researching and making available the image of Colin Turnbull; Roby Moulton, a 2008 intern at Smithsonian Folkways Recordings, for assisting in locating images from the archives; and George Pickow, John Pickow, and Jean Ritchie, for opening their wonderful archive of folk imagery to me.

For general assistance and guidance, thanks to Perry Werner, who took the author photo and also helped with researching imagery at David Gahr's house and elsewhere; and to Paul Prestopino for his knowledge about the 1960s folk movement and for helping me track down Tony Martin.

Complete source notes for this book and other materials are available at the Web site, www.folkways.si.edu/worldsofsound.

Special thanks, as always, to my family: Jessica, Tunnicliff, and Flannel; to my brother, Bob Carlin, who introduced me to traditional music and continues to challenge and inspire me, and his family, Rachel Smith and Benjamin; and to my parents, the late Benson Carlin and Vivian F. Carlin, with my heartfelt apologies for ruining their collection of Asch label 78s when I was too young to know better.

DIRECTOR'S INTRODUCTION

A passion for recorded sound technology, a commitment to cultural egalitarianism, an enduring legacy of human expression, an unending project to compile an aural encyclopedia portraying the breadth of humanity—the sixty-year history of Folkways Records embodies all of this and more. Just as writers have devoted themselves to the pen, photographers to the camera, and painters to their brushes and palette, Folkways founder Moses Asch etched his life's work in the phonogram—capturing, curating, and stubbornly distributing a world of sound that he insisted was of vital importance to humankind.

The Folkways Records and Service Corporation came into being in 1948, at the brink of a post–World War II surge in the availability and affordability of the phonograph. A few years previously, recording on tape replaced the more cumbersome wire and disc media, and a few years later, the radical improvements in sound recording technology yielded the high-fidelity long-play recording and further bolstered the medium's burgeoning popularity. Asch had begun his aural masterpiece a decade earlier—emboldened by a chance conversation with Albert Einstein—recording songs of ordinary Americans who in his heart of hearts he knew were anything but ordinary. Two attempts at launching record labels—Asch and Disc—failed, but served as the training ground for Folkways, and as Asch hit his stride, he ended up producing close to twenty-two hundred albums over its thirty-six-year span, nearly one album per week!

In 1987, the year following Asch's death, the Folkways Records collection passed to the Smithsonian Institution—with conditions. First, the Smithsonian must conserve the collection and hire an archivist. Second, Smithsonian insisted that the label should pay its own way if any public outreach was to occur. Third, the Asch family required that the entire Folkways catalog remain available to the public, in keeping with Asch's policy of keeping the entire catalog in print. Fourth, Smithsonian needed to raise funds to purchase the performance rights to the Folkways catalog; it did so, with the help of Bob Dylan, Bruce Springsteen, U2, Emmylou Harris, Willie Nelson, and other notable artists who offered a fundraising concert that led to a film and Grammy-winning recording. With the collection in hand, Smithsonian brought on anthropologist and archivist Anthony Seeger, who became the first director of the newly minted

Smithsonian/Folkways label. Smithsonian/Folkways published its first recording in 1988, and it made the historic Folkways Records holdings available, first as cassettes and later as custom CD-R copies. Two decades later, Smithsonian Folkways (the slash was dropped) had launched over 400 albums—either new recordings or compilations drawn from the Folkways Collections—and, through adding the capacity to offer digital downloads in 2005, the entire collection of close to forty thousand tracks was made available via the Web, expanding the reach of Asch's vision exponentially.

For me, as an ethnomusicologist, sound has no intrinsic meaning whatsoever. *People* vest sound with meaning, whether they be the creators, the performers, or the consumers/participants. The meaning and effect evoked by a song, for example, might change according to the person listening to it, the moment in which it is sung, and the social circumstances in which it is performed. Likewise, the fullest meaning of the Folkways sound collection is found in its relationship to the people who create the music and sounds, to the people who listen to them, and to the social/cultural circumstance that surrounds them over time.

In *Worlds of Sound*, Richard Carlin weaves multiple threads into the story of Folkways: Moses Asch's personal experiences and motivations; the New York City intellectual community in which he operated; collaborations with contributors; relationships to the artists he recorded; and the evolution of sound recording technology and business practices. Then Carlin takes us twenty years further, tracing the intrigues and accommodations of the "Revolution for Two Institutions," the recasting of Folkways Records as Smithsonian Folkways, a living "Museum of Sound." Carlin tells his tale with the authority of a Folkways artist and compiler, music scholar, and editor of many dozens of music publications. Each chapter is replete with audio references, all available—as Asch required—from Smithsonian Folkways. The Smithsonian Institution's mission is "the increase and diffusion of knowledge," and in *Worlds of Sound*, Richard Carlin has contributed enormously to this mandate, crafting an elegant, meaning-laden frame around the remarkable accomplishments of an extraordinary man and his Folkways fellow travelers.

Daniel Sheehy, Ph.D.
Director & Curator
Smithsonian Folkways

AMERICA SINGS FOR ASCH

★

ASCH RECORDS AND ALBUMS, SIGNATURE AND STINSON LABELS, FOR FALL DELIVERY

AMERICAN FOLK MUSIC
ASCH LABEL

ALBUM NO.

330—SONGS OF THE LINCOLN BATTALION. Contains 3-10" records.

432—FOLKSAY (Cowboy Mountain Songs and Dances). Contains 4-10" records.

343—SONGS BY LEAD BELLY (Blues). Contains 3-10" records.

344—COUNTRY DANCES (Reels and Squares). Contains 3-10" records.

345—BURL IVES, the Wayfaring Stranger (American Folk Songs). Contains 3-10" records and book by Alan Lomax.

346—SONGS FOR VICTORY (Music for Political Action). Contains 3-10" records.

347—WOODY GUTHRIE (Popular Favorites). Contains 3-10" records.

348—SONGS BY JOSH WHITE (Popular Favorites and Blues). Contains 3-10" records.

550—BLUES (Traditional). Contains 3-12" records.

HOT JAZZ
ASCH LABEL

ALBUM NO.

350—JAZZ VARIATIONS. 3-10" records and book.

450—MARY LOU WILLIAMS AND HER FIVE. 3-12" records and book (Exclusive Artist).

351—MARY LOU WILLIAMS TRIO (Bill Coleman, Al Hall) (Exclusive Artist) Album of Popular Favorites. Contains 3-10" records.

551—JAMES P. JOHNSON and Orchestra (N. Y. Jazz). Contains 3-12" records.

452—ART TATUM TRIO. Contains 2-12" records.

352—MEADE LUX LEWIS. Contains 6 original compositions, 3-10" records.

353—STUFF SMITH TRIO. Contains 6 original compositions, 3-10" records.

RECORD NO.

1001—12" BOOGIE WOOGIE PIANO SOLO. James P. Johnson.

500—10" RAINBOW BLUES. GIRL OF MY DREAMS. Jerry Jerome and His Cats and Jammers.

501—10" ARSENIC AND OLD FACE BOOGIE. WHEN I GROW TOO OLD TO DREAM. Jerry Jerome and His Cats and Jammers.

502—10" SATCHEL MOUTH BABY. Mary Lou Williams and Her Five. MISTY BLUES. Jerry Jerome and His Cats and Jammers.

HILLBILLY
ASCH LABEL

RECORD NO.

2001—SOLDIER OVER THERE. Cactus Cowboys. KICKING MY LOVE AROUND. Cactus Cowboys.

2002—I GOT A GAL. Cactus Cowboys. RIDING ALONG. Cactus Cowboys.

2003—WORRIED AND ALONE. Cactus Cowboys. OVER THE RIVER JORDON. Cactus Cowboys.

2004—LONELY, SAD AND BLUE. Wallace Fowler and Orch. IF I HAD MY LIFE TO LIVE OVER. Wallace Fowler and Orch.

2005—LIVING IN SORROW. Wallace Fowler and Orch. YOU'RE MY DARLING, YOU'RE MY SUNSHINE. Wallace Fowler and Orch.

FOREIGN - RUSSIAN
STINSON LABEL

Outstanding Russian Record Albums.

75 USSR records in addition to the following albums:

ALBUM NO.

210—RED ARMY SONGS. Contains 6-10" records and text.

250—RED ARMY SINGS. Contains 2-12" records and text; 8 songs including the famous Meadowland.

252—GYPSIES. Contains 3-12" records; 12 songs.

260—ARIAS FROM RUSSIAN OPERAS. Contains 2-12" records; solo artists and chorus of the Bolshoi Theatre.

FOREIGN - JEWISH
ASCH LABEL

ALBUM NO.

400—TRADITIONAL JEWISH FOLK SONGS AND DANCES. Contains 3-12" records and text.

604—JEWISH FOLK SONGS. Contains 4-10" records and text

RECORD NO.

6010—12" KOL NIDRE, ELI ELI. Cantor Leibele Waldman.

6031—12" DUDELE. A CHASEND'DL OIF SHABOS.

6027—10" LIEBE FREILACH, MIRELLE. Seymour Rechzeit.

6028—10" RUCHELE, ROSZENKES AND MANDLEN. Seymour Rechzeit. 50 additional selections.

TALKING BOOKS
ASCH LABEL

ALBUM NO.

101—IN THE BEGINNING by SHOLEM ASCH. Contains 3-10" records and text; biblical; for children.

354—POEMS BY LANGSTON HUGHES. Contains 4-10" records and text; recitation.

SIGNATURE LABEL

RECORD NO.

28101—10" VOODTE. HAWKINS' BARRELHOUSE. Coleman Hawkins and Orch.

28102—10" HOW DEEP IS THE OCEAN? STUMPY. Coleman Hawkins and Orch.

28103—10" SQUEEZE ME. Yank Lawson and Orch. THE SHEIK OF ARABY. Yank Lawson and Orch.

28104—10" GET HAPPY. CRAZY RHYTHM. Coleman Hawkins Swing Four.

90001—12" THE MAN I LOVE. SWEET LORRAINE. Coleman Hawkins Swing Four.

90002—12" I GOT RHYTHM. I'M FOR IT, TOO. Dicky Wells and Orch.

90003—12" FLAMINGO. NIGHT AND DAY. Shelly's Trio.

9004—12" ON THE SUNNY SIDE OF THE STREET. TIME ON MY HANDS. Shelly's Trio.

ALBUM NO.

SI-1—FATS WALLER MEMORIAL ALBUM. Contains 4-10" records and book, with Earl Hines Trio, Oscar Pettiford, Al Casey and Nat Jaffe—Sid Jacobs.

For addresses of our eleven distributors and complete catalogue—write to

Stinson Trading Co., 27 Union Sq. W., N. Y. C.

Records

The Billboard 1944 Music Year Book   Page 161

PREFACE

THE FOLKWAYS MOMENT

This book is about a record label—originally known as Folkways Records and Service Corporation and then, for the last two decades, as Smithsonian Folkways Recordings—and the many people who have helped shape it over its sixty years of existence. It is a book of stories, culled from aging scrapbooks and ledgers, yellowed carbons of correspondence, recorded interviews with Moses Asch—Folkways' founding father—and his legion of creative collaborators, and many, many new interviews and discussions with those who are preserving and enlarging the Folkways legacy, and the listeners who have been influenced by its varied recordings.

These stories often share a common theme, something that Dan Sheehy and Atesh Sonneborn—currently Director and Associate Director of the Smithsonian Folkways label—have astutely called a "Folkways Moment": the first encounter with a Folkways recording that affects the listener significantly. New sounds are heard; ears are opened; lives are transformed. While they may sound like exaggerations, I was repeatedly amazed by how many stories I heard that began, "When I heard that record of folksongs from Trinidad, I suddenly realized there was a world of music beyond what I could hear on the radio . . ." or "My parents played Pete Seeger records for me when I was a kid, and I just have had that sound in my head as long as I could remember . . ." or "I heard that record of African Pygmies in college, and I was ready to jump on a tramp steamer and give up my academic career forever. . . ." The shock of hearing something totally new offered a glimpse into deeper possibilities, life beyond the American mainstream, worlds where human expression in all its variety could freely interact.

But for the true believers it went beyond the sounds themselves. The physical presence of a Folkways album—which looked totally unlike a commercial LP—was itself a source of wonder. The front "cover" consisted of a paper wrapper glued over a plain sleeve, the black cardboard textured like aged leather. The wrapper only reached about one-third of the way around the back of the

"America Sings for Asch," advertisement, *Billboard Yearbook*, 1944.

album, and a list of the tracks to be heard within sometimes was printed on the back to give you a clue of what you were buying. Inside the sleeve, a heavy piece of cardboard was inserted to create two pockets. In one, a booklet of notes was inserted, sometimes as little as four pages but more often expanding to thirty or more pages of background notes, photographs, and song lyrics; in the other pocket, the record was placed, somewhat heavier than a typical vinyl album. Folkways albums were decidedly different; difficult to find in record stores outside of major cities, priced higher than normal albums, treasured, and passed eagerly from listener to listener, their very obscurity making them that much more desirable.

Sometimes the pressings were noisy; or the photos in the booklet notes were printed too dark and were hard to decipher; sometimes the central hole in the record was miscalibrated so the recording sounded wobbly and distorted. No matter; these were all part of the difference that made Folkways releases so alluring. You had to try hard to listen to a Folkways record; it wasn't something that you could just slap on the turntable without a second thought.

You'd find these odd records first in libraries. They'd have them stacked up, sounds of steam locomotives, Shakespeare plays and Latin language instruction discs, the expected Woody Guthrie and Pete Seeger albums, and the unexpected music of carousels, insects, and computers. Battered by passing through hundreds of hands, scratched and sometimes unplayable, they offered enticing glimpses into new aural worlds. And the hunt was begun: Where could you find these albums? What other sound secrets might they hold?

You'd hear rumors, almost like sightings of meteors or far-off stars. There was this store on 43rd Street in New York where you could buy Folkways records for as little as ninety-nine cents. It was an odd record shop, hidden down a half-flight of steps, below street level, that few found without first hearing about it in whispers from other true believers, who didn't want the secret spread too far for fear that the supply would be exhausted. "Check out Record Haven," they'd say, "but don't tell anybody else about it!" Sure, these discs came without the covers or notes, and an extra hole was drilled through the record label, but at least you could open the door a crack on that special sound world. Or you might hang out in Sam Goody's bargain store, believing the oft-repeated story that—in a fit of generosity—Moses Asch would slip his unsold inventory into the bins, selling off the odd African music record to make room for the newer releases in his warehouse.

Folkways records were different because Folkways artists and producers stood out. Label founder Moses Asch said he preferred to record artists who had something to say, and were unafraid to say it, whatever the consequences. Pete Seeger led the way, stubbornly performing anywhere he could when facing the blacklist in the 1950s and early 1960s, singing songs of "social significance" long before anyone thought a song could change the world. But there were countless others, equally outside of the commercial music system, who spoke through Folkways releases. Kentucky mountaineer Roscoe Holcomb with his high, tenor voice, so biting that it would make the hairs in your ears leap to attention; Elizabeth Cotten's sure-fingered guitar picking, juxtaposed against her imperfect and yet perfectly appropriate voice; Tony Schwartz's documentary recordings of children's voices in urban playgrounds, echoing off the brick and concrete; not to mention the multitudes of world music performers, strangely compelling because their voices could be heard nowhere else. As Dan Sheehy told me, "The recording has a certain power, to move people, to break people out of their old modes. Each one of these recordings of less-familiar music is an opportunity to build a new window in our metaphoric house of how we view the world."

When you talk to Folkways fans, those who grew up with the label in the 1950s and 1960s, and newer listeners just discovering this material on CDs or through online downloads, you can tell that these recordings have meaning that transcends their musical value. The life stories that were transformed through the Folkways moment are truly impressive. Here are just three of many stories that I heard:

Len Chandler was a college student studying classical clarinet when a teacher played him a Lead Belly recording. Although he was African American, Chandler was totally unaware of the blues tradition, and was immediately transfixed by the power of Lead Belly's music. Soon after, he abandoned his dream of a classical career to pursue a new one: to perform and record his own music. Chandler became one of the outstanding singer-songwriters of the Civil Rights era.

Ruth Stone was just another student pursuing a degree at Hunter College when she heard an album of Liberian music on Folkways. Soon, she was visiting the country that was the source of this music, to dig deeper into its traditions and styles. She became one of this country's most important scholars of African music based on this "chance" encounter with a Folkways record.

Ken Bilby was a comfortable suburbanite listening to rock radio when he discovered two early albums of Jamaican music in his local library. Bilby was excited by the strong marriage of African rhythms with Spanish, French, and other European traditions. He was so inspired that he decided—as a teenager—to go to Jamaica to record more of this music. These recordings became the basis for further Folkways releases, and so the early albums inspired the creation of new material.

My own Folkways moment began when I was just five or six years old. My parents gave me a copy of *Birds, Bugs, Beasts and Little Fishes* by Pete Seeger, and I played and played that record until the vinyl was nearly worn off the disc. When I was twelve years old, I took the bus into New York City and naively showed up at Folkways' offices, asking to buy a copy of Elizabeth Cotten's first album. An old man came out of a back room and said, "Oh no, we don't sell records here," and then told me to go to Sam Goody's on 47th Street. Five years later, I returned to the Folkways offices with a tape of concertina players I had recorded in England as part of a Youthgrant to document this tradition. I didn't hear a thing for about six months. So I returned to the offices, asking for my tape back. After digging around in the back, the same old man—who I now knew was Moses Asch—came back and said, "Oh no, I want to put this record out!" and so began a five-year relationship with this difficult and endearing man. If I could make a record for the $200 budget he was willing to pay, he'd put it out, often within three months of receiving the finished tapes. This amazing process was built on personal trust that I would do my very best to present the unvarnished voice of the people who I recorded.

When Moses Asch began his mission to document "all the sound of the world," he could hardly have envisioned the impact that his off-beat enterprise would have. Through his work and countless collaborators, he was able to capture the soundscape of a century, so now we can know what a mid-twentieth-century office sounded like, relive a sit-in at a Nashville lunch counter, hear the voices of poets, statesmen, and agitators speaking of what were once front-page concerns, or follow the vision of an original artist or producer whose unique production might otherwise be lost.

The eccentric record collector Harry Smith, who created for Folkways the landmark *Anthology of American Folk Music* set, perhaps put it best in 1991 when he was awarded a Chairman's Merit Award at the Grammy ceremonies. "I'm glad to say my dreams came true," he said. "I saw America changed by music." I hope that this book can inspire you to return to the Folkways catalog to hear again—and anew—the riches that are contained within it. Perhaps, in its small way, this book can add another room to the house of how you view the world.

Richard Carlin
April 2008

Worlds of Sound

Chapter 1

CREATING WORLDS OF SOUND

The Extraordinary Career of Moses Asch

A picturesque village in the Cotswolds; a Pygmy camp in the Congo; a tiny settlement deep in the Brazilian rain forest; a platform of the New York City subways. Most of us will never visit these places to hear their music and sounds. But we *can* hear British ballad singers, Pygmy leaf orchestras, Brazilian Indian musicians, and the howl of the metal subway wheels as they rub against the tracks, thanks to the vision of a recording engineer working in a closet-sized studio in New York City. His name was Moses Asch; his legacy, about twenty-two hundred albums of music and sounds from around the world released over a period of thirty-eight years on the Folkways label. For the last twenty years, this mission has been upheld and expanded by the Smithsonian Folkways label, a nonprofit record company formed shortly after Asch's death to maintain and build on his vision.

Worlds of Sound celebrates Asch's outlandish plan to document every possible human musical expression (and many nonhuman sounds, too). Over the years, Folkways would become influential for several generations of folk revivalists, from Pete Seeger to Bob Dylan to Lucinda Williams. But Folkways also issued recordings of poets Langston Hughes and Nikki Giovanni, North American tree frogs, sounds of steam locomotives, electronic music by John Cage, traditional Irish music recorded live in pubs, Indonesian gamelan and African kora players, civil rights marches and the Watergate hearings, and much more. Asch's worlds of sound were expansive and all-inclusive, and this book will carry forward that spirit.

> "I'm not interested in individual hits. To me a catalogue of folk expression is the most important thing."
>
> —Moses Asch

How did Asch build his "encyclopedia of sound" and still keep his business—albeit small—afloat? Asch's strategy for success contradicted what most businesspeople would call common sense. As early as 1946, Asch told a reporter from *Time* magazine, "I'm not interested in individual hits. To me a

David Gahr captured Moses Asch at work in the closet-sized control room of Cue Studios in the late 1950s. (© David Gahr)

catalogue of folk expression is the most important thing"—and he meant it. No Folkways record ever cracked the top 10 of any chart—or the top 100, for that matter. Yet the influence of Folkways' records has lasted long after many once-successful pop labels have been forgotten.

MOSES ASCH, THE INDEPENDENT

Asch's philosophy and career choice were colored by his background as an Eastern European émigré, albeit one far better off than most of his contemporaries. His father was a well-known writer named Sholem Asch. The family was originally from Poland, but thanks to Sholem's success as an author, settled outside of Paris in 1912. Sholem left his family in Paris for work in New York City in 1914; a year later, he sent for his wife and children, including young Moses.

Asch rarely wrote about his childhood or spoke of it in public. However, in a letter written to Pete Seeger's daughter Mika when she was jailed in Mexico following a protest march held at the 1968 Olympics, he uncharacteristically opened up about his childhood experiences:

From left, Moe, Nathan (Moe's older brother, who was a well-known writer), Frances (Moe's wife), Nathan's son, David, and Moe and Nathan's father, Sholem, with two unknown women, greeting Sholem on his arrival in the United States, c. 1935. (Courtesy of Michael and Margaret Asch)

> At the age of 6–7 (1911) I became very ill this was in Paris, the suburbs, we had our own house with separate bed rooms. . . .

The four of us [Asch and his siblings] were taken care of by my aunt Basha, mother's revolutionary sister, who had fled from a train taking her to Siberia. . . . I was confined to bed for a period of 6 months with nothing to do. . . . Basha taught me many fundamental things. The one that has always stayed foremost was that one cannot be a progressive person interested and dedicated to social justice and reform if one lived a lie or did not tell the truth. . . .

With the outbreak of WWI (1914) Basha brought the four of us to America. Father and mother were already here. Father was being published and his plays were shown on Second Ave. Father being not very clear as to our legal names and ages did not declare my name and age properly. So I was left behind at Ellis Island. For four days without communication I remained behind bars. . . . It exposed me to the immigrants their way of life and the way official dome acts in relation to people's lives. When a custom officer could not make out a person's name he gave him one that was Americanised. etc. Every one had a tag on them and were herded and treated like cattle. [Original punctuation and spelling]

AMERICAN LABOR PARTY

Caravan

COMES TO TOWN

HELLO, EVERYBODY! HELLO, EVERYBODY!

ROOSEVELT LEHMAN

Radio Labs built a sound truck for the Roosevelt/Lehman campaign that was used for outdoor rallies and political events. (Courtesy of Gary Kenton)

Whether Asch was actually confined on Ellis Island for several days or just several hours, this frightening experience was seared into his memory, leaving him feeling vulnerable in a foreign world where immigrants were lumped together and treated like "cattle." This feeling of being judged because of one's group identity rather than one's individual achievements is something that Asch struggled to overcome. As he told Israel "Izzy" Young in a 1970 interview, "For what I stand for, I'll die, but for what somebody else tells me I stand for, I object."

Sholem Asch believed in using literature to instruct and educate his fellow man. While not gifted as a writer, Moses would follow in his father's footsteps in his chosen career of audio engineering. In the mid-1920s, he studied radio engineering in Germany, a center for the new science. On his return to the United States, he worked for various electronics firms before opening his own small radio repair business, called Radio Labs, during the Depression. Asch branched out into installing sound systems for rallies and events, which led to a job at New York's left-leaning radio station, WEVD (named for socialist leader Eugene V. Debs and owned by the Yiddish-language paper *The Forward*, which also employed Sholem Asch as one of its columnists). A major part of his job was to record programs on acetate discs for later broadcast, inspiring him to enter the record business.

Moe (second from left) with his coworkers in the workshop of his business, Radio Labs. The firm specialized in installing PA systems and building custom amplifiers.

ASCH RECORDS *present-*

AN OUTSTANDING RECORD ALBUM OF JEWISH AND HEBREW SONGS
A-610 3-12" Records

Kol Nidre   -   Eli - Eli
(Sung by the celebrated Cantor Leibele Waldman)
Dos Yiddishe Lied Part 1 & 2
A Chasendel Auf Shabes
A - Dudele

And the following famous masterpiece ASCH Record Albums of Songs, Dances, Prayers.

| A 600A-4-10" Record assorted songs and dances | A 601P- 4-10" Records Palestinian songs and dances incl. Hatikvah, Techezakna | A 602C 4-10" Records Cantorial prayers by outstanding cantors of today | A 604F 4-10" Records Jewish Folk Songs, old and new | H605D 4-10" Records Jewish Dances, Freilachs |

ASCH *Famous Jewish Artists include:* Cantor Leibele Waldman, Menashe Oppenheim, Max Kletter, Saul Meisels, Chaim Tauber, Dave Tarras, Pesach Burstein, M. Yordeini, Harry Lubin, Oscar Julius Quartet, and Cantor M. Ganchoff.

Among Asch's first releases on his new label were cantorial and Hebrew-language recordings; this early poster was designed for in-store display.

Pee Wee Russell, Cliff Jackson, and Muggsy Spanier recording in the Asch studios. Note how the office door opens directly into the studio and how Asch tried to make the musicians more comfortable by hanging paintings in the small space.

In 1940, Sholem invited his son to travel with him to Princeton, New Jersey, to meet the physicist and humanitarian Albert Einstein. When Einstein asked the young man what he did for a living, Asch responded that he was working in radio and recording. Einstein was intrigued by this career choice, and encouraged the young man to record and document all the sounds of the world, to create an "encyclopedia" of man's musical expression. Asch took this as a life calling, and the idea was germinated to use his talents to capture a world of sound.

With limited resources, a tiny staff, and a closet-sized recording studio, Asch began his quest in early 1940, when he founded his first record label. As the major labels withdrew from special-interest recording, Asch recognized a gap in the marketplace. WEVD's listeners began requesting Jewish cantorial records that the major labels had stopped issuing; Asch responded by buying masters and recording new selections for this market.

Asch had open ears—and also open doors— for all types of musicians. His studio was located in midtown Manhattan and he was there day and night, ready to record, at no charge, anyone willing to play for his microphones. He told Gene Bluestein:

My studio . . . was very open. There was a window, and my equipment [desk and files] was against it . . . on the other end was a studio that I insulated and built, about 15 by 10 feet. The door was on the other side and you walked into the studio . . . so we were always in the place . . . [when] people used to come in and say "I want to record," all I had to do was get off the desk and put the equipment on.

This open-door policy was in stark contrast to bigger studios that charged fees to would-be artists, if they could get past an often surly receptionist. To make the atmosphere more "homey," Asch hung several works of art in the tiny space.

Fred Ramsey, an early associate of Asch's who brought many African American musicians to the studio in the 1940s, remembered how Moe could elicit a good performance through his natural sympathy with the artists:

Moe could make musicians comfortable: Usually he would be warm and welcoming. He would ask them questions about their backgrounds, asking where they come from . . . and when did you start playing music—anything that would get them to thinking that someone was interested in what they were doing.

One day, a scruffy folksinger with a battered guitar showed up on his doorstep. Asch looked him over and said, "Who are you?" The singer responded, "I'm Woody Guthrie." Asch gruffly responded, "So what?" Guthrie was not put off, but simply stated he had come to record, hearing that Asch would record anyone, anytime. A deep friendship was born, with Guthrie recording hundreds of discs for Asch, and Asch commissioning Guthrie to write songs for children and topical songs. Other regulars at the Asch studio during this period were the twelve-string guitarist Lead Belly, the banjo player Pete Seeger, and jazz pianists James P. Johnson and Mary Lou Williams. Williams quipped about the freedom that Asch gave his artists: "If you only burped, Moe recorded it."

The 1942 American Federation of Musicians' strike against the major labels was a stroke of good fortune for smaller operators such as Asch. Desperate for

SONGS TO GROW ON

"Act out" albums for American children, recorded under the supervision of Beatrice Landeck of Hunter College, New York University, and Mills School.

NURSERY DAYS

written and sung by WOODY GUTHRIE
3-10" Discs, Album No. 605
$3.15

SCHOOL DAYS

Charity Bailey, singing songs from the Little Red School House.
3-10" Discs, Album No. 604
$3.15

WORK SONGS TO GROW ON

Make play out of work. Sung by Woody Guthrie and Cisco Houston.
3-10" Discs, Album No. 603
$3.15

SONGS TO GROW ON invite children to "act out" simple patterns of work, play and personal care. The traditional ballad forms impart the spirit of America. They entertain while teaching both independence and co-operation. These participation albums are ideal to occupy children while mother is busy. For home, school, and wherever children are.

Early advertisement for *Songs to Grow On* featuring Woody Guthrie.

records, the distributors would buy nearly anything. Many folk and jazz performers were not welcomed by the union anyway—because folk and jazz weren't considered to be either "serious" or "commercial" enough for the unions to pay much attention to them—so they were free to work for Asch. His little label grew, and he began making deals with other producers, including Norman Granz (who was just beginning his career producing jazz concerts on the West Coast). Together Granz and Asch issued the first-ever live jazz recordings, and the concept of the live concert recording was born (see Chapter 2). For Asch, it was a natural outgrowth of documenting "real" sound. Plus, it had the added advantage of not costing the label much for the artists, and there were no studio costs.

Granz's friendship with Asch led to a near-catastrophe for the young engineer. Granz obtained some recordings of an up-and-coming West Coast pianist named Nat Cole and passed them to Asch. Lured by the possibility of breaking into the pop charts, Asch decided to issue the record in fall 1946. He invested heavily in publicity and advertising, and pressed thousands of discs. But disaster struck when—according to Asch—an early-season snowstorm crippled transpor-

Insert notes for the ill-fated King Cole Quintet album.

IN THE RECORDING BOOTH. MOE ASCH
OPERATES HIS RECORD MAKER—

Don Freeman, a noted newspaper columnist and artist, sketched Asch recording vocalist Stella Brooks using a disc-cutting machine in 1946.

tation on the East Coast and the discs could not be delivered in time to reach dealers for the Christmas rush. Asch was left holding the bag. Over the following months, bills mounted, and although Asch struggled on for about another year or so, the legacy of his attempt to have a pop hit eventually led to his bankruptcy. As part of the bankruptcy settlement in 1948, he was banned from participating in the record business until his creditors were paid.

Asch took from his bankruptcy an important lesson: he decided that he never wanted to record another hit record. In early 1949, he commented to an unnamed writer from *People's Songs* (the newsletter of left-wing folk music) that he had "focused too much time and money on popular jazz" and from this point forward he would focus on "good records," which would be "sold to a small circle of people who will buy them."

After his bruising experience with the Nat Cole record, Asch came up with a new formula for survival: he would record artists who, in exchange for freedom to record as they wished, would work for little up-front payment. The records would appeal to small audiences but—unlike pop recordings that quickly went out of date—would have a long shelf life. By recording most of the performers in his own studio, Asch could produce his records much more economically. After World War II, the new technology of tape recording cut recording expenses greatly, and portable models made it possible for recordings to be made outside of the studio.

Folkways Records and Service Corporation

In July 1948, a new record company was born—Folkways Records and Service Corporation. Its president was Marian Distler. Due to his bankruptcy, Asch was barred from starting a new label; Distler had been his assistant at his previous labels, so she incorporated the new firm, hiring Asch as her "consultant." This fiction was maintained for several years, with Asch calling himself "production director" for Folkways, rather than its owner or president, through the 1950s. But it was clear that Folkways was an extension of Asch's previous labels and that he was the shaping force behind its catalog.

Why was the label called "Folkways Records *and* Service Corporation"? Perhaps Asch planned to return to doing public-address system and sound installation work. Or maybe he was interested in booking artists or sponsoring concerts in addition to making records. An article that Asch wrote circa 1946–47 gives some insight into what he meant by "service." Called "The Independent," the article not only is a statement of Asch's operating philosophy but also makes an argument for the dozens of other small, often specialized labels that were blossoming in the period immediately following World War II. Just as he had done in his radio days, Asch was positioning himself as a spokesperson for the industry, showing the majors that they could not dominate what the country was allowed to hear.

In this article, Asch explained that small labels thrive by providing a service to specific communities:

> The man [who] . . . will render service in exploiting local talent and issuing records for that community finds a customer for his product, by servicing that community. If times are hard so that not enough local people can afford to buy records or if other and more progressive companies come into the picture and give better service or exploitation or more variety, then the need for the original producer disappears and he is forced out of business . . .

This idea of providing a "service" to small communities foreshadowed the idea of micro or niche marketing by several decades. Asch criticizes the major labels not for being "big" but for trying to impose from above their taste on the record-buying public:

> In order to function as a business the record industry must support and help the development of new labels with new ideas; otherwise the life-blood of a young, interesting and needed medium of expression will be lost and buried in mediocrity. New customers cannot be developed by the archaic method of standardizing performer and composition as the [major labels] tend to do: on the one hand limiting the customer as to his wants and on the other, tying up money in an inventory that "THEY" chose.
>
> The dealer that displays and talks up new labels, albums and records will find that he is helping to promote those companies that will keep him in business.

In other words, it is both good business and socially sound to service new interests and markets, and not just support mass-market products.

Just as Folkways served its audience and artists, Asch expected them—in return—to serve the label. When times got tight, Asch recognized that it was more important for the label to survive than to always keep current with royalty payments or other obligations. The mission of Folkways—to provide a service by documenting the sounds of the world—was always foremost in his mind. As John Cohen recalled in a 1991 interview with Asch biographer Peter Goldsmith: "Moe taught me [that] the importance of keeping the place going was even more important than keeping the artist going. It was more important to keep Folkways alive and not pay the artists, than let Folkways sink."

10 INCH 33 1/3 RPM LONG PLAY RECORDS

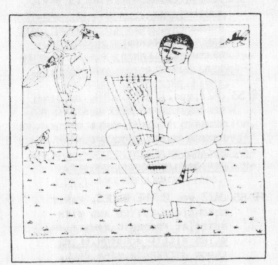

FOLKWAYS RECORDS

FP 1 SQUARE DANCES WITH PIUTE PETE AND HIS COUNTRY COUSINS. EASTERNS, WESTERNS, PLAYPARTYS. CALLS&INSTR. DESCR. BOOKLET. BUFFALO GALS, RED RIVER VALLEY, STEAM BOAT, LOOBY LOU, SHOO FLY, STEP RIGHT BACK, RICKETTS HORNPIPE, DUCK FOR OYSTER.

FP 2 WHO BUILT AMERICA WITH BILL BONYUN, GUITAR ACC. AMERICAN HISTORY THRU FOLKSONGS. INTRO BY BEATRICE LANDECK. WALY WALY PRAETES, SANTY ANO, AUCTION BLOCK, BOLL WEEVIL, HAPPINESS SONG, CHISHOLM TRAIL, MICHACRA SALANGADOU, GREEN MOUNTAIN BOYS ERIE CANAL, GOVERNMENT CLAIM, DRILL YE TARRIERS, JESSE JAMES SHOOT THE BUFFALO, SO LONG, SHLUF KIND, KLEINE JONGES.

FP 3 DARLING COREY WITH PETE SEEGER AND HIS FIVE STRING BANJO IN FAVORITE FOLKSONGS. NOTES BY ALAN LOMAX. ILL. BY CUNNINGHAM. JOHN RILEY, DEVILISH MARY, EAST VIRGINIA BLUES, CRIPPLE CREEK, PENNY'S FARM, DANVILLE GIRL, DARLING COREY, RISSELTY ROSSELTY IDA RED, OLD JOE CLARK, MY BLUE EYED GIRL, COME ALL FAIR MAIDS, JERRY'S ROCKS, SKILLET GREASY, I HAD A WIFE.

FP 4 TAKE THIS HAMMER WITH LEADBELLY AND HIS TWELVE STRING GUITAR. MEMORIAL ALBUM OF HUDDIE LEDBETTER SINGING NEGRO FOLKSONGS BY HIMSELF AND WITH OTHERS. NOTES BY ALAN LOMAX. ILL. BY CUNNINGHAM. GREEN CORN, YELLOW GAL, BIG FAT WOMAN, GRAY GOOSE, LAURA, PICK A BALE OF COTTON, MEETING AT THE BUILDING, GOOD MORNING BLUES, YOU CAN'T LOSE ME CHOLLY, LEAVING BLUES, IRENE GOOD NIGHT, TAKE THIS HAMMER, WE SHALL WALK THRU THE VALLEY BRING ME A LI'L WATER, SILVY.

FP 5 SONGS TO GROW ON WITH WOODY GUTHRIE PRIZE WINNING ACTIVITY ALBUM SUPERV. B. LANDECK. PUT YOUR FINGER IN THE AIR, COME SEE, RACE YOU DOWN THE MOUNTAIN, CAR SONG, DON'T YOU PUSH ME DOWN, MY DOLLY, HOW DOO DO, PICK IT UP, MERRY GO ROUND, SLEEPY EYES, WAKE UP, CLEAN-O, DANCE AROUND.

Early Folkways catalog, c. 1950, showing the first releases on the new label.

Asch also decided to buck the industry standard by keeping all of his recordings in print. The major labels would keep a record available only if there was enough demand for it. Asch reasoned that if he could produce recordings of value, demand, while small, would continue for decades—which is what occurred. Asch's basic philosophy supported this idea; as he once remarked, "Just because the letter *J* is less popular than the letter *S*, you don't take it out of the dictionary." Although he said all of his albums were always "available," he didn't have a warehouse bulging with thousands of discs. Instead, Asch reasoned that he could press albums when demand reached a sufficient level (sometimes as few as twenty-five orders) and that his customers would be happy to wait for an album to become available again because of its unique quality and content. He could escape the cycle of boom and bust that plagued his competitors.

> "Just because the letter *J* is less popular than the letter *S*, you don't take it out of the dictionary."
>
> —Moses Asch

The new world of LPs opened another door for Asch, who had always been more interested in presenting and documenting a group of songs than in producing individual hits. His 1940s 78s were usually packaged in "albums," which held six to ten 78s along with a small booklet giving background information and song lyrics. He drew on the pool of New York's radical young artists—including Ben Shahn, David Stone Martin, and many others—to create his album cover art, which was pasted onto a thick black jacket. This packaging gave Asch flexibility, in that he could print albums in tiny (by industry standards) quantities, producing just enough cover "slicks" and booklets as needed.

Asch continued this practice in the new world of LPs. By printing his liner notes separately in individual booklets, Asch could present fuller documentation than the typical release of his day. Often, the majors would simply print brief information—really no more than ad copy—on the back of an album. Asch felt strongly that his recordings required fuller documentation, and he insisted that he would not release an album without proper notes. Advertising—if any—was limited to the back of the booklet, if space allowed. When he ran out of a booklet, he would insert a small card into the record jacket, giving the listener the opportunity to request a copy when the booklets were again available. In this way, he also built a mailing list (see Chapter 10).

LPs were cheaper to produce and provided more flexibility in allowing for longer performances than 78s, as Moe noted to Izzy Young in 1970:

Three 78 records, both sides, could fit on one 10-inch LP. So here I had one economic cost, not three economic costs. Instead of a [78 rpm] album with 3 pockets I had an album with one pocket. And then we always had that trouble with a good folk song: By the time you come to the meat of the matter, then you end up [at the end of] the 78. . . . So it helped the kind of thing I was interested in.

LPs also created a market for more "serious" recordings, such as classical music and world and folk music. While 45s were aimed at the pop market, producing disposable hits for young listeners, LPs were for the connoisseur who wanted to build a collection of great recordings. Folkways' recordings appealed to this collector mentality.

With the postwar baby boom, Asch discovered another new market: children's and educational records. He had had an unlikely success in the 1940s by marketing an album of Lead Belly's recordings for children; after all, the blues singer was a convicted murderer, hardly someone one would think likely to appeal to suburban parents. But Asch recognized the PR potential in choosing an ex-convict as a children's artist:

> I recorded him singing children's songs that he knew, because I had had some success with recordings for children. Walter Winchell [the famous gossip columnist] got a hold of that and wrote: "Here is this convict, this murderer, and he's associated with a record company that puts out children's records!"

The engaging warmth of Lead Belly's performances won over parents across the country, and suddenly suburban children were singing "Go Tell Aunt Rhody" as they learned it from the ex-convict.

Asch discovered that educators valued content over sonic quality or fancy presentation. His open-door policy in the studio extended to politicians and businessmen, who came in to record their memoirs. His interest in documentary recording led him to reissue radio programs and recordings of government hearings not originally envisioned as material for records. One of his earliest collaborators, Tony Schwartz, elevated the aural documentary to a new level of sophistication through the thematic albums he created (see Chapter 11).

Finally, the folk revival that began with the Weavers' 1949–50 pop hit "Goodnight Irene" (a Lead Belly song that ironically reached number one on the pop charts six months after the singer's death) laid the groundwork for four decades of Folkways product. The folk revival was largely an urban and college-campus-based phenomenon; places such as New York's Washington Square, Boston's Harvard Square, Chicago's Old Town School of Folk Music, and liberal-leaning campuses including Oberlin, Swarthmore, and the University of Chicago became hotbeds of folk music. This underground movement lasted well beyond the pop hits of the Weavers and the Kingston Trio; its energy in performing folk music,

Bob Dylan accompanies Karen Dalton and Fred Neil at Cafe Wha? in Dylan's first New York City club appearance, 1961. (© Fred W. McDarrah)

researching its roots, and rediscovering and recording older singers culminated in the early career of singer-songwriter Bob Dylan.

Like Guthrie before him, Dylan showed up at the Folkways office hoping to record an album. The similarly scruffy singer was turned away, and complained bitterly to friends that he'd thought that Folkways' mission was to record anyone: "I went up to Folkways. I says: 'Howdy. I've written some songs.' They wouldn't even look at them. . . . I never got to see Moe Asch. They just about said, 'Go.'" A few months later, following a legendary solo show at a Greenwich Village club, Dylan was given a rave review by the *New York Times* critic Robert Shelton, and John Hammond of Columbia Records signed him to make an album.

Despite the currency of this story, it's unlikely that Asch was unaware of Dylan or his songs. After all, Pete Seeger was an early champion of Dylan's and must have told his close associate about this exciting new talent. Plus, Dylan's songs had appeared in *Broadside* magazine, and Asch had begun releasing on the Broadside label records made from the audition tapes for these songs, including Dylan's work. After signing with Columbia, Dylan actually participated in two sessions that were produced by Asch for Broadside albums, as a gesture of gratitude to the magazine that first published his songs. Asch recognized Dylan's talent, but also realized that he was not the kind of artist who should be recording for Folkways. Dylan's mannered vocal style bothered Asch, as he told Gary Kenton some twenty years later:

> You know the twang that many folk singers developed after Bob Dylan? This is false, it is not common to the man. With Dylan, of course, it was the poetry that counted rather than the rendition. His popularity was a combination of the rendition *and* the poetry, but that style wouldn't work for Folkways. On my *Broadside* sessions with Dylan, he was dealing with specific political and economic problems, so he didn't falsify his voice. He stated it as he felt it. This is my main criteria.

Recording engineer Mel Kaiser recalled that when Dylan was finished, Moe whispered to him, "That's Bob Dylan. That's not for me, but mark my words this kid is really going to make it."

Throughout the 1950s and early 1960s, Asch prospered by running a "lean and mean" operation. However, the lure of popular success again led him briefly astray in the early 1960s, when the folk revival was in full bloom. Asch found his recordings of artists such as Pete Seeger, Woody Guthrie, and the New Lost City Ramblers suddenly in high demand. Again, record distributors were banging down the door. For a while, it seemed as if Asch could bridge the gap between his artistic vision and commercial success. However, the folk revival ran out of steam almost as quickly as it occurred, and for a while it looked as though Folkways would collapse, a victim of its own success.

Yet somehow he scraped by, relying on his team of tried-and-true producers to keep him afloat during the tough years of the late 1960s. Asch went into a final period of productivity in the 1970s, just as a new folk revival was occurring. This new revival was broader-based, with interests in Irish, Jewish, Cajun, and other "ethnic" musics. Once again, the Folkways back catalog came into play; Asch had some of the best recordings of these musical styles, and his flexibility and speed allowed him to quickly meet market demand. New distributors such as Rounder Records opened markets for Folkways' product. While many faulted Asch for his sometimes low-quality 1970s recordings, minimal packaging, and inexpensive pressings, no one could ignore his presence.

The Art of Collaboration

Asch took a very Eastern European attitude toward business. He had little respect for larger organizations, whether governmental or corporate. Corporations stood between the people and their right to knowledge and self-expression, in Asch's view. This extended even into the area of electronics; bandwidth on early AM radio was carefully rationed so that more stations could be heard (and more money made) at the sacrifice of sound quality; records were produced with artificially boosted frequencies so that they'd sound better on cheaper equipment (but in turn distort the real sound that they purported to reproduce). All of this galled Asch, who maintained a purist view that any limitation on the free flow of information—whether it be thoughts, words, or electrons—impeded the people's right to knowledge.

Despite his inclination toward independence, Asch recognized that in order to create his "encyclopedia of world sound" he would need collaborators. These collaborators would become for Asch very much like an extended Jewish family, whose members might argue incessantly but always were pursuing a common goal. Folkways was built through personal relationships and trust; lacking the money to attract major talent, he gave his artists something more important, freedom to create.

Almost every Folkways release can be traced back to a regular contributor, through either direct involvement or recommendation. Once Asch accepted someone's integrity, he rarely questioned the material that person submitted. This is a common theme in interview after interview given by Asch's collaborators over the decades: once Moe took you into his inner circle, he trusted your judgment and taste. As Ken Goldstein commented in 1991: "He liked very good people and once you produced something that was successful—not that it sold, that wasn't a criterion for

him—then you could produce anything you wanted." Even those artists or producers who had a falling-out with Asch would continue recommending him to others. The genius of Folkways was the way Asch built on these associations while at the same time guarding his own freedom.

Asch extended his own sense of integrity to his collaborators. If he believed in someone's vision and trusted him or her to do good work, he had no problem issuing that person's records; it was only the fake or phony that he didn't want to be associated with. When Izzy Young asked him how he judged material for issuing, he replied:

> First of all, who is the guy who collected it? Do I have confidence in him as a person of integrity? That's number one. Chet Williams, for example did the songs of Somaliland and he just gave me another one, but he was one of the most astute human beings who was living with the people and recording the people. Anything he would put his name on would be worth preserving, because not

Cover for *Baijun Ballads: Somali Songs in Swahili*, edited by Chet Williams.

only of the content but because the guy did it. In many cases the man who recorded it is as important as the content because he stands for something in the field.

How did Folkways survive financially? Canadian scholar Tony Olmsted has written an entire book addressing this question, showing how Asch cleverly created various entities—from Folkways and related labels to a distribution company, Pioneer Record Sales, a book publishing company, Oak Publications, and alliances with various other resellers and distributors—to protect Folkways' mission. The mission was always first; finances followed. Nonetheless, Moe insisted in interview after interview that he was not a "philanthropist" but had a well-reasoned way of measuring the success of each project, as he told Izzy Young:

> The criteria [for selecting a Folkways release], outside of the content which I am the sole judge, is that the thing has to pay for itself. In some cases, that is as few as 3–400 records, in some cases—take Ella Jenkins, my top children's artist—she gets $6000 for recording, but I sell 10,000 of her records a year. So the amount I anticipate return depends on the amount I've invested.
>
> It is not a gamble, as such. I—more or less—can anticipate the sales of any one of my albums, 2 years, 3 years, 4 and 5. Each item stands by itself, depending upon its content. And I can pretty well predict the volume that each record, its potential.

It is interesting to note that Asch was paying Ella Jenkins an advance of $6,000 in 1970—the same time he was typically paying most of his collaborators $200 to $500 per issue, including all of the studio costs.

In the 1950s, he had paid Ken Goldstein "$50—for writing the notes, recording the album, editing the tape," and, Goldstein added wryly, "suffering from working

with Moe." But, like most Folkways collaborators, Goldstein noted: "I didn't care—I wanted the material to be released." John Cohen also made this distinction:

> I never felt that Folkways was unfair. I had deep respect for Moe. And also Moe gave me something that was so much more than [money]. Moe gave me the right, total responsibility for what I did. I could go out somewhere and record, if I wanted to have photographs with it, I would photograph, I would edit it, I would design the cover, I would write the notes, I would design the booklet. . . . to me, it meant much more than payment.

"What was the return for us in working for Folkways, for very little money and for very little distribution? One, he put them out. The other was we had almost a free hand to create our own material."

—Sam Charters

Sam Charters echoed the others as he explained how he made just $150 from producing the landmark *Music of the Bahamas* albums, featuring the first recordings of master guitarist Joseph Spence:

> The essence of the Folkways operation was, you have to understand, there was no money. . . . When Annie [his wife, Ann Charters] and I did the 3 volumes on the Bahamas in 1958, we went down, went to Miami, went over on the ship, hung out, stayed in native everything . . . So I sent the 3 [finished albums] to Moe and got the check: $50 each. So, for our whole summer, everything, we received a total of $150. But that's, you understand, how it worked: we wanted to do those recordings in the Bahamas, and the only way we could do them was by taking advantage of Moe saying, "I'll put it out."

Joseph Spence with his wife and his sister in New York City, 1962.
(Photo by Ann Charters)

As longtime friend and collaborator Harold Courlander put it in a 1989 interview with Gary Kenton, Moe pursued his dream despite the many obstacles in his path:

> He was a man who *loved* his work and he thought he was doing something worthwhile. And he was willing to do it for nothing as long as he could pay the rent. . . . He was always wrestling with the problem of insolvency, beating back creditors, or something like that. I never knew for sure [if] he'd figured out the system of business, and that's the way it worked, or whether it was what it appeared to me, that he was simply out of money, he couldn't pay the bills.

A telling anecdote by John Cohen illustrates how Asch felt his small enterprise was—literally—under the knife of competition, the government, and financial realities:

> [The office was in] a loft building, and it had wooden beams. Above Moe's desk was one of these African swords, shaped like a letter "C," you know, sharp on both sides, and it just rested over a beam, right above his chair. "Moe," I said, "that could fall down." "You want to sit here? You want to sit in my seat?" That was his answer. Oh my God!

Was Moe tempting fate or defying it? No one could ever be certain.

As he aged, Asch became increasingly deaf and suffered several heart attacks. Nonetheless, his bullish temperament combined with his vision to preserve and build his encyclopedia of world sound kept him at his desk until the mid-1980s, when he physically could no longer report to work. Latter-day successes include the first two albums by Texas singer-songwriter Lucinda Williams and dulcimer player Kevin Roth. Yet Asch also continued to produce albums of African kora music, Georgia Sea Islands singers, sound effects, electronic music, and even English concertina music, all guaranteed to sell in tiny numbers. He never abandoned his basic working philosophy and continued to issue records in the same plain packaging he had used for decades.

Moses Asch on West 61st Street, c. 1979. (© David Gahr)

Around 1980, he wrote a "Declaration of Purpose" for the label that summed up his philosophy:

> As Director, I have tried to create an atmosphere where all recordings are treated equally regardless of the sales statistics. . . . The real owners of Folkways are the people that perform and create what we have recorded not the people that issue and sell the product. . . . Folkways succeeds when it becomes the invisible conduit from the world to the ears of human beings.

One of the people who came out of the folk revival and had been influenced by Folkways was folklorist, performer, and festival organizer Ralph Rinzler. Through a series of twists and turns in his own career, Rinzler found himself at the Smithsonian Institution. As Asch aged, it became clear that Folkways would need a permanent home, a place where his vision could be carried forward. Rinzler encouraged the Smithsonian to negotiate with Asch, who—true to his independent ways—had difficulty giving up the collection that he had so lovingly built. These negotiations were still ongoing when Asch passed away on October 19, 1986. Luckily, the groundwork had been laid, and within a year the Moses and Frances Asch Collection came to Smithsonian (see Chapter 12).

Although the Smithsonian had agreed to keep all of the Folkways recordings available, there was not at first the idea of continuing the label. However, it soon became clear that the Folkways mission was not completed, that building an encyclopedia of the world of sound was still an important task. Although working in a fundamentally different way than Asch did—who else could have run a record label in his way?—the outcome has been a series of reissues and new recordings that very much maintain the spirit of Folkways' mission. Asch always balanced his aesthetic goals with the need to keep the Folkways ship afloat. So, too, the Smithsonian has balanced academic quality and the need to maintain and grow the Folkways mission.

JAZZ IS

FOLK MUSIC

Chapter 2

JAZZ IS FOLK MUSIC

When Moses Asch opened his tiny recording studio in 1940, New York was in the midst of a musical renaissance. Working across the hall from the studios of progressive radio station WEVD, Asch had access to a variety of artists. Unlike more pop-oriented stations, WEVD attracted progressive singers and performers, or those who were "unemployable" in more commercial settings (notably, black jazz musicians). Asch was a record collector and fan of jazz—he first heard the music around 1920 while working one summer picking apples on a farm outside of Kingston, New York—and so it was only natural that he would record these musicians along with the folk performers who would later make him famous.

NEW YORK JAZZ: THE 1940S

In New York City in the 1940s, the lines between folk and jazz music were not as strongly drawn as they are today. Progressive nightspots, including Café Society, presented folksingers such as Lead Belly and Brownie McGhee side by side with performances by Thelonious Monk and Billie Holiday. The audience was the same: left-leaning white and black New Yorkers (Café Society was one of the first interracial clubs) who admired these artists as much for their biographies as they did for their music. And, musically speaking, there wasn't that much difference between Billie Holiday's "Strange Fruit" (written by left-leaning high school teacher Lewis Allen) and Josh White's "One Meat Ball," as both songs addressed social issues: "Strange Fruit" attacked racial segregation and lynching, while "One Meat Ball" at least implicitly addressed poverty.

Jazz pianist Mary Lou Williams' longtime friend and manager, Father Peter F. O'Brien, described the importance of Café Society to the 1940s-era jazz world in New York City in this way:

> [Mary Lou enjoyed a] more or less constant "gig" at Café Society [in the 1940s]. . . . Many of the most brilliant players from the era found employment at Café Society: Teddy Wilson, Eddie Heywood, Billie Holiday. Some of them [recorded with Mary Lou for Asch during this time]: Vic Dickenson, Edmund

Spread from Disc Records' 1946 catalog proclaiming "Jazz is folk music," reflecting Moses Asch's belief that all human expression is by its nature "folk" music.

"To me there was no difference between jazz and folk music. It is all part of the contemporary scene."

—Moses Asch, 1983

Hall, and Frankie Newton who led the house band there for awhile. Then there's Josh White who, in another category, was one of Café Society's biggest stars.

A key event occurred in 1938 when jazz promoter, journalist, and record producer John Hammond presented his "From Spirituals to Swing" concert at New York's Carnegie Hall, featuring folk performers such as Josh White and Sonny Terry. This concert drew a direct line from folk music styles to popular jazz, emphasizing the African American contribution to the music. Among younger jazz critics, there was a new interest in recovering jazz's earliest roots, which would lead to the New Orleans revival of the postwar years.

It is not surprising, then, to discover that jazz musicians were frequent performers at Moses Asch's small studios. Blues and jazz performers often came to the 46th Street building to play over radio station WEVD; when they were finished with their broadcast, they could simply cross the hall and pick up some extra cash by cutting a few sides for Asch. Asch kept late hours and rarely required musicians to make an appointment for studio time, so players could wander in after a club date for a session.

Asch was particularly sympathetic to African American musicians and culture, recognizing kindred spirits among the creative outsiders who formed the jazz world. He was also open to less-popular musicians and styles, for both financial reasons—it was cheaper to record musicians who did not command high playing fees—and philosophical ones. From about 1941 to 1947, a surprising range of musicians passed through his studio, including pianists Mary Lou Williams, James

Log sheet from 1944–45 showing the many different jazz and folk musicians who showed up at all hours (mostly afternoons and evenings) to record for Asch.

P. Johnson, Joe Sullivan, and Art Tatum and small ensembles led by Muggsy Spanier, Sidney Bechet, and Pee Wee Russell.

BUILDING THE CATALOG: CHARLES EDWARD SMITH AND FREDERIC RAMSEY JR.

Asch was aided in his quest by two young jazz enthusiasts, Charles Edward Smith and Frederic Ramsey Jr. Both were interested in jazz's early history, particularly the oral histories of the players themselves. They coedited the influential anthology *Jazz Men* in 1945, which was among the first books to champion New Orleans and other "roots" jazz styles. Although occasionally their informants inflated their own stories and worth—most notably trumpeter Bunk Johnson, who made a considerable career out of being a New Orleans "relic"—the book presented the real voices of the jazz performers with dignity.

Fred Ramsey in the 1950s. (Courtesy of the Historic New Orleans Collection, Museum/ Research Center, acc. no. 2006.0257)

Fred Ramsey was in many ways a perfect partner for Asch in his early years: both were record collectors with a long interest in blues and jazz, and both had a lifelong fascination with recording techniques, particularly by the new opportunities offered by portable tape recorders in the early 1950s. (Ramsey proposed at one point basing a record series on the sounds heard outside of his rural New Jersey farmhouse, each record devoted to a single season.)

Like many of Asch's collaborators, Ramsey recalls being "hired" by Moe in a rather informal way—although it is clear that Moe was aware of Ramsey's scholarship and had targeted him as a potential collaborator, subtly drawing him into the Folkways orbit:

I had met [Moe] through Charles Edward Smith [around 1940] . . . The beginning of the real relationship with Moe was when Moe was starting the record company. And Moe asked me to come up and help them get organized. That was 117 W. 46th Street. It was a little tiny place, just filled with newspapers, there were shelves from here to there. . . .

Charlie Smith had been a pioneer for Moe, and he had written some of the very first notes. And Moe said, "I know what you been doing. Do you want to come down and do some work for me?" and I said, "Sure." His reputation was already good, but he had only put out a few records. That's how I really began to record for Moe, and also to scout a little bit.

This was the time when everybody who ever wanted to start a record company tried to jump into it. It became very competitive, and there was an awful lot of hard feeling between the people who were not making it. Well, it was obvious that Moe was going to make it. . . . From the beginning, the guy had a real conscience, he never recorded junk. He had a real sensitivity for talent, even if it was down-and-out talent. He gave them initial tryouts and pressings and recordings in a period when some of these people wouldn't be touched by anyone. Like Woody Guthrie, who had a message, but he never sold very much. But Moe was right that Guthrie was a person who should have been recording. And Moe did just about as good a job as anyone could have done.

. . . He didn't make any promise of paying me and as a matter of fact I don't think he *did* pay me. . . . I don't feel I was wronged by Moe in the least. He said, "The most I can pay is $25 a week, but you won't have to work here every day." I felt it was a fair thing, I was used to living on not very much money.

Along with Smith, Ramsey was responsible for "supervising" (what today we would call "producing") many of the jazz sessions held at Asch's small studios in

Baby Dodds at the drums.

the 1940s, as well as writing liner notes for the 78 albums. Asch apparently gave Ramsey full freedom to select musicians and shape the albums. The result was a series of unusual experiments for the time, including a 78 set documenting New Orleans drummer Baby Dodds' technique (including interviews with Dodds and demonstrations of his drum patterns) and rehearsal sessions by Mary Lou Williams and Art Tatum. It was unheard of to issue what was essentially raw, working material like this on record, and many accused Asch of issuing second-rate material, missing the point that the records were documenting the jazz process, not the finished product.

Many years later in an NPR interview, Fred Ramsey and Moses Asch recalled how Asch sensitively got Dodds to re-create for him the music he had played in the brothels and bars of New Orleans:

Ramsey: I was there with Baby Dodds [when] I began to have a sense of Moe's method of operation. Because you gave him a great deal of time and asked him questions that really made him come alive. You asked him about the first playing he ever did and the different kinds of acts he played for which were really not pure music, but he backed hoofers and cabaret girls. Then he started beating out the different rhythms. You got the guy in a mood of total recall.

Asch: Baby Dodds played something. I asked him "Was this the way this was done in a whorehouse that you played in and was this the beat that the girls walked in when they stripped?" . . . He was a very quiet man . . . but we got him to feel that he belonged. Usually these people feel "What does the

white man want here—he wants something and [he] pays [me] and that's it."
Baby felt entirely different and I came out with a terrific session.

Ramsey could follow his enthusiasms freely; if he heard an artist whom he thought worthy of being recorded, Moe would simply say, "Bring him in," and the deal was done. Ramsey recalled for Peter Goldsmith how Asch came to record an unusual pop-gospel group, the Two Gospel Keys:

> That was the period right after the War when there were great, enormous halls in Harlem, filled with performers. The Two Keys, these were two ladies who came up from the South. And I think every Sunday these Two Keys would perform, and they had guitar, mandolin . . . They filled this enormous hall with music, and they had people falling out just like in church, and they had tremendous demonstrations. And I got on to this within their first or second performance. And I got hold of Moe, and told him about those ladies, and he said, "Bring them in." . . . Moe was very much taken with them, and, as he could do, drew the best possible performance from them. [Their album] might have sold somewhat, but I doubt it sold much.

HOT IVORIES: JAMES P. JOHNSON AND MARY LOU WILLIAMS

Two jazz pianists were regular visitors to Asch's studios and became close to the engineer-entrepreneur. One was composer James P. Johnson, who recorded a wide range of solo material for Asch, from early stride piano instrumentals to Broadway show tunes from the 1920s and 1930s to his more experimental pieces that showed the influence of modern composition. The pianist is relaxed in his performances, as if he were playing in his own living room simply for his own pleasure. Asch encouraged Johnson to record more ambitious works, including a piano reduction of his *Yamekraw* suite, a jazz-classical hybrid that had been rarely performed in its full orchestral form at the time.

The jazz player with whom Asch had the longest relationship was pianist, composer, and arranger Mary Lou Williams. Williams was exceptional in many ways: a female musician in a male-dominated world, she began her career arranging for Andy Kirk's band in the 1930s, creating many innovative big-band arrangements. In the 1940s, she was an early and enthusiastic

Newspaper clipping showing Mary Lou Williams in the Asch studios with Josh White.

Part of recording session at Asch Studio Eddie Dougherty, drums; Jimmy Butts, bass; Bill Coleman, trumpet; Mary Lou Williams, piano; Josh White, guitar. Tunes recorded were "Adelaide" with vocals by Bill Coleman; "Froggy Bottom," with vocals by Josh White and Jimmy Butts; and "The Minute Man" with vocals by Josh White. To be released on Asch records. Pix by Morgan Smith.

Sketch of Mary Lou Williams by David Stone Martin. (Reproduced courtesy of the Estate of David Stone Martin)

supporter of the nascent bebop movement and younger players such as Thelonious Monk. Always a deeply spiritual person, she converted to Catholicism in the 1950s and for a while retired from jazz performance. She returned to touring in the 1970s (and continued to play until her death) and was named a professor of music at Duke University in the 1980s.

Williams recorded piano solos and in small group settings for Asch in the 1940s. Like his folk sessions of the time, the music has a spontaneity and charm that makes up for the occasional missed note or technical problem. As Johnson did with *Yamekraw*, Williams recorded a small trio version of her extended work *Zodiac Suite* in 1945; that same year, Café Society's owner, Barney Josephson, underwrote a performance of the work by an eighteen-piece orchestra, its only full-scale performance in its original form.

Thanks to her friendship with Asch and the loose atmosphere at his sessions, Williams also turned up on various other recordings that he made, accompanying blues singers Nora Lee King and her fellow Café Society star Josh White on a few sides. On her own recordings, Williams felt free to experiment, as she recorded both her own works and her unique arrangements of standards. As she said, "Moe would turn on the tapes, go downstairs, and leave us alone." He never interfered with her playing.

Mary Lou was important to Asch for another reason: early on, she brought into his orbit the artist-illustrator David Stone Martin. Martin was a self-taught illustrator who had worked in the Depression years on several Works Project Administration (WPA) projects, and then settled in New York City around 1940, where he met artist Ben Shahn. His work was greatly influenced by Shahn's in both its political content and its use of line and color. Martin lived close to Café Society and became a regular at the club, sketching the many musicians who worked there, including Williams. She liked his work and recommended that Asch use Martin to illustrate an album of her piano solos. Asch subsequently made Martin his prime cover artist for dozens of albums.

Norman Granz and *Jazz at the Philharmonic*

Cover of the first *Jazz at the Philharmonic* album drawn by David Stone Martin; the drawing of the trumpeter became a symbol for the Festival through the 1950s. (Courtesy of the BenCar Archives)

Asch's most famous jazz releases of the 1940s were not made at his own studios. They came about through serendipity and his openness to new ideas. In Los Angeles, a young jazz enthusiast and concert promoter, Norman Granz, organized a unique concert at the city's Philharmonic Hall in 1944. Called "Jazz at the Philharmonic," it was the beginning of an annual concert series—and eventually world tours—that brought together for informal onstage jam sessions musicians who normally did not perform together. The concert was recorded for Armed Forces Radio broadcast, and Granz tried to attract interest from a major label. However, at the time, issuing live recordings with audience noise, applause, and spoken introductions was unheard of, not to mention the fact that these were not studio-quality recordings.

A close friend of Moe's was record distributor George Mendelssohn, a Hungarian refugee who settled in the United States just before World War II. Mendelssohn had distributed Asch's records and quickly became close friends with him. Asch introduced Mendelssohn to jazz, and the two sometimes visited Café Society Downtown together to hear James P. Johnson or Mary Lou Williams. In 1945, Mendelssohn was laying the groundwork for starting a classical label, and traveled to Los Angeles to scout out material. He also kept his eyes open for good jazz recordings, knowing that Asch might be interested. He was directed to Granz by a local record distributor.

Mendelssohn recounts that Granz was so broke at the time that he couldn't afford to keep his telephone going:

> Norman Granz's sitting on the floor; he had absolutely no furniture, his telephone was blocked for all outgoing calls . . . He said, "George, I have three items. I believe in them, listen to them, they're yours if you can send me $2000." I did. Came back to New York and I wired him $2000, and I got the first, second, and third [discs] of *Jazz at the Philharmonic*. . . . Now I made up my mind to have classics, so I [wasn't interested in issuing this material myself]. So I said to Moe, "How about you taking it?" Moe said, "I don't have $2000." "All right, you'll pay me back eventually."

Asch recognized that these recordings documented a unique event, and entered into a partnership with Granz to distribute them. Asch asked the artist David Stone Martin to create the cover art and special label—featuring a drawing of a trumpeter—for the series. However, as many others would too, Granz found it difficult to collect his portion of the profits from Asch. By 1948, Granz took back the master recordings to start his own jazz label, which eventually became Verve Records. Although he was sorry to lose these best-selling records, Asch was most annoyed that Granz also took with him David Stone Martin, who would create dozens of distinctive album covers for Verve and other jazz labels through the 1950s. Still, he could not blame the young promoter for going out on his own.

FREDERIC RAMSEY'S SEARCH FOR THE ROOTS OF JAZZ

As many more jazz labels cropped up in New York in the late 1940s and early 1950s—including Alfred Lion's Blue Note, Bill Grauer's Riverside, and Bob Weinstock's Prestige—Asch could no longer compete for talent. His interest had always been in older styles rather than contemporary jazz anyway, so it's not surprising that his first jazz project for Folkways was an ambitious one: an eleven-volume history of jazz, with songs to be selected by Frederic Ramsey Jr. Beginning in 1950, the albums featured historic commercial recordings by major jazz artists, most of which were no longer available on 78 or LP from the original labels. The idea of recovering these recordings for a new generation was a fresh one, part of Asch's belief that all recordings should be available for listeners, not just those that were commercially successful or maintained by the big labels. It would also spawn the idea that Asch was a musical "pirate," profiting off material produced by others (see Chapter 4). Nonetheless, both major labels and independents would quickly jump on the idea of reissuing classic 78s on LP, inspired by Asch's initial experiments.

Ramsey used the set not only to establish a list of great pieces and master performers but also as a way of organizing jazz history. The notion of different eras of jazz was just beginning to form, and the set gave body to these eras in its own organization. The set also established certain genres—such as jazz piano—that ran across eras. Ramsey also freely mixed recordings by black and white bands, showing the interplay between the races that was part of his democratic vision of jazz.

Ramsey received a Guggenheim Foundation fellowship to travel through the South in 1954 to research the roots of jazz music, recording as many traditional singers and bands as he could locate. Helped by other scholars and the musicians he met, Ramsey took a peripatetic route from the upper South through Georgia, Alabama, Mississippi, and finally to New Orleans. The result was the landmark ten-LP set *Music of the South*, issued by Folkways literally as quickly

TOP: Fred Ramsey's wife, Amelia, designed the first full cover for the *Jazz* series.

BOTTOM: Ronald Clyne redesigned the *Jazz* series covers to create this striking type treatment. Each volume had the same cover with a different background color.

as Ramsey could edit the tapes, in 1955 and 1956. One of Ramsey's most important finds of this trip was a country songster named Horace Sprott. Sprott sang traditional field hollers, blues, and play party songs in what Ramsey described as "a 'straining voice.' A high degree of personal feeling, considerable skill in handling his voice, and a remarkable memory. . . . It is the old way, the country way, the way they had it before 'they had the time increasin',' as he tells us."

Ramsey wrote a remarkable series of letters to Asch as he gathered the material that would go into the record series. They offer on-the-spot reports about how he uncovered the artists, as well as his initial reaction to them. On April 11, 1954, he reported from Greensboro, Alabama, his first encounter with Sprott:

> I traced Horace down to a really remote spot in the lowlands, way out in the Pinetucky beat. He was working with two other fellows and a mule, chopping down pine trees, trimming and sawing them; the driver was cussing the mule. As I came on them in the woods, it seemed the sounds of their work, and of the birds and the trees, were worth recording. So I sat the Magnamite [a portable tape machine] down in the bush, and set it going. Just about then, they chopped down a tree, and it made a wonderful short sequence.
>
> Saturday morning was the big day. I went out early and gathered Horace, and he took me to Mattie Daniels' cabin where they had electricity. I set up the [recording equipment]. Horace started off with a spiritual, and right

"There were many men like [Horace] Sprott . . . [who] passed from one hard time to another, never forgetting the song. . . . This poetry, and the music that went with it, was their heritage and their trust."
—Frederic Ramsey Jr.

Horace Sprott and his family on their farm. (Photo by Frederic Ramsey Jr.)

away I began to feel better. He's a fine singer, with a deep, grainy voice. As the morning went on, over 30 people squeezed into the one tiny room. Then Horace had a beer, and he started in on a really beautiful blues—"Smoke Like Lightning"—using the false, or high voice . . . He called it one of "them old cornfield songs." Then we were off. Some buck dancers came in, and one of them started a dance right in the middle of the cabin floor. Well, the tape recorder was set up on an ironing board, and the floor boards were real springy, and in 2 seconds everyone in the room was clapping and tapping, and the tape machine was jumping up and down with every beat. I had to lean all my weight on it to keep it down—I never thought it would go on working.

On May 9, Ramsey raved to Asch about his final session with Sprott, proclaiming the singer to be "as significant to American folksong as was Leadbelly." Ramsey hoped to be able to raise funds for a New York concert to introduce Sprott to a larger audience, but apparently this never occurred.

The excitement of recording in the field—and being able to capture a real evening of music as it unfolded—is vividly captured in Ramsey's correspondence. On April 19, he described his working methods and how they captured the way the music really sounded:

I am recording outdoors, putting the mike in front of the porch. Singers sit up there and perform out at it. In the open fields, or when there are woods, when a singer really gets going, there's a natural echo that really gives the feeling of the open country. This is really the way the music actually sounds. . . . Of course, at a shindig, you get all sorts of background noises—children, roosters (you can add Alabama to your rooster collection, I've some good ones), cows, and sometimes a car. But I'm recording everything absolutely realistically, with no attempt to "dampen out" the extraneous sounds.

SAM CHARTERS: NEW ORLEANS JAZZ AND RAGTIME

In the mid-1950s, Fred Ramsey introduced Asch to a younger jazz scholar who would become one of his key collaborators: Samuel B. Charters. Initially interested in New Orleans jazz and its antecedents, Charters would produce dozens of albums for Folkways of early jazz and blues performers (see Chapter 6). In many cases, these recordings introduced an artist to the folk revival audience, serving as a stepping-stone to performance opportunities and more lucrative recording arrangements with other labels. Charters shared Asch's love of documenting passing styles. Among his initial releases were recordings of New Orleans brass and parade bands.

In 1956, Ramsey wrote the introductory notes for Charters' first Folkways release, a recording of the Six and Seven-Eighths String Band from New Orleans. The band formed in the early teens at Tulane University, and its members were young white students who were emulating the jazz sounds that were bursting all across the city. Although black string bands were known in and around the city, the more formal white bands grew out of university banjo and mandolin clubs. When Charters recorded the band in the 1950s, it was led by a New Orleans doctor named Edmond Souchon and featured mandolin, guitar, steel guitar, and bass. Its repertoire ranged from light classical and pop material to jazz-flavored material drawn from the New Orleans repertory. Charters correctly notes that this style of string band music did not predate jazz so much as exist side by side with it, a fact that is often overlooked by historians who like to make neat chronologies showing how one musical style developed out of another.

Charters followed this release with several other albums of traditional New Orleans bands, notably an LP of music by the Eureka Brass Band, originally

"We were literally surrounded by bands. Never a day went by without either a parade or a funeral and with these came those wonderful marching bands."
—Edmond Souchon, leader of the Six and Seven-Eighths String Band

Eureka Brass Band, 1954. (Photo by Sam Charters)

Sam Charters carries the tuba with the Eureka Brass Band, 1959. (Photo by Ann Charters)

formed in the 1920s. Like most of the bands, it was associated with one of the fraternal lodges that provided assistance and a meeting place for their membership. One of the last of the parade bands, the group survived the Depression and World War II, which had decimated earlier bands. They maintained the same repertory—a mix of hymns and dirges appropriate for funeral processions, popular songs, and jazz-like instrumentals—that had been a staple of New Orleans bands since the turn of the century. Charters recorded them in their lodge headquarters, which he described as a "ramshackle frame building" where the band would rehearse and gather on Sunday afternoons for their weekly parades.

Sam Charters' wife, Ann, brought a new interest to the Folkways label: ragtime piano. Long before the ragtime revival of the mid-1970s, Charters recorded a collection of classic rags herself and, along with her husband, helped locate one of the key figures of the ragtime era, Joseph F. Lamb. Among the legendary group that also included Scott Joplin, Arthur Marshall, and James Scott, Lamb was the only white pianist-composer to write "classic" ragtime pieces. Modeled on the popular four-part marches of the day, these compositions were scored and meant to be played as serious compositions, not in the "rinky-tink" style of barroom pianists.

Lamb was a particularly interesting figure because he came from a middle-class background, raised just outside of New York City in the well-to-do suburb of Montclair, New Jersey. Always an enlightened town, Montclair boasted a large "colored" population, but it was still unusual for a son of one of its professional white families to be aware—let alone in awe—of a black musical style such as ragtime. Ragtime had about it the whiff of bawdy houses and barroom brawls; Joplin struggled to escape this negative image throughout his career, and certainly Lamb's family wouldn't have approved of his interest in this musical style. Nonetheless, Lamb managed to meet Joplin around 1906–7 and play him one of his own compositions, "Sensation."

Like many Folkways releases, Lamb's album was made under less-than-ideal circumstances—in his front parlor, while the normal family activities of cooking and cleaning went on. Unlike the showy commercial pianists of the ragtime revival—such as Knocky Parker—Lamb's playing was graceful and stately. The record captures Lamb's playing and his unique speaking voice—another remnant of earlier times—as he tells the story of how he first met Joplin and how this meeting transformed his life. Sadly, Joseph Francis Lamb died at his home in Brooklyn a little over a year after making these recordings.

In the liner notes, Charters tells in detail how he found and recorded Lamb:

[Brooklyn's] East Twenty-First Street . . . is in a substantial, middle class neighborhood not far from Coney Island. The houses are crowded together along the sidewalk, most of them two story, but there are small yards and trees; so it's a pleasant street to walk along. . . . The neighbors who have lived near the Lambs for nearly forty years know Joe as a sincere, friendly man, busy with his family. . . .

[But] there had been another side to Joe's life—a side that most of his neighbors in Brooklyn didn't know anything about. Between 1908 and 1919 Joe Lamb had written some of the most brilliant ragtime compositions published in America. . . . Sometimes Joe would play the piano for friends in Brooklyn and sometimes the neighbors would hear him working over a new composition, but his family and his children took most of his time. In the Twenties and the Thirties ragtime seemed to have been almost forgotten. Joe didn't even talk about his years as a composer. He kept copies of his rags in the piano bench, but they were piled in with a lot of other music and he didn't play them regularly. . . .

Since then Joe has had occasional visits from young enthusiasts, he has been playing again. . . . Even the neighbors have heard most of his rags. Until he began the long hours of practice that went into this recording the only recording he had ever done of himself was a tape he had made of several of his newer rags. He hasn't written them down, and he was afraid he might forget them if he didn't get them recorded. . . .

Joe's hearing difficulty made it very difficult for him to hear the music clearly, but he felt that it was very important to have the recording finished and he worked very hard during the weeks it took to get the final versions of his rags. . . . Joe not only did not improvise when he was playing, he played from the music to be sure of every note. His rhythm was almost classical in style, with the gentle glide of dance music rather than the exhibitionist flurry of the vaudeville ragtime that is still popular. After nearly sixty years of playing and writing ragtime, Joe still found it as fresh and exciting as ever.

Sometimes sitting over dinner it was hard to remember that the elderly man sitting beside me was Joe Lamb. Sometimes we talked about ragtime, but usually it was about the grandchildren or about people he had known during his life. . . . Joe said of himself, "I didn't want to be in the music business—I hardly met any musicians except Scott Joplin—I wanted to keep my music in my private life. I didn't want to make any money on my things. I only wanted to see them published because my dream was to be a great ragtime composer."

There have been few men who have so fully realized their dreams as Joe Lamb.

"Maybe You Can Do Something with This":
Dave Jasen and Recovering the Legacy

By the early 1970s, the jazz recordings that Asch made at the beginning of his career were known primarily to collectors and enthusiasts, particularly those interested in the early development of jazz piano. But the general jazz listener was unaware that great jazz players had recorded for Asch, and the recordings were rarely heard. Plus there were piles of unissued acetates among Asch's collection that remained to be discovered.

Asch didn't give this older material much thought until around 1969–70, when he was temporarily unable to issue recordings under the Folkways name due to unresolved issues around the distribution deal he had made. Reviving the Asch label naturally led him to recall his very first recordings for Asch and Disc. Old friends and collaborators Charles Edward Smith and Sam Charters were called on to cull through some of this material for two 2-LP sets, called *The Asch Recordings*, focusing on the jazz, blues, and folk material that was recorded in the 1940s.

However, it took a new collaborator to unearth much of the unissued and forgotten jazz material in the Asch vaults. Argumentative, burly, and gruff, Dave Jasen was every bit a match for the often argumentative, burly, and gruff Asch. Jasen was a member of a loose-knit fraternity of early jazz and blues record collectors who met for regular dinners in New York City. Among them were Nick Perls, the son of an art dealer who used his inheritance to start Yazoo Records, the most important early blues reissue label of the 1960s and 1970s; Bernard Klatzko, another blues enthusiast who founded the short-lived Herwin label; Carl Seltzer, friend of Eubie Blake, who managed the pianist's later career and recordings; and Richard Nevins, a collector with far-flung tastes who now runs Shanachie Records. Jasen had collaborated with Nick Perls on a few reissues of early ragtime 78 recordings; however, Perls could only issue a few albums of this material, and Jasen knew he had enough material for dozens more. Perls was happy to introduce him to Moe Asch.

The year 1974 was an ideal time to begin a ragtime reissue program. It was one year after the hit film *The Sting* had made Scott Joplin's "The Entertainer" a major hit. Plus, classical pianist and scholar Joshua Rifkin had just issued the first modern collection of recordings of Joplin's major works, which became a surprise best-seller. Jasen owned hundreds of 78s of this material; Asch had his RBF series (the initials stood for "Record, Book, and Film") dedicated to reissuing early material. It was a match made in ragtime heaven, and one project happily followed another.

Jasen would gather the 78s, take them to Nick Perls for remastering (he wouldn't trust his valuable originals to just anyone, and he knew that Asch did not have a specialist in 78 mastering), type up the notes on his trusty 1950s-era Royal typewriter, and submit everything to Asch in a matter of weeks. After the first successful release, Asch was quick to ask, "What's next?" as soon as Jasen completed a project.

But the real prize for Jasen was Asch's own recordings. Knowing that Asch was not particularly forthcoming, Jasen waited patiently for an opportunity to ask about this material. In 1977, Jasen stopped by the Folkways offices to drop off a ragtime piano collection and, sensing an opening, asked Asch about his recordings of James P. Johnson, a hero to Jasen for his blending of ragtime and jazz piano influences. Asch went into a back room and returned with some old 78 albums and—even more tantalizing to Jasen—unissued acetates. "Maybe you can do something with these," he said to Jasen. Indeed he could. The result was an LP of issued and previously unknown recordings by the pianist, and a near carte blanche for Jasen to explore Asch's archives.

From the late 1970s through Asch's death, Jasen culled the archives to reissue or discover recordings by pianists, small combos, and vocalists who had visited the Asch studios in the 1940s. His interest was in recovering the music;

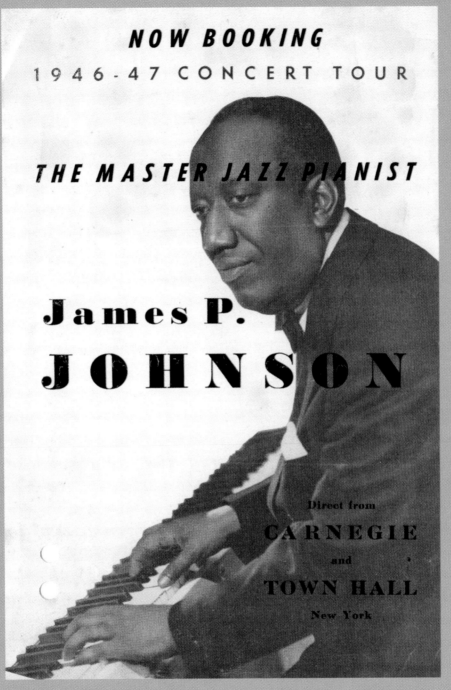

NOW BOOKING
1946-47 CONCERT TOUR

THE MASTER JAZZ PIANIST

James P.
JOHNSON

Direct from
CARNEGIE
and
TOWN HALL
New York

Publicity flyer for James P. Johnson, c. 1946.

his documentation was often brief, but the music was lovingly assembled and remastered. For Jasen—as for most of Asch's collaborators—Moe offered a perfect partner: he trusted Dave to handle the original recordings with the attention and care that they deserved, and in return he issued the albums exactly as Jasen envisioned them. After Asch died, Jasen could never find another commercial label that was willing to reissue his early recordings.

LISTEN UP!

MARY LOU WILLIAMS

Jazz Rehearsal, I • FW02292 • 1950

Mary Lou Williams • FW02843 • 1964

The History of Jazz • FW02860 • 1978

Mary Lou Williams: The Asch Recordings 1944–47
• FW02966 • 1977

Mary Lou's Mass • SFW40815 • 2005

Zodiac Suite • SFW40810 • 1995

Zoning • SFW40811 • 1995

Mary Lou Williams Presents Black Christ of the Andes
• SFW40816 • 2004

BABY DODDS

Baby Dodds Talking and Drum Solos • FW02290 • 1951

MUSIC OF THE SOUTH

Vol. 1: Country Brass Bands • FW02650 • 1955

Vol. 2: Horace Sprott, 1 • FW02651 • 1955

Vol. 3: Horace Sprott, 2 • FW02652 • 1955

Vol. 4: Horace Sprott, 3 • FW02653 • 1955

Vol. 5: Song, Play, and Dance • FW02654 • 1956

Vol. 6: Elder Songsters, 1 • FW02655 • 1956

Vol. 7: Elder Songsters, 2
• FW02656 • 1956

Vol. 8: Young Songsters
• FW02657 • 1956

Vol. 9: Song and Worship
• FW02658 • 1956

Vol. 10: Been Here and
Gone • FW02659
• 1959

SIX AND SEVEN-EIGHTHS STRING BAND

Six and Seven-Eighths String Band of New Orleans
• FW02671 • 1956

JOSEPH LAMB

Joseph Lamb: A Study
in Classic Ragtime
• FW03562 • 1960

JAMES P. JOHNSON

The Original James P.
Johnson: 1942–1945,
Piano Solos • SFW40812 • 1996

1940S JAZZ RECORDINGS REISSUED BY DAVID A. JASEN (SELECT)

Jazz Piano Greats: From Original Piano Solo Recordings
by Moses Asch,
1944–1945
• FW02852 • 1974

Dixieland of the Forties
• FW02853 • 1978

Jazz Violin of the Forties
• FW02854 • 1981

WOODY GUTHRIE

THIS LAND IS YOUR LAND
THE ASCH RECORDINGS VOL. 1

Smithsonian Folkways

FOLKWAYS RECORDS FA 2454

THE RAINBOW QUEST
PETE SEEGER

lead belly sings for children

Smithsonian Folkways

Chapter 3

LASTING FRIENDSHIPS

Lead Belly, Woody Guthrie, and Pete Seeger

When Moses Asch founded his tiny record label in 1940, he began a nearly five-decade odyssey of documenting the world of sound. Little could he have known that within the next five years he would forge relationships with three of the most important folk performers of the time: Lead Belly, Woody Guthrie, and Pete Seeger. In each case, Asch played a key role in shaping their careers, as a patron, gadfly, banker, and personal friend.

LEAD BELLY: TAKE THIS HAMMER

The story of the discovery of Lead Belly in Angola State Prison by father-and-son folklorists John and Alan Lomax in 1934 has often been told—how they heard the singer perform and provided him a job after his parole (as a driver and companion for their field work); brought him to New York, where he was an immediate sensation; and then had a falling-out with the singer, who longed for popular success and the prestige and income that came with it. After Lead Belly arrived in New York and went out on his own, he became a key figure in the nascent folk revival; his apartment on East 10th Street was often the center of impromptu sing-alongs, and many artists—including Josh White, Brownie McGhee, Sonny Terry, Woody Guthrie, and Pete Seeger—became his close collaborators and companions.

Lead Belly recording his *Last Sessions* at Fred Ramsey Jr.'s apartment. (Photo by Jim Chapelle, courtesy of the Historic New Orleans Collection, Museum/Research Center, acc. no. 2006.0257)

Lead Belly Remembered by Pete Seeger

Many memorial concerts have been staged to commemorate Lead Belly's life and music. In 1964, a hootenanny in his honor was held in New York's Town Hall, sponsored by *Sing Out!* magazine. In the program notes, Pete Seeger recalled the time in the 1940s when he, Woody Guthrie, and others played and sang with Lead Belly for New York's progressive folk audience.

I was seventeen, in New York City, when I first met Huddie Ledbetter. He was not tall—perhaps five feet seven or eight—but compactly built, and he moved with the soft grace of an athlete. He was grey-haired—in his late fifties, I'd say. Always neatly dressed. There I was, trying my best to shed my Harvard upbringing, scorning to waste money on clothes other than blue jeans. But Lead Belly always had a clean white shirt and starched collar, well-pressed suit and shined shoes. He didn't need to affect that he was a workingman. His powerful ringing voice, and his muscular hands moving like a dancer over the strings of his huge twelve-stringed guitar, his honesty and pride, showed he was a workingman.

He and his wife Martha had a little flat on the lower east side. Woody Guthrie and I visited him often there, and made music together with him, till the neighbors complained of the noise. I was proud that he accepted me. Perhaps he wondered at my earnestness, trying to learn folk music. . . .

He was an expert at country-style buck-and-wing clog dancing. In one number he would imitate the gait of all the women of Shreveport—high and low. And another dance accompanied the story of a duck hunter. His guitar became the gun. Pow!

He'd sometimes get on a rhyming kick. For a couple hours on end every sentence that came out of his mouth was rhymed. Sitting in the car, on our way to bookings, he'd go on fanciful flights of poetry and imagination.

Huddie! How we miss you. Sometimes audiences couldn't understand your Louisiana accent. Sometimes young people thought your style of music was old-fashioned. But you were always honestly yourself, never trying to pretend you were someone else, never trying to be a chameleon for the fashions of the day.

He was not the cleverest guitar player; he didn't try and play the fanciest chords, the trickiest progressions, or the fastest number of notes. Rather, the notes he played were powerful and meaningful. . . .

Looking back, I think that the most important thing I learned from him was the straight-forward approach, the direct honesty. He bequeathed to us also, it is true, a couple hundred of the best songs any of us will ever know. I wish people would stop trying to imitate his accent, and rather learn from his subtle simplicity, and his powerful pride.

Well, one year, in 1949, he started having to use a cane to go on stage. His voice, always soft and husky when speaking, still rang out high on the melodies, but his hands grew stiffer and less certain on the guitar. Then one day he was gone, and we were left with regrets that we had not treasured him more.

Lead Belly and his wife, Martha Promise, in their East Village apartment, c. 1948. (Photo by Jim Chapelle, courtesy of the Frank Driggs Collection)

Lead Belly's recording career in the 1930s had been sporadic and frustrating. Alan Lomax had tried to help by arranging sessions at Columbia's and Victor's blues subsidiary labels; the Victor sessions paired him with the modern harmonizers the Golden Gate Quartet, who didn't quite know what to make of his rough-hewn country style. Attempts to market him as a modern blues performer failed, and the big labels didn't know how to reach the growing folk market.

Lead Belly was brought to Asch's attention early in his recording career via a contact he had made in the 1930s. Asch had overseen the sound for the garment workers' famous revue *Pins and Needles*, and the show's producer, Sy Rady, raved to Asch about the twelve-string guitarist. From the moment Asch met Lead Belly, he was impressed; unlike the comic-book depiction of the singer in the newspapers as a "blood-soaked balladeer," Lead Belly was a soft-spoken, immaculately dressed man and a serious musician. His vast repertoire from years of entertaining ranged from field hollers to spirituals to blues and pop songs. Asch had an immediate rapport and sympathy for Lead Belly, who often had been caricatured by the media—and even by some folk fans.

Even the progressive Musicraft label gave its Lead Belly album the rather racy title *Negro Sinful Songs*, although exactly how "Go Down Old Hannah" and "The Gallis Pole" (as it is titled on the 78) reeked with "sin" is unclear. The notes to the album continue the salacious title theme, stating that "Lead Belly early on decided that he preferred frankness, flesh, and the devil to sanctimoniousness without a guitar." This kind of pulp description of a serious artist galled those who valued Lead Belly's musicianship.

However, Asch recognized Lead Belly's deep sense of self-pride and dignity, as he recalled to Izzy Young in the early 1970s:

Cover of *Negro Sinful Songs*, released by Musicraft Records. (Courtesy of the BenCar Archives)

Lead Belly was the most formal human being that ever existed. His clothing was always the best, pressed the best. His shoes were $60 shoes in those days, when he may not have had much money to come home with. He had to have a cane. He treated himself as a noble person. And when he recorded, knowing that this was for people to understand what he stood for, he recorded in exactly that same way. He became a human being who expressed himself in a certain fashion.

Cover of *Work Songs*, Asch's first Lead Belly release, 1941.

When Lead Belly appeared in a solo concert at New York's Town Hall in 1948, he wore a tuxedo onstage—not the overalls that John Lomax had once presented him in.

In January 1941, Lead Belly made his first recordings for Asch, a selection of work songs and spirituals. Sales were not brisk and reviews were scanty, although the *New York Times* cited the album among a grab bag of notable "1942 recordings [that are] not easily classified"—including an album of American bird songs.

In fall 1941, Asch asked Lead Belly to record an album of children's songs—a radical idea, considering Lead Belly was a twice-convicted felon. The recordings were successful enough that New York's Metropolitan Museum of Art invited the singer to give a children's concert. As Asch recalled in 1960:

> "In the early days at Asch you knew Lead Belly by that powerful twelve-string guitar, the crease in his pin-stripe suit and the shine on his shoes."
> —Charles Edward Smith

[The concert] was jam-packed, children all over the place, frantic parents. But the moment Lead Belly started to play and sing, the audience hushed, the children grouped around him as though it was grandfather singing for them, some sang with him, others danced, parents were bewitched.

Unlike the *Work Songs* set, the children's set sold (relatively) well, underscoring for Asch the importance of the children's market.

Typical of the way he treated artists who he admired, Asch often advanced Lead Belly small amounts of money—$20 here, $50 there—with little attempt to reconcile these "advances" against income made from recordings. Because Lead Belly recorded far more songs than were released at the time, and also participated in hootenanny-like sessions with several performers, it was probably impossible to keep track of exactly what he was owed. This eventually led the singer to complain about lack of compensation. In a testy exchange of letters, Asch argued that in fact he had over-paid the singer—which may have been true based on actual sales of discs to that date. Eventually, the Lead Belly recordings would be an extremely valuable part of the Folkways catalog, so the small investment that Asch made at the time in the singer was amply repaid.

Lead Belly serenades a group of children, c. 1943. (Courtesy of the Frank Driggs Archives)

Through this period, Lead Belly was a regular performer at Café Society and, later, newer clubs such as the Village Vanguard. He attracted a devoted following among the left-leaning crowd who frequented these spots. Frederic Ramsey described a typical club date for the British fan magazine *Jazz Music* in 1946:

His guitar snaps around into position as he faces his audience. He places his foot on a chair, tunes the 12 strings. While he tunes, fingering lightly, running through "Easy, Mr. Tom," he talks to his audience. "Good evenin' ladies an' gentlemen . . ." His eyes roam around the silent room, picking out friends. "Little girl over there in the red dress, she wants a reques'—." The fingers pluck easily, but he's not ready yet. He smiles, and his face shines . . . as the light picks up the rich, beautiful pigment of his skin. "—an' if it's a request, then you know that's best . . . Now this is the 'Rock Island Line.'"

Not all of the audience appreciated Lead Belly's talents. For many, the Vanguard was a place to meet and gossip about the latest left-wing news, and Lead Belly's performance merely provided a pleasant soundtrack for drinking. Recalled Mike Alegria, a fan who befriended Lead Belly:

Huddie's effect on New York audiences varies greatly. At times the entire place is silent while he sings and on the choruses of his "group" songs everybody joins in with tremendous gusto . . . [one] song that always got a huge response from [the] audience was "Irene," which everyone got a kick out of singing with him.

On the other hand, at times he has no effect on the audience whatsoever. In some instances where the crowd is especially uninterested and overly drunk, the talking and general noise is so loud he can't be heard at all. Nobody seems the least bit interested in whether he sings or what he's singing about.

Apparently, the life of a folksinger was no easier in this fondly recalled "golden age" than it is today.

From the mid-1940s, Frederic Ramsey was one of the most vocal champions of the singer. Toward the end of the 1940s, as the signs of Lou Gehrig's disease—which would take the singer's life—were beginning to manifest themselves, Ramsey held several marathon sessions at his apartment, armed with a relatively new machine: a tape recorder. Thanks to this new technology, the singer was not limited to the three minutes or so that could be recorded on a 78 rpm disc. This would be his last significant recording session.

Ramsey realized that the new technology of magnetic tape and the LP format would finally offer the opportunity to record Lead Belly's repertoire along with his own comments about these songs in a coherent way. As he said in an article in *High Fidelity* about the recording of *Last Sessions*: "No longer would each separate selection have to be cut on a disc that, at its longest, could play only five minutes . . . No longer would artist and recorder have to labor over exact timing for each selection. And if Lead Belly wanted to talk between his selections, we could leave the microphone open and pick that up, too." Lead Belly shared Ramsey's enthusiasm once he heard the initial takes. "Man, you got something there," Ramsey reports he said. "You can just let that thing run. Now let's try some more."

Lead Belly loved to perform, so the recording sessions at Ramsey's apartment went very easily, with very few breaks, as Ramsey later recalled:

You couldn't stop that guy from performing. I mean, you could have paid him nothing, and he'd come there and have a good time, and he would play. We wouldn't do that, but some people did. We *were* friends, and Lead Belly came and wanted to play, we always saw that he not only had whatever he wanted to drink or should drink and also would pay him something. . . .

I had just gotten new equipment, and it had always been a dream to record Lead Belly in an informal atmosphere, not in a studio, and with friends around. . . . He followed a kind of stream of preference of his own things, one suggesting another. And he could go on forever. This was also typical of Lead Belly when he played for a group of friends . . . he was really turned on by the fact that he could play any darn thing that came into his mind . . . I felt that was very creative.

Lead Belly's disease caught up with him and he passed away in late 1949. Ironically, six months later the Weavers had a number one hit with his song "Goodnight Irene." Suddenly, Ramsey's tapes were of interest to major record labels, who wanted to extract the songs from them. Ramsey felt the tapes should be kept intact, as an important document of the singer's life and repertory; as he said:

Frederic Ramsey Jr. (center) and Lead Belly (left) listen to a playback of the *Last Sessions* tapes in Ramsey's apartment, 1948. (Photo by Jim Chapelle, courtesy of the Historic New Orleans Collection, Museum/ Research Center, acc. no. 2006.0257)

> Several [record companies] wanted to bring out part, or some of the material that Lead Belly had recorded on tape, but not one of the major companies cared to preserve the sequence which is so vital a part of the feeling of these recordings. The only person in the entire record industry who would go along with this idea was Mr. Moe Asch. . . . But in 1948, when the tapes were made, he had a very small list, and had to proceed with caution.

It wasn't until 1952 that Asch felt he had the wherewithal to take on the project. On first examining the tapes, however, he realized he'd have to issue six LPs of the normal twenty minutes or so per side to contain all of the material. Sensitive to getting this important material to the public, Asch came up with a way of fitting an extra ten minutes per side by eliminating "tracks" between songs and tightening the space between the grooves. *Lead Belly's Last Sessions* appeared in two 2-disc sets in 1953. The original cover simply had a dramatic photograph of the singer's face, eyes closed, with no title or indication of who was performing. (Later issues had a box added that gave this information.)

Woody Guthrie, c. 1942.
(Courtesy of the Frank Driggs
Archives)

WOODY GUTHRIE: THIS LAND IS YOUR LAND

Unlike the well-dressed, large-framed Lead Belly, Woody Guthrie looked like a wiry hobo. As previously noted, when he first appeared at the Asch studios, he announced, "I'm Woody Guthrie," and Asch supposedly grunted in reply, "So what?" Yet from nearly the start, Asch recognized a quality in Guthrie that few others saw. Beneath the rough-hewn exterior was a man of considerable intellect; behind the aw-shucks Okie accent and I'm-just-a-hillbilly act, Guthrie was well educated, sensitive, and unusually gifted as a poet, artist, and performer. And—best of all—he was full of energy, prolifically turning out songs, writings, and illustrations in a seemingly endless stream. For example, while on leave from the merchant marines in 1944, Guthrie and his wartime pal Cisco Houston cut some 160 sides, many of which went unissued for decades.

Asch took Guthrie under his wing, nurturing his talents, suggesting topics, and even paying him to review all of his other releases. Guthrie took the job seriously, writing lengthy correspondence about each set, including the classical recordings that at the time Asch was licensing from the Soviet Union. Guthrie was said to have particularly enjoyed Prokofiev, and played the record incessantly around his Brooklyn home.

Many years later, in 1974, Guy Logsdon asked Moses Asch about his relationship with Guthrie. Usually taciturn, Asch gave his longest statement about Guthrie's talent and why he was well suited to nurture it:

Woody wasn't anxious to meet recording people; he was anxious to meet people he could communicate with. He was very uncommunicative; he was very anti-social. He didn't want to be bothered by society or people. I guess his mind was constantly working like a poet . . . He was not interested in writing for the sake of publishing.

One day, Woody comes in and squats himself on the floor. He squats himself before the office door and just sits there—very wild hair, clean shaven, and clothing one would associate with a Western person. . . . He started to talk—a person of broad English, and then you wonder if that was a put-on. When he lets himself go, his English becomes more common English, with Western or Oklahoman accents. And that's when I know he's not putting on or making fun. If you listen to those Library of Congress recordings, you can hear all the put-on he wanted to give Alan Lomax. This is the actor acting out the role of the folk singer from Oklahoma.

With me, he wasn't at all that way. He spoke without any put-on; he spoke straight. I began to realize . . . that this was a very serious . . . and . . . articulate person. The simplicity of his speech was so deep that you start to remind yourself of Walt Whitman. The words were clear, simple, but the meanings were deep and very well thought out and philosophized. So we became friends. . . .

He did two things for me. He wrote the most important critiques of my records that I ever had. He would spend a whole page or two pages of typed

> "Woody [Guthrie] would come to the studio, fall down on the floor, wild hair and everything . . . full of jokes and everything else. Get him in front of a microphone . . . his style was free, but his presentation was formal. You knew that the man had a statement to make, and he made it."
>
> —Moses Asch

Cover of Woody Guthrie's first Asch 78 album, drawn by Guthrie himself.

From left, Lee Hays, Burl Ives, Cisco Houston, and Woody Guthrie rehearse for a radio broadcast. (Copyright Woody Guthrie Publications, Inc. Used by permission)

observations of the contents, whether it was Greek or Indonesian or African or American folk; he would sit down and study the recordings that I issued and write me a critique. The other area was that we would sit together and plan projects. Like authors, he would be interested in ideas from others. He planned at least forty different albums, and he would even put thirty titles for each of the forty albums.

Asch recognized that Guthrie was serious about his art. He also realized very quickly that Woody knew exactly what he wanted to achieve in each recording session, and quickly adjusted his work style to accommodate him. He told Izzy Young:

Woody was using me like a pen, I was just an instrument. And once we had Woody set in front of a mic, he knew exactly what the guitar was going to sound like, what he was going to sound like. He was using the instrument for himself; all I was doing was handling the machine.

Asch was more than willing to be the "machine" that captured Woody's creative spark. This openness and sympathy to the artist's vision was striking at a time when most recording sessions were run by the clock and little was done to make the artist feel comfortable or in control.

One of Guthrie's closest associates in the war years was guitarist-singer Cisco Houston. Born in Delaware, Houston was raised from age two in Southern California. In 1932, at the height of the Depression, his father died, and Houston began "rambling," working odd jobs and entertaining with his guitar. In the late 1930s, he was introduced to Woody Guthrie—who had come to California to escape the poverty and dust storms of his home state of Oklahoma—through actor Will Geer, and the two began performing together. Houston came east and in 1940 enlisted in the merchant marine, where he was soon joined by his close friend Guthrie.

In April 1944, when the two were on leave in New York City, Guthrie and Houston worked the Eighth Avenue bars, playing for tips. Before hitting the bars, they visited Asch at his studios, and over a series of days recorded dozens of songs, including Guthrie originals and traditional folk songs and Western ballads. This was Guthrie's most concentrated period of recording in his life, and thanks to his easy friendship with Houston, the sessions overall have a relaxed feeling of two buddies swapping songs (and competing with each other).

One of the projects that Asch suggested to Guthrie was to write a series of songs that would tell the story of Sacco and Vanzetti, the famous labor activists who were the victims of anti-union and anti-Communist feelings following World War I. In 1945, Asch commissioned the songs, and Guthrie struggled for the next two years to produce material he felt would capture both the history and meaning of the famous 1920 trial. Guthrie had hoped to complete the work in time to be recorded for the Christmas season of 1946, but he didn't feel the songs were finished yet. Asch hoped to inspire the singer by underwriting a trip for him and Cisco Houston to Boston, so he could absorb the atmosphere of the city and find out more about the events leading up to the trial. In fall 1947, the results were finally committed to acetate disc; ironically, Asch soon went bankrupt, and the recordings were not issued until 1960.

Guthrie was a talented and playful artist. This quick watercolor sketch was probably a design for a song sheet or record sleeve for one of his children's songs. (Copyright Woody Guthrie Publications, Inc. Used by permission)

The Dust Bowl Ballads

Thanks to his Oklahoma heritage, Guthrie is best known for his association with the devastating dust storms of the 1930s that led tens of thousands of Okies to leave home in search of a better living in California. However, Guthrie's two-album set *Dust Bowl Ballads*, originally issued by RCA Victor in 1940, was directly inspired not by personal experience but by the film of a best-selling novel, John Steinbeck's *Grapes of Wrath*. Guthrie correctly felt that these songs—including "Dusty Old Dust (So Long, It's Been Good to Know Yuh)," "Tom Joad," "Do Re Mi," and "I Ain't Got No Home"—were among his best, so it was devastating to him when Victor allowed the records to go out of print in the late 1940s.

Building on the fame of the original set, in 1946 Moses Asch issued *Ballads from the Dust Bowl*, which included another Guthrie classic, "Pastures of Plenty." Soon after, Guthrie wrote a letter to Asch and his assistant, Marian Distler, with praise and anxiety about how it would be received:

> dear moe: asch's crashes,
>
> > dear marian, distler's discs,
>
> > I HAVE LISTENED to the album, BALLADS FROM THE DUST BOWL, and I like the cover better than I thought I did. I think this cover will look better to the customer on the shelf or in a window than it does to me. . . .
>
> THE LETTER AND WORDS TO THE SONGS on the inside front cover are too small to read. It is like hunting back into the archives of folk songs [at the Library of Congress] for something that is right there in front of you. . . . But I know that it takes practice to get very good at anything and even after you get good it takes money. . . .
>
> > I guess I can criticize other folks records lots plainer than I can my own. I would for this and similar reasons get a big kick out of looking at all comments favorable and not so favorable that you stir up with Ballads from The Dustbowl.

Still, Guthrie wished he could get Victor to reissue his original Dust Bowl songs, so he wrote the label in 1948. He received a curt reply saying that Victor could not reissue them at this time, due to lack of commercial interest. Using this as a "release," he asked Asch to put them out on Folkways, and Asch—who believed that this major corporation had no right to deny the people the right to hear these songs—agreed to do so. The album was issued in 1950 under the name *Talking Dust Bowl*. (See Chapter 4 for a further discussion of Asch's fight with RCA over this material.)

Guthrie's liner notes made it clear that he viewed the songs to be just as relevant in postwar America—when the Depression was quickly fading from memory—as they had been when he wrote them.

> I've lived in these dust storms just about all of my life. (I mean, I tried to live). I met millions of good folks trying to hang on and to stay alive with the dust cutting down every hope. I am made out of this dust and out of this fast wind and I know that I'm going to wind out on top of both of them if only my government and my office holder will help me.
>
> > I wrote up these eight songs here to try to show you how it is to live under the wild and windy actions of the great dust storms that ride in and out and up and down.
>
> > That old dustbowl is still there, and that high dirt wind is still there. The government didn't fix that and Congress couldn't put a stop to it. Nobody tried very hard.
>
> > That's why FOLKWAYS is putting out these BALLADS FROM THE DUSTBOWL, to let you listen to these songs and to ask your own heart what kind of work you can do to help all of the refugees which you hear of in this Album.
>
> > Woody Guthrie

Guthrie's relations with Moe soured in the later 1940s when money came between them. Additionally, Guthrie was already showing symptoms of Huntington's disease, which many—including Asch—mistakenly believed were caused by heavy drinking. In fact, the disease was beginning to take its physical toll, and within a few years Guthrie would be virtually unable to perform or write.

During the long period of Guthrie's inactivity (he was hospitalized on and off through the mid-1950s and then permanently until his death in 1967), Asch was central in keeping Guthrie's music alive through his recordings. For several decades, Folkways was the only source for some of Guthrie's best-loved songs. Meanwhile, Asch continued to draw from his collection of unissued acetates to issue songs—such as "This Land Is Your Land" (the title track of a 1950 Folkways collection)—that would become world-famous. Finally, after Asch's death, the Smithsonian Institution, led by archivist Jeff Place and Guthrie scholar Guy Logsdon, meticulously rescued and restored all the known recordings that Guthrie made for Asch, and released most of them on a four-CD set. This monumental work stands alongside Guthrie's Library of Congress recordings as his definitive artistic statement.

Jack Elliott and Woody Guthrie, 1961. (© John Cohen)

PETE SEEGER: RAINBOW QUEST

Unlike Lead Belly and Woody Guthrie—both of whom had recorded for major labels—Pete Seeger was a relative unknown when he met Moses Asch. After dropping out of Harvard, Seeger had worked for Alan Lomax briefly in 1939 as an intern at the Library of Congress' Archive of Folk Song. Within a few years, Lomax would be at the nerve center of progressive music—he moved to New York City to host two radio programs on CBS, organized concerts, acted as a scout for Decca Records, and generally encouraged, prodded, and otherwise egged on young singer-performers who he thought had potential to spread the word about folk music. He gave Seeger a mountain of books and records to absorb, introduced him to Dust Bowl balladeer Woody Guthrie, and encouraged him to pursue a career as a banjo player—Seeger had originally studied to be a journalist.

> "It wasn't until I got back from hitchhiking out west in 1940 that I made this for me great discovery: as long as I knew how to play a banjo, I'd never starve."
> —Pete Seeger

Seeger first met Asch in 1941, just before he enlisted in the army. He was invited with a group of other singers to record an album of Spanish Civil War songs; however, the rehearsals collapsed and it wasn't until a year later that

Charles Seeger on a camping trip with his family, 1921. Seeger plays a portable pump organ with his youngest son, Peter, in his lap while his wife, Constance, plays the violin. (Courtesy of the Library of Congress, National Photo Company Collection, npcc.04250)

Seeger—now in an army camp outside Washington, D.C.—revived the idea with Tom Glazer, Bess Lomax Hawes, and Butch Hawes. Seeger phoned Moe, who was happy to arrange a session, and he took a weekend pass to come to New York City. One day was spent rehearsing, and a few hours on Sunday recording, before Seeger had to return to his base. The result was *Songs of the Lincoln Brigade*, issued on Asch-Stinson Records in 1942.

On a second leave in 1944, Seeger came to New York at the invitation of Alan Lomax. Lomax had convinced Decca to record a cantata of folk songs called *The Lonesome Train*, asking Seeger to be one of its performers. Late at night, after the Decca sessions were complete, Seeger and Lomax dropped in on Asch, and Seeger recorded a few solo numbers (which went unreleased at the time). In 1947, Seeger traveled to Los Angeles for work in a play; there, a friend named Ernie Landau arranged for Seeger to record several old-time banjo songs. Landau tried to interest a West Coast label in the recordings but failed to find any takers. He sold the acetates to Moses Asch; two years later, the recordings appeared on a 10-inch LP called *Darling Corey*. This was Seeger's first solo collection, and also among the first folk-revival recordings of banjo songs; it was highly influential in the 1950s, inspiring countless players to take up the instrument. The liner notes were written by Seeger's mentor, Alan Lomax.

Pete Seeger entertaining at the opening of the Washington labor canteen during World War II. (Photo by Joseph A. Horne, United States, Office of War Division, 1944, Library of Congress fsa.8d41983)

In fall 1948, Seeger and a group of friends formed a folk quartet called the Weavers, and within a year were playing at Greenwich Village's Village Vanguard club (see Chapter 9). Signed to Decca, they had a major hit with Lead Belly's song "Goodnight Irene" in 1950. The timing could not have been better for the fledgling Folkways label, which owned a back catalog of Lead Belly recordings.

The Weavers and Seeger quickly ran into trouble for their "progressive" political pasts. Seeger was listed in the infamous book *Red Channels*, as was Alan Lomax. Unable to find nightclub work, the group disbanded in 1952, and Seeger returned to the life of an itinerant solo performer. Unable to place his recordings anywhere else, he became by default an "exclusive" Folkways recording artist, recording a string of children's albums, song collections, and an innovative collection of classical and popular songs adapted for five-string banjo called the *Goofing Off Suite*. Seeger had developed short instrumental pieces, usually under a minute in length, that he performed in concert in impromptu medleys; he mentioned the idea of recording these to Asch, who was as always ready and willing to try something new. The album was a major influence on a new breed of guitar and banjo instrumentalists.

Pete Seeger on Pete Seeger

Pete Seeger wrote this biography for his *Sampler* album, issued in 1954. It was not used, but it offers a charming early life story from the banjo player and performer.

Like a lot of other people who sing folk songs these days, I was born in New York City (35 years ago). Father a musicologist, mother a violinist. Went to school most of my life in the Connecticut countryside. Never intended to be a musician, but always liked to make music in some way for the fun of it . . . musical glasses, whistles, and so on. Played the ukulele at eight, and tenor banjo in the school jazz band at 14. When 16, was smitten by a 5-string banjo played at a square dance festival in Asheville, North Carolina. Three years later, upon quitting college in mid-term, took banjo with me, used it as a calling card, and visited all 48 states within a few years. Took intermittent jobs such as a porter at the New York World's Fair, roving puppeteer playing to dairy farmers during milk strike of '39, and assistant to Alan Lomax in the Archive of American Folk Song.

Failing to make an honest living in any normal way, I found myself picking up change singing songs. Feeling in addition that it was an occupation useful to mankind, have done it ever since, through 2 years with the Almanac Singers, 3½ years in the army, 3 years as director of People's Songs, and 3 years with the Weavers.

Having sung on street corners, back porches, in churches, union halls, in all kinds of saloons ranging from Ciro's and the Palmer House to places better left unmentioned. On radio stations, TV, a few movies, schools, colleges, camps, and other places respectable and disrespectable. Hope to continue thus. Feel myself very fortunate to have been able to lead such a life, and envy no one except children, because they have so many years ahead of them.

Feel very grateful to my family, then and now, for what they taught me; also thanks to Woody Guthrie, Aunt Molly Jackson, and Huddie Ledbetter, for their instruction of music and life; to literally thousands of other musicians and singers . . . who showed me how music can help shape a healthy life.

Look forward to the day when folk music will be recognized as art, as much as any other kind; when singers will be songwriters and songwriters singers; when folksingers can whistle Bach if they want, and when composers will not disdain to try and write a folk tune, when the heritage of Asia and Africa will be as well known as that of Europe. Toward these aims, would like any person who likes folk music to consider: *There are as many different kinds of songs in the world as there are people.* In our land we have an extraordinary variety, brought here by the sons and daughters of every continent under the sun. You can pick your favorites from blues to ballads in a dozen different languages. Sing not with an eye on an audience, but rather for your friends and family. Sing with them. Let us each be proud of our heritage. Our heritages.

The apex of a pyramid is as high as the base is broad; we will have great music in our country when many people are able to make their own music, when every household will have a guitar as well as a radio or camera.

And the music of the future will not be simple imitation of the past, but will be honest combinations of many traditions.

Seeger signed this letter and then added, in handwriting, a short note: "I wish the hell I was a writer like Woody. But perhaps there is something here you can use."

There are as many different kinds of songs in the world as there are people. In our land we have an extraordinary variety, brought here by the sons and daughters of every continent under the sun. You can pick your favorites from blues to ballads in a dozen different languages. ~~XXX~~ Sing not with an eye on an audience, but rather for your friends and family. Sing with them. *Let us ~~all~~ each be proud of our heritage. Our heritages.*

The apex of a pyramid is as high as the base is broad; ~~and~~ we will have great music in our country when many people are able to make their own music, when every household will have a guitar as well as a radio or camera.

And the music of the future will not be a simple imitation of the past, but will be honest combinations of many traditions.

Yours
Pete Seeger

Marion — I wish the hell I was a writer like Woody. But perhaps there is something here you can use —
Pete

P.S. — tapes are mailed under sep. cover

Last page of typed liner notes for the *Pete Seeger Sampler,* with Seeger's characteristic banjo signature and his brief note to Marian Distler.

The Government Versus Pete Seeger

On August 18, 1955, the House Un-American Activities Committee was meeting in New York to investigate Communism in the media. Pete Seeger had been a target of witch-hunters for years; his name had appeared in *Red Channels*' list of liberal performers, and he made no secret of his progressive beliefs. Seeger refused to answer a series of questions put by the committee, mostly relating to different groups for whom he had performed in the 1940s, and was cited for contempt of Congress two years later.

In 1961, Seeger's trial was finally held. The folk world rallied to his defense, with Seeger's manager heading a committee for his defense. Seeger held a singing press conference before the trial began, with newsmen said to be "tapping their feet" while he sang his famous "Hammer Song," according to the *New York Times*. Moses Asch was one of four character witnesses called in the trial. Seeger's defense was based on his First Amendment right of free speech and also on the claim that the committee was not legitimately working on legislation but was merely interested in blacklisting performers. The presiding judge rejected these arguments, saying the committee had a legitimate right to ask questions and that Seeger had "breached one of the most serious obligations of United States citizenship" by refusing to answer them. In his response, Seeger said he had never engaged in any subversive activities or refused to play before any group that asked him to perform. Seeger was sentenced to serve ten 1-year terms in prison (based on the ten questions he refused to answer), to run concurrently, and to pay court costs of the prosecution.

A year later, however, the conviction was overturned. The appeals court agreed that the committee had not had a clearly defined mission, and therefore made it impossible for Seeger to adequately prepare himself to answer its questions. The judge pithily stated: "We are not inclined to dismiss lightly claims of Constitutional stature because they are asserted by one who may appear unworthy of sympathy. Once we embark upon shortcuts by creating a category of the 'obviously guilty' whose rights are denied, we run the risk that the circle of the unprotected will grow."

Although this reversal should have ended all blacklisting of Seeger, it had mixed results. Seeger was signed by a major label, Columbia, in 1961, and his career greatly benefited from the label's ability to market his recordings. However, many of his concerts were still boycotted, and in 1964 when ABC launched a new television show called *Hootenanny* to cash in on the folk revival, the network refused to book the singer for the program. It wasn't until 1967 that Seeger played on network television, appearing on the *Smothers Brothers Comedy Hour*. Even then, his desire to sing the antiwar song "Waist Deep in the Big Muddy" was initially refused by the network's censors; however, the Smothers Brothers themselves lobbied for a second appearance, where the singer dramatically presented the song.

Should Pete Seeger go to jail?

"I would put Pete Seeger in the first rank of American folk singers. I think he ought to be a free man, roving the American landscape, singing for the audiences who love him — Republican, Democrat, and Independent."

Carl Sandburg

". . . THE NOTION THAT THE REPUBLIC IS A SAFER PLACE BECAUSE THE JUSTICE DEPT. HAS CAUGHT UP WITH HIM IS THE KIND OF FANTASY TO WHICH WE HAVE BEEN SUBJECTED TOO LONG. NO ONE HAS REMOTELY SUGGESTED THAT SEEGER IS A SPY OR A SABOTEUR, OR THAT HE POSSESSES ANY KNOWLEDGE OF SUCH DREARY AREAS. THE COMBINED POWER OF THE HOUSE COMMITTEE AND THE JUSTICE DEPT. THAT SHOULD BE RALLIED TO IMPRISON HIM IS A BITTER BURLESQUE. SOME JAIL WILL BECOME A MORE JOYOUS PLACE IF HE LANDS THERE, AND THINGS WILL BE BLEAKER OUTSIDE".

From an editorial NEW YORK POST March 31, 1961

After Pete Seeger's conviction in 1961, his manager Harold Leventhal mobilized an effort to have the conviction overturned. This brochure was one of many that were distributed at the time in defense of Seeger.

Pete Seeger and Moses Asch at the Folkways offices, mid- to late 1950s. (© David Gahr)

Asch became "not just an employer, but a close friend," as Seeger told me. Through the 1950s, Seeger could literally drop in on the Folkways offices at any time and record as few as one or as many as an album's worth of songs:

> We got to be on such good terms, that if I heard a new song—and I found myself walking somewhere near [the Folkways offices]—I'd stop in and say, "Moe, I've learned a new song. Would you like to hear it?" And he'd put a mic up in front of me, I'd record it, and be on my way 15 minutes later. And 3 months later it would come out as a new record.

Seeger rarely chose the material that appeared on individual albums, letting Moe pull together the various sessions as he wished, titling and packaging the albums without consulting the singer. Seeger proudly noted that albums appeared fairly consistently through the period, sometimes one every three months, based on these impromptu sessions.

There were thematic albums that were more planned and usually resulted from discussions between the performer and producer. In the latter part of the 1950s, Asch conceived of recording a series of albums to be called *American Favorite Ballads* and turned to Seeger as the ideal performer for it. Ultimately, five albums were issued, and became in many ways the aural equivalent of

such classic publications as Francis James Child's five-volume ballad collection, which had appeared about a century before. Seeger noted to me, with a chuckle, that many of the songs were not strictly ballads, but nonetheless the series established a "standard" collection that would be drawn on by performers for decades to come. To mention only one recent example, the repertory for Bruce Springsteen's *Seeger Sessions* albums was drawn largely from these albums. Smithsonian Folkways has recently reissued them in remastered form for a new generation of listeners.

Another interesting experiment was *Rainbow Quest,* which extended the collagelike idea of linking short songs into medleys that was first used on the all-instrumental *Goofing Off Suite.* One of the short songs that was featured in these medleys was Seeger's original, two-verse version of "Where Have All the Flowers Gone?"; younger folksinger Joe Hickerson (see Chapter 9) was inspired to expand this into a full song that became one of the anthems of the civil rights and anti–Vietnam War era of the 1960s.

With the folk revival in full swing, Seeger suddenly found himself a hot property in the early 1960s. He left Folkways to sign with major label Columbia, with the proviso that he could continue to record for Folkways for special projects. Meanwhile, there was enough material in the Folkways vaults for Asch to issue Pete Seeger albums regularly through the 1960s. In 1978, Seeger returned to Folkways with the album *Banks of Marble,* recorded in the garage-studio of his old friend (and ex-Weaver) Fred Hellerman. Typical of the Folkways philosophy, no special advertising was done for the album, and its placement in the catalog was the same as other new releases, including the usual range of music, literature, and sounds. Seeger released a few more albums through the early 1980s on the label.

Arlo Guthrie and Pete Seeger mugging for the camera in 1978. (© Fred W. McDarrah)

LISTEN UP!

LEAD BELLY

Where Did You Sleep Last Night: Lead Belly's Legacy, Vol. 1 • SFW40044 • 1996

Bourgeois Blues: Lead Belly's Legacy, Vol. 2 • SFW40045 • 1997

Shout On: Lead Belly's Legacy, Vol. 3 • SFW40105 • 1998

Lead Belly's Last Sessions • SFW40068 • 1994

WOODY GUTHRIE

Long Ways to Travel: The Unreleased Folkways Masters, 1944–1949 • SFW40046 • 1994

This Land Is Your Land: The Asch Recordings, Vol. 1 • SFW40100 • 1997

Muleskinner Blues: The Asch Recordings, Vol. 2 • SFW40101 • 1997

Hard Travelin': The Asch Recordings, Vol. 3 • SFW40102 • 1998

Buffalo Skinners: The Asch Recordings, Vol. 4 • SFW40103 • 1999

Ballads of Sacco and Vanzetti • SFW40060 • 1996

Dust Bowl Ballads • FW05212 • 1964

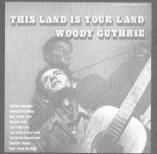

PETE SEEGER

American Favorite Ballads, Vol. 1 • SFW40150 • 2002

American Favorite Ballads, Vol. 2 • SFW40151 • 2003

American Favorite Ballads, Vol. 3 • SFW40152 • 2004

American Favorite Ballads, Vol. 4 • SFW40153 • 2005

American Favorite Ballads, Vol. 5 • SFW40154 • 2007

American Favorite Ballads, Vols. 1–5 • SFW40155 • 2009

American Industrial Ballads • SFW40058 • 1992

Broadside Ballads, Vol. 2 • FW05302 • 1963

Goofing Off Suite • SFW40018 • 1993

Gazette, Vol. 1 • FW02501 • 1958

Gazette, Vol. 2 • FW02502 • 1961

Headlines and Footnotes: A Collection of Topical Songs • SFW40111 • 1999

If I Had a Hammer: Songs of Hope and Struggle • SFW40096 • 1998

Rainbow Quest • FW02454 • 1960

Singalong Sanders Theater, 1980 • SFW40027 • 1992

The Pete Seeger Sampler • FW02043 • 1954

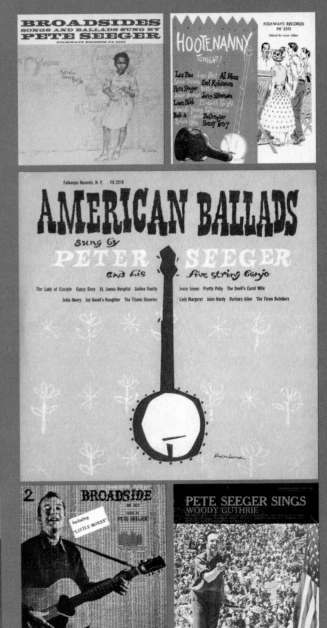

(photo By D. Garr)

To Moe Asch and the staff of   10-14-64
Folkways Records (Mr. Asch. is an Artist)

Chapter 4

"I SAW AMERICA CHANGED BY MUSIC"

Harry Smith's *Anthology of American Folk Music*

Moses Asch had a high tolerance for eccentrics; he valued those people who had a strong sense of individuality, who refused to conform to "group" standards. A loner himself, he understood that it took considerable nerve to live by your own standards and to create your own aesthetic world.

Of all the eccentrics who came to work with Asch over the years, none was more eccentric than legendary filmmaker, anthropologist, folklorist, and philosopher Harry Smith (1923–1991), who created the legendary *Anthology of American Folk Music* (1952)—although his intentions upon meeting Asch were somewhat less grandiose.

Smith was born and raised in the Pacific Northwest. His parents were students of Theosophy, a turn-of-the-century quasi-religious movement that included a fascination with folk rituals and spiritualism. His mother taught on an Indian reservation, and Smith developed a lifelong interest in Indian culture. (Smith's 1964 recording of an all-night peyote ritual was issued by Folkways as a two-LP set.)

After briefly attending college as an anthropology major, Smith settled in San Francisco. He became interested in filmmaking and painting, and befriended many other avant-garde artists. As a hobby, he also began collecting early 78 recordings, which were available cheaply in junk shops and secondhand stores throughout the Bay Area. (The recent introduction of the LP and the end of wartime rationing had led to large-scale dumping of earlier 78s.) Smith was particularly interested in foreign and American regional musics that he had never heard before.

In 1950, Smith was awarded a Guggenheim fellowship to study painting in New York. He spent all of his money on travel and had little cash left on arrival. However, he did have a major asset, his 78 collection, and he began to

Harry Smith in 1964, photographed by David Gahr, and signed by Smith as a gift to Moses Asch. (© David Gahr)

ask around to see if he could find a buyer for it. A fellow collector recommended that he visit Moses Asch, who was known for buying 78s of folk and blues music. When Asch first met Smith, he was reminded of a somewhat quieter—but no less strong-willed—Woody Guthrie. Asch wasn't interested in buying the collection, but he recognized almost immediately its value as a document of American music. He urged Smith to consider compiling it into a series of records. He provided workspace for Smith and a small stipend, and set him free to conceive of the albums in any way he thought fit. As Asch later recalled:

> He came to me and said: "Look, this is what I want to do. I want to lay out the book of notes. I want to do the whole thing. All I want to be sure of is that they are issued." Of course I was tremendously interested. Harry did the notes, typed up the notes, pasted up the notes, did the whole work.

> "Harry Smith's anthology was a collaboration . . . Moe took from Harry, Harry took from Moe."
> —Sam Charters

Smith had a slightly different memory of how it all came about. In an elliptical and often amusing interview with journalist Gary Kenton conducted in the early 1980s, Smith described how he showed up at the tiny Folkways offices, hoping to sell some of his extra 78s to help himself. He tried vainly to explain this to Asch, who apparently didn't understand what Smith was after:

> Mr. Asch is getting more and more puzzled, and he said something like, "What are you doing this for?" Well, I need the money. I've got the records. I'm sleeping on somebody's sofa. He said, "Why don't you bring out an album of these things?" . . . He said, "You'd make more by bringing out this stuff," because he'd evidently shown it to someone—I don't know who—and they knew I was selling him the cream of the crop.

Ever the iconoclast, Smith evolved his own method of selecting and organizing the material. Smith didn't believe in the artificial divisions propagated by the music industry as well as the fans themselves. As Smith recalled to John Cohen in 1968:

> Before the *Anthology* there had been a tendency in which records were lumped into blues catalogs or hillbilly catalogs. . . . That's why there's no such indications of that sort [color/racial] in the albums. . . . It took years before anybody discovered that Mississippi John Hurt wasn't a hillbilly.

AMERICAN FOLK MUSIC

SELECTIONS IN THIS ALBUM

57. THE COO COO BIRD
58. EAST VIRGINIA
59. MINGLEWOOD BLUES
60. ONE MORNING IN MAY
61. JAMES ALLEY
62. SUGAR BABY
63. I WISH I WAS A MOLE
64. MOUNTAINEER'S COURTSHIP
65. MERCHANTS DAUGHTER
66. BOB LEE JUNIOR
67. SINGLE GIRL
68. LE VIEUX SOULARD
69. RABBIT FOOT BLUES
70. EXPRESSMAN BLUES
71. POOR BOY BLUES
72. FEATHER BED
73. COUNTRY BLUES
74. 99 YEAR BLUES
75. PRISON CELL BLUES
76. TWO WHITE HORSES
77. C'EST SI TRISTE
78. DOWN PLANK ROAD
79. ROLL DOWN THE LINE
80. SPIKE DRIVER BLUES
81. K. C. MOAN
82. TRAIN ON THE ISLAND
83. LONE STAR TRAIL
84. FISHING BLUES

VOLUME THREE SONGS

ARTISTS IN THIS ALBUM

57. CLARENCE ASHLEY
58. BUELL KAZEE
59. CANNONS JUG STOMPERS
60. DIDIER HERBERT
61. RICHARD BROWN
62. "DOCK" BOGGS
63. BASCOM LUNSFORD
64. MR. & MRS. STONEMAN
65. STONEMAN FAMILY
66. MEMPHIS JUG BAND
67. THE CARTER FAMILY
68. C. BREAUX & J. FALCON
69. BLIND LEMON JEFFERSON
70. JOHN ESTES
71. RAMBLIN' THOMAS
72. CANNON'S JUG STOMPERS
73. "DOCK"BOGGS
74. JULIUS DANIELS
75. BLIND LEMON JEFFERSON
76. BLIND LEMON JEFFERSON
77. C. & O. BREAUX & FALCON
78. UNCLE DAVE MACON
79. UNCLE DAVE MACON
80. JOHN HURT
81. MEMPHIS JUG BAND
82. J. P. NESTOR
83. KEN MAYNARD
84. HENRY THOMAS

EDITED BY HARRY SMITH

FP 253

FOLKWAYS RECORDS & SERVICE CORP. N. Y.

The original cover for the *Anthology*, showing the "Celestial Monochord" that Smith chose as its central image.

Instead, Smith drew on his beliefs in Theosophy, color theory, and his sense that music had the power to unify mankind to come up with a unique four-volume scheme. The first set would be devoted to "ballads," the second to "social music," and the third to "songs"; the fourth set was left uncompleted. Each set was assigned a color representing the four elements: earth, air, fire, and water.

Although today known as the *Anthology of American Folk Music*, the original covers for each two-LP set simply stated across the top *American Folk Music*. (The full, more familiar title appeared on the spine of the original sets.) The song titles appeared in one column, with the name of the artist in a second. Behind this type, Smith placed a Renaissance drawing of a monochord—a single-string instrument—implying that all music could be reduced to a single, unifying force: the primal vibrating string. Smith described it to John Cohen as "the Celestial Monochord . . . forming earth, air, fire, and water, and the different astrological signs." The idea of the unity of sound—and the importance of its preservation—would have appealed strongly to Moses Asch.

The fourth set was not issued in Smith's lifetime; Asch claimed Smith was never able to complete the notes for the set, while Smith gave conflicting reasons, from an argument with Asch's assistant, Marian Distler, over its contents to an inability to complete the "content analysis" that he felt the material needed (as he told John Cohen). To Gary Kenton, Smith gave a more down-to-earth reason revolving around an argument about a single recording, showing how strongly he viewed the interrelationship of each song to the project:

> I'd had an argument with Miss Distler. She wanted to include a particular song that's called . . . "We've Got Franklin D. Roosevelt Back Again." I think it's by the Delmore Brothers [actually it was recorded by Bill Cox in 1936]—it was not a good performance, so far as that set was concerned. The first criterion was excellence of performance, combined with excellence of words. Now, the fourth volume . . . had "No Depression in Heaven," by the Carter Family, which is not only beautifully sung but has excellent words. I didn't like that record ["Back Again"], and so they decided not to issue the album.

Perhaps Distler resented the growing partnership between Asch and Smith; at the very least, the office was so small that it was difficult sharing space with the eccentric painter, who might arrive drunk and whose dress and personal hygiene were—by 1950s standards—outrageous.

Smith continued:

> Well, I had such arguments with Miss Distler that after the *Anthology* . . . came out . . . for a long time I didn't contact Mr. Asch . . . he got in touch with me through somebody else after a year or two, because I stomped out of the office in a huff.

Although Smith's original vision of a four-volume set was not achieved initially, the *Anthology* had a kind of internal logic. The idea of structuring the material around topical categories was one found in many folk song collections; the Lomaxes had classified songs as "work songs," "children's songs," "story songs," and so on. But Smith took it to a new height, because he freely mixed performers from different races and musical genres; the only unifying conception was that the source material was all recorded roughly between the coming of electric microphones (c. 1925) and the Depression, when the recording industry collapsed (c. 1934). Smith's categories were sufficiently vague to allow for a wide range of material and performers to be included in each set. The result was a kind of musical collage, where white southern performers such as the Carter Family rubbed shoulders with black blues guitarists and Cajun string bands.

Smith described the *Anthology* as a kind of collage or mosaic, with each part interrelated yet separate; Moses Asch described the Folkways catalog in almost identical terms, with its individual albums placed within this larger constellation.

Like Woody Guthrie and Pete Seeger, Smith felt that music had the power to change society; however, he split with them when it came to how music could effect that change. To him, Guthrie and Seeger were too didactic; their songs were transparently meant to uplift "workingmen" through instilling in them the values of peace and love of their fellow man. Smith heard Woody Guthrie perform only once, and, as he recalled to John Cohen, he was less than impressed:

> Someone had taken me to hear [Guthrie in the late 1940s when Smith was living in Berkeley]. . . . In the hall I suddenly met a lot of people who had interest in records and stuff. Being naive, I didn't realize they were revolutionaries trying to blow up the state capitol or something. But I didn't like his singing. It was too sophisticated and too involved with social problems, I felt. It wasn't the sort of stuff I was interested in.

The cover of the booklet that appeared with the original *Anthology*. Note that Folkways charged an extra dollar for this booklet.

Like the proto-hippie he was, Smith was more interested in how music affected the underlying psyche of mankind and thus made social change occur:

> I felt social changes would result from it. I'd been reading from Plato's *Republic*. He's jabbering on about music, how you have to be careful about changing the music because it might upset or destroy the government. Everybody gets out of step. You are not to arbitrarily change it, because you may undermine the Empire State Building without knowing it. Of course, I thought it would do that. I thought it would develop into something more spectacular than it did, though. . . . I imagine[d] it having some kind of a social force for good.

The booklet that Smith created for the albums was also unique. Like Asch, he strongly believed that documentation was important to the understanding of the music, but he took a different approach than the more prosaic booklets that appeared with Folkways releases. Smith included the kind of discographic

OVERLEAF: A few typical entries from the booklet's text. Note how each entry resembles a three-by-five card, giving basic information on each track and Smith's often humorous descriptions of the material.

Death of John Henry

Featured by Sam Kirk McGee

1. The prisoner out-ran that John Henry was dead, Could - n't hardly stay in
2. They took John Henry to that grave-yard, They looked at him good and
3. John Hen - ry's wife wore a brand new dress, It was all trimmed in
4. John Hen - ry told her she could, Lord she cried I
5. John Hen - ry told his cap - tain, I am a Ten-nes-see
6. John Hen - ry ham - mered in the moun-tain, Till the ham-mer caught on

bed ____ Mon - day morning on the East - bound train Home-ward John
long ____ Very - last words that his wife said to him, My husband he is
blue ____ Very - last words she said to him, Hen-ry I've been
think ____ Who-lays a hammer from the should - er, Bound to hear her
man ____ Be - fore I'd see that stranger beat me down, God to have a ham-mer
fire ____ Very - last words I heard him say, "Cool drink of wa-ter

Hen - ry's dead. ____ Home-ward John Hen - ry's dead.
dead and gone. ____ My husband he is dead and gone.
good to you. ____ Hen-ry I've been good to you.
when she rings. ____ Bound to hear her when she rings.
in my hand. ____ Got to have a hammer in my hand.
fore I die." ____ "Cool drink of wa-ter 'fore I die."

18

GONNA DIE WITH MY HAMMER IN MY HAND
BY WILLIAMSON BROTHERS AND CURRY
VOCAL SOLO WITH DUET CHORUS
WITH VIOLIN AND TWO GUITARS.
RECORDED IN 1927.
ORIGINAL ISSUE OKEH 45127(w80757)

JOHN HENRY VOWS TO DEFEAT MECHANIZATION; QUESTIONS
CAPTAIN, WARNS SHAKER AND SON, WIFE STRONG TOO

GUY B. JOHNSON IN HIS "JOHN HENRY" LISTS THE FOLLOW-
ING (P. 18) AS FACTS: 1. JOHN HENRY REALLY LIVED
2. HE BEAT A STEAM DRILL DOWN AND DIED DOING IT.
3. LI'L BILL WAS HIS BUDDIE OR HELPER 4. HE WORKED
FOR A RAILROAD CONSTRUCTION CONTRACTOR 5. HIS WIFE'S
NAME WAS LUCY. THE FOLLOWING ARE PROBABILITIES:
1. HE DIED IN THE EARLY 70'S 2. HE WAS A VIRGINIAN
3. HE WORKED ON THE C & O OR A BRANCH OF THAT SYSTEM
4. HIS CAPTAIN WAS TOMMY WALTERS; PROBABLY AN ASSIST-
ANT FOREMAN. (SEE THE ABOVE REFERENCE FOR MORE COM-
PLETE DETAILS).

DISCOGRAPHY:
BILL WILSON. BIRMINGHAM JUG BAND. OKEH 8895. JOHN
HENRY BLUES. JOHN CARSON. OKEH 7004. DEATH OF JOHN
HENRY. DAVE MACON. VOCALION 15320. JOHN HENRY. HENRY
THOMAS. VOCALION 1094. AAFS 15. JOHN HENRY WAS
A LITTLE BOY. J. E. MAINER. BLUEBIRD 6629.
BIBLIOGRAPHY: BOTKIN-235;COX-184;HENRY-441;JOHNSON-II-
180;JOHNSON-I-84;LOMAX-II-3;LOMAX-V-258;LOMAX-IV-258;
LUNSFORD-32;MORRIS-182;ODUM-II-221;PERROW-VOL.26-163;
SANDBURG-24;TALLEY-105;WHITE-189

19

STACKALEE
(HUTCHISON)
BY FRANK HUTCHISON
VOCAL SOLO WITH HARMONICA, GUITAR.
RECORDED IN EARLY 1927.
ORIGINAL ISSUE OKEH 45106(w80-359A)

THEFT OF STETSON HAT CAUSES DEADLY DISPUTE. VICTIM
IDENTIFIES SELF AS FAMILY MAN

THE MURDER MENTIONED HERE PROBABLY TOOK PLACE IN
MEMPHIS IN ABOUT 1900. STACK LEE SEEMS TO HAVE BEEN
CONNECTED BY BIRTH OR EMPLOYMENT WITH THE LEE FAMILY
OF THAT CITY WHO OWNED A LARGE LINE OF STEAMERS ON
THE MISSISSIPPI.

DISCOGRAPHY: STACKERLEE. MISSISSIPPI JOHN HURDT.
OKEH 8654. STACKOLEE AND BILLY LYONS. FURRY LEWIS.
VOCALION 1132.
BIBLIOGRAPHY: BOTKIN-122; JOHNSON-II-194; LOMAX-II-93;
ODUM-I-196; ODUM-II-245; SCARBOROUGH-I-92

FRANK HUTCHISON
Exclusive Okeh Artist

20

WHITE HOUSE BLUES
BY CHARLIE POOLE WITH THE
NORTH CAROLINA RAMBLERS
VOCAL SOLO WITH VIOLIN, BANJO, GUITAR.
RECORDED IN 1926.
ORIGINAL ISSUE COLUMBIA 15099D(w142658)

McKINLEY SWEARS, MOURNS, DIES. ROOSEVELT GETS WHITE
HOUSE AND SILVER CUP

ON SEPTEMBER 6, 1901, WILLIAM McKINLEY, 25TH PRESIDENT
OF THE UNITED STATES WAS SHOT AT CLOSE RANGE BY A YOUNG
ANARCHIST, LEON CZOLGOSZ. THIS MURDER TOOK PLACE AT A
GREAT RECEPTION AT THE PAN-AMERICAN EXPOSITION IN
BUFFALO, NEW YORK WHERE THE PRESIDENT HAD GONE TO DE-
CLARE HIS VIEWS ON THE TARIFF.

DISCOGRAPHY: CANNON BALL BLUES. CARTER FAMILY.
VICTOR 40317. THE ROAD TO WASHINGTON. ERNEST V.
STONEMAN. OKEH 45125. MR. McKINLEY. HOMER BRIAR-
HOPPER. DECCA 5588. SEE ALSO THE BATTLESHIP OF
MAINE, RED PATTERSONS PIEDMONT LOG ROLLERS, VICTOR
20936 FOR A RELATED COMPOSITION.
BIBLIOGRAPHY: LOMAX-IV-256

21

FRANKIE
BY MISSISSIPPI JOHN HURT
VOCAL SOLO WITH GUITAR.
RECORDED IN 1928.
ORIGINAL ISSUE OKEH 8560(w400221)

ALBERT DIES PREFERRING ALICE FRY, BUT JUDGE FINDS
FRANKIE CHARMING AT LATTER'S TRIAL

ALLEN BRITT SHOT FRANKIE BAKER OF 212 TARGEE STREET,
ST. LOUIS MISSOURI, OCTOBER 15, 1899. THE SONG WAS
FIRST SUNG BY, AND PROBABLY WRITTEN BY, "MAMMY LOU"
A SINGER AT BABE CONNER'S FAMOUS CABARET IN THAT CITY.

DISCOGRAPHY: FRANKIE AND JOHNNY. JIMMY ROGERS.
VICTOR 22143. FRANKIES GAMBLIN' MAN. WELBY TOOMEY.
GENET 3195. FRANKIE DEAN. TOM DARBY AND JIMMY
TARLTON. COLUMBIA 15701D. FRANKIE. DYKES MAGIC
CITY TRIO. BRUNSWICK 127.

BIBLIOGRAPHY: BELDEN-330;EDDY-245;GORDON-46;HENRY-338;
HUDSON-189;LOMAX-II-103;LOMAX-III-192;LOMAX-V-312;
MORRIS-126;ODUM-I-228;PERROW-VOL.28-178;RANDOLPH-II-125;
SANDBURG-76;SCARBOROUGH-80;WHITE-213

22

WHEN THAT GREAT SHIP WENT DOWN
BY WILLIAM AND VERSEY SMITH
VOCAL DUET WITH TAMBORINE, GUITAR.
RECORDED IN 1927.
ORIGINAL ISSUE PARAMOUNT 12505B(4685-728)

MANUFACTURERS PROUD DREAM DESTROYED AT SHIPWRECK.
SEGREGATED POOR DIE FIRST

AT 2:20 A.M. APRIL 15TH, 1912 THE WHITE STAR LINER
TITANIC THE LARGEST SHIP AFLOAT, ON HER MAIDEN VOYAGE,
STRUCK AN ICEBERG AT FULL SPEED, GOING DOWN WITH
1513 PERSONS. SEE BRITISH PARLIAMENTARY PAPERS NO.
2253, SHIPPING CASUALTIES (TITANIC) 1912 [ED. 6352]
FOR DETAILS.

DISCOGRAPHY: THE TITANIC. ERNEST V. STONEMAN. OKEH
40288. SEE ALSO (SINKING OF) THE TITANIC BY RICHARD
"RABBIT" BROWN (VICTOR) AND GOD MOVES ON THE WATER
BY BLIND WILLIE JOHNSON (COLUMBIA) FOR DIFFERENT
BALLADS OF THE SAME THEME.
BIBLIOGRAPHY: HENRY-426; JACKSON-II-210; RANDOLPH-IV-
145; WHITE-347

CARTER FAMILY

Furry Lewis

23

ENGINE ONE-FORTY-THREE
(A.P. CARTER)
BY THE CARTER FAMILY
VOCAL SOLO (BY SARA CARTER) WITH
AUTOHARP, GUITAR.
RECORDED IN 1927.
ORIGINAL ISSUE VICTOR 40089B

GEORGIE RUNS INTO ROCK AFTER MOTHER'S WARNING. DIES
WITH THE ENGINE HE LOVES

GEORGE ALLEY WAS BORN IN RICHMOND, VIRGINIA, JULY 10TH,
1860; MARRIED NOVEMBER 10TH, 1881, AND HAD FOUR CHILDREN.
THE WRECK ON THE C & O IN WHICH HE WAS KILLED OCCURED
AT 5:40 A.M. OCTOBER 23RD, 1890, WHILE HE WAS RUNNING
TRAIN NO. 4, THE F.F.V. ("FAST FLYING VESTIBULE"),
ENGINE 134. HE LIVED FIVE HOURS AFTER BEING HURT. THE
WRECK OCCURED THREE MILES EAST OF HINTON, AND WAS
CAUSED BY A LANDSLIDE. THE BALLAD WAS PROBABLY COMPOSED
BY A WORKER IN THE ROUND HOUSE AT HINTON, WEST VIRGINIA.
(COX)
DISCOGRAPHY: WRECK ON THE C & O ROAD. BRADLEY
KINCAID. CHAMPION 54098. THE C. AND O. WRECK. GEORGE RENEAU.
VOCALION 14897.
BIBLIOGRAPHY: COX-221; LOMAX-II-31; MORRIS-III;
RANDOLPH-IV-129; THOMAS-II-115

24

KASSIE JONES (TWO PARTS)
(F. LEWIS)
BY FURRY LEWIS
VOCAL SOLO WITH GUITAR.
RECORDED IN 1928.
ORIGINAL ISSUE VICTOR 21664A&B

CRACK ENGINEER JONES IN FATAL COLLISION. KNEW ALICE
FRY. WIFE RECALLS SYMBOLIC DREAM, LATER CONSOLES
CHILDREN

JOHN LUTHER JONES (KNOWN AS "CASEY" FROM THE TOWN
OF CAYCE, KENTUCKY, NEAR WHERE HE WAS BORN) WAS
KILLED A LITTLE AFTER 4 A.M., APRIL 30TH, 1900
WHEN THE ILLINOIS CENTRAL'S NO. 638 PLOUGHED INTO A
FREIGHT TRAIN THAT EXTENDED INTO THE MAIN LINE
FROM A SIDE TRACK NEAR VAUGHN, MISSISSIPPI. WHEN
THEY TOOK CASEY'S BODY FROM THE OVERTURNED CAB, THEY
FOUND ONE HAND ON THE WHISTLE CORD AND THE OTHER
ON THE AIRBRAKE LEVER. ACCORDING TO HIS WIDDOW,
CASEY ESTABLISHED A TRADEMARK FOR HIMSELF BY HIS
INIMITABLE METHOD OF BLOWING THE WHISLTE IN A KIND
OF LONG DRAWN OUT NOTE, BEGINNING SOFTLY, THEN RIS-
ING, THEN DYING AWAY ALMOST TO A WHISPER. PEOPLE
LIVING ALONG THE RIGHT OF WAY WOULD TURN OVER IN
THEIR BEDS LATE AT NIGHT AND SAY "THERE GOES CASEY
JONES". "I REMEMBER", SAYS SIM WEBB, CASEY'S ENGIN-
EER, "THAT AS I JUMPED FROM THE CAB CASEY HELD
DOWN THE WHISTLE IN A LONG, PIERCING SCREAM". THE
BALLAD WAS WRITTEN A FEW DAYS AFTER THE WRECK BY
WALLACE SAUNDERS AN ENGINE WIPER OF MEMPHIS, MISS-
ISSIPPI, WHO HAD BEEN A CLOSE FRIEND OF JONES.
(SEE ERIE RAILROAD MAGAZINE, APRIL 1928 AND APRIL,
1932.

DISCOGRAPHY: CASEY JONES. JOHN CARSON. OKEH 40038.
ON THE ROAD AGAIN. MEMPHIS JUG BAND. VICTOR 38015.
SOUTHERN CASEY JONES. JESSE JAMES. DECCA 7213.

BIBLIOGRAPHY: BOTKIN-241; HUDSON-214; JOHNSON-II-182;
LOMAX-II-34; LOMAX-V-264; MORRIS-109; ODUM-I-207; ODUM-II-
126; PERROW-VOL.26-165; POUND-56; SANDBURG-366; SCARBOROUGH-
I-249; WHITE-374

25

DOWN ON PENNYS FARM
BY THE BENTLY BOYS
VOCAL SOLO WITH BANJO, GUITAR.
RECORDED IN 1929.
ORIGINAL ISSUE COLUMBIA 15565D(W149254)

RENTERS CAUGHT BY POVERTY ON GEORGE PENNY'S FARM
PICTURE LANDLORD AS MISER, THIEF, AND LIAR

THIS RECORDING IS A REGIONALIZED RECASTING OF AN
EARLIER SONG "HARD TIMES". A TRANSCRIPTION OF THE
"BENTLY BOYS" VERSION IS FOUND IN LOMAX -IV, P. 287.
BIBLIOGRAPHY: GARDNER-443; HUDSON-215; LOMAX-II-332;
LOMAX-IV-287

26

MISSISSIPPI BOWEAVIL BLUES
BY THE MASKED MARVEL
VOCAL SOLO WITH GUITAR.
RECORDED IN 1929.
ORIGINAL ISSUE PARAMOUNT 12805B(15211,P1337)

BOLLWEAVIL SURVIVES PHYSICAL ATTACK AFTER CLEVERLY
ANSWERING FARMERS QUESTIONS

A TEXT SIMILAR TO THIS RECORDING DOES NOT SEEM TO
HAVE BEEN PRINTED IN ANY EASILY AVAILABLE SOURCE.
ALL OF THE REFERENCES GIVEN BELOW REFER TO A COMPO-
SITION CONTAINING A NUMBER OF PHRASES AND RHYMES
IN COMMON WITH THIS VERSION, BUT IN A TOTALLY DIFFER-
ENT METRICAL PATTERN.

DISCOGRAPHY: AAFS 16.

BIBLIOGRAPHY: BOTKIN-916; HANDY-3; HUDSON-199; LOMAX-II-
112; LOMAX-III-184; LOMAX-V-236; MORRIS-188; SANDBURG-8-
252; SCARBOROUGH-I-77; WHITE-352

information that would appeal to hard-core collectors—but that was rarely noted in reissues at this time. Instead of providing song lyrics, he provided witty headline-like summaries of the song's contents. These became legendary among folk fans for their telegraphic, almost Zen-like statements—and their tongue-in-cheek humor. Who can forget his pithy description of the contents of "King Kong Kitchie Kitchie Ki-Me-O" (also known as "Froggy Went a-Courtin'"): "Zoologic miscegeny achieved in mouse frog nuptials, relatives approve"?

The booklet also included illustrations from early phonograph advertisements, catalog clippings, and a mélange of medieval- and Renaissance-style wood-block art. The collage of words and images mirrored the assembly of the music itself. Yet each entry was also squared off with ruler lines, resembling a stack of three-by-five cards that had been dropped whimsically into this order (but could have been reshuffled by Smith into another sequence). You could almost imagine these as catalog cards for some wonderful, imaginary sound library.

> "The *Anthology* made the familiar strange, the never known, and the forgotten into a collective memory that teased any single listener's conscious mind."
>
> —Greil Marcus

Few noticed the *Anthology* on its first release, although Ken Maynard, writing in the *New York Times*, reviewed it at the time. Although primarily a descriptive review, Maynard began his piece with some prescient comments on how ephemeral pop culture can be:

For the very reason that they are so readily discarded, the things that people throw away often become in succeeding eras the most valuable. Gramophone records of apparently transient music rendered by little-known performers are a case in point. So many of them have been thrown out that the disks that cost practically nothing when new now fetch good prices as "collectors' items."

Another of life's ironies is that often items which are not especially interesting in themselves become extremely interesting when they are laid side by side. . . . Thus Harry Smith's collection of early phonograph records has become both valuable in a monetary sense and interesting in what it reveals about American popular music before it became standardized by coast-to-coast radio programs, nationally distributed talking pictures, and phonograph releases that blanket the country.

Maynard captured two key ideas behind the *Anthology* long before other critics did: the importance of preserving otherwise forgotten musical styles; and the extra resonance that occurs when these "items" are "laid side by side" to complement and comment on each other.

The *Anthology* as Touchstone: Folk and Blues Rediscoveries

Many of the blues and old-time music artists rediscovered in the 1950s and 1960s never would have been searched out if their work hadn't been featured first on the *Anthology*. Smith had the remarkable ability to select their signature work, and often the songs that he chose for the *Anthology* remain their best-known recordings. Among the artists who Smith was the first to recognize and reissue were:

Dock Boggs. This banjo player from Virginia made a handful of 78 recordings in 1927 and 1929 and had ceased playing after his marriage (his wife disapproved of "sinful" banjo music). Boggs' blues-tinged vocals and driving two-finger picking style are both features of the recording that Smith chose for the *Anthology*, "Sugar Baby." Hearing this recording led Mike Seeger to seek out Boggs, finding him in his hometown of Norton, Virginia (see Chapter 8).

Recording Tom Ashley at his home shortly after his rediscovery. (Photo by Ralph Rinzler, courtesy of the Ralph Rinzler Archives, Smithsonian Institution)

Mississippi John Hurt. Like Boggs, Hurt recorded only a few 78s during the blues boom of the 1920s, and then returned to a life of farming. His "Spike Driver's Blues" is a unique interpretation of the John Henry myth and among the best of these early recordings. Unlike the Delta bluesmen who sang in an intense, gospel-influenced style, Hurt's vocals were relaxed and his guitar playing rhythmic and propulsive.

Clarence "Tom" Ashley. Again, Smith selected one of Ashley's best solo recordings, "The Coo Coo Bird," to feature on the *Anthology*. The song was much covered in the folk revival, notably by Peter Stampfel of the Holy Modal Rounders, who gave it a slightly psychedelic spin while still honoring the spirit of the original. Ralph Rinzler rediscovered Ashley during a performance at the Union Grove Fiddlers' Convention in 1960. In turn, Ashley led Rinzler to guitarist-vocalist Doc Watson. Watson probably never would have had a career beyond his native area if it hadn't been for this connection (see Chapter 8).

Blind Willie Johnson. The great, gruff-voiced gospel singer is represented by his wonderful version of "John the Revelator." This song-sermon, half sung, half preached, and half growled, marries the hard edge of the Delta blues with the fervor of gospel music. After hearing this one cut, Sam Charters was influenced to seek out more recordings by Johnson, and arranged for the first full LP reissue of his work on Folkways (see Chapter 6).

Charlie Poole and the North Carolina Ramblers. Banjoist-singer Charlie Poole was among the most popular of old-time recording stars of the mid-1920s. Smith chose the topical "White House Blues" to include in his collection, which was typical of the style of the Poole group, a much less rowdy ensemble than their best-known contemporaries, Gid Tanner and the Skillet Lickers. Poole's group became one of the models for the old-time revival trio the New Lost City Ramblers, who covered many of their songs (see Chapter 8).

Moses Asch and Allen Ginsberg, c. 1970. (© David Gahr)

Smith's relation with Asch was typical of many who worked for the volatile label head; awe, fear, frustration, and affection were all part of his reaction to Asch's sometimes abrupt changes in mood. ("I don't like being yelled at," Smith told Gary Kenton describing why he went "for years at a time" without contacting Asch.) It is clear that both saw an opportunity to be gained from working together: the always near-destitute Smith saw that he could make easy money by working for Asch; Asch saw a man who had an amazing collection and knowledge about musical styles. Smith told Allen Ginsberg that Moe "dreaded his coming" to the Folkways offices, because he knew Smith would "hit [him] up" for ready money. Smith often dumped half-finished projects at Folkways in return for an "advance." Eventually, most of these projects were completed, although not always by Harry; a pile of tapes of Allen Ginsberg chanting his poetry to his own harmonium accompaniment was left with Asch in 1971 and was eventually edited for release ten years later by Ann and Samuel Charters.

> "Wherever I go, the first thing they ask me is: 'Is it still in print? Is the *Anthology of American Folk Music* still in print?' Yes!!!"
>
> —Moses Asch, 1970

Yet, despite all of these difficulties, each had a deep affection for the other that comes forth in their memories of working together. As Smith told Kenton:

He's a very humorous person, you know. Despite his—as Izzy Young says, and I won't apply it to Mr. Asch, but it's applicable to the general situation, "Within that rough exterior beats a heart of tinsel." But within Mr. Asch beats a heart of gold, actually.

Harry Smith in his room at the Chelsea Hotel; the Wollensak tape machine (just visible next to him on the floor) was purchased for him by Moses Asch to record the Fugs, among others, in the 1960s. (© John Cohen)

After storming out of the Folkways offices when Asch refused to issue the fourth volume of the *Anthology*, Smith fell out of touch with Folkways for nearly a decade. He came back to Asch in 1964 with his recordings of an all-night peyote ritual among the Kiowa in Oklahoma. This led to a renewed period of recording. Befriending the Beat poets of New York's East Village, Smith recorded the first album by the proto-punk band the Fugs in 1965, which originally appeared as *The Village Fugs* on Folkways. As late as the early 1980s, he was still producing recordings for Asch, including an album of flute music by Charles Compo.

The ever-eccentric Smith became a permanent fixture in New York's Chelsea Hotel, longtime home to many artists. He focused most of his energy on avant-garde filmmaking, and became somewhat of a legend among the New York radical arts community. Allen Ginsberg was particularly important in supporting Smith, both financially and artistically, in his later decades. Ginsberg hired Smith as a "Shaman-in-Residence" for his Colorado-based Naropa Institute.

It took several years for Smithsonian Folkways to issue the *Anthology* on CD. Unlike Smith and Asch, the Smithsonian could not reissue the material without the permission of the original labels, and wanted to document the history of the set. When the set finally appeared in 1997, it was a surprise success. Previously, at the 1991 Grammy ceremonies, Smith was awarded a Chairman's Merit Award for his original work on the *Anthology*. True to his long-held beliefs, Smith simply acknowledged this honor by stating, "I'm glad to say my dreams came true. I saw America changed by music." He died a few months later.

MUSIC SHOULD BE FREE!

Asch's decision to reissue early jazz recordings on Frederic Ramsey's ten-volume *Jazz* series and then to issue the *Anthology of American Folk Music*, both consisting of commercial recordings made by the major labels, angered many in the music industry. They labeled him a "musical pirate," something that irritated him no end, because Moe didn't feel he was stealing anything. Rather, by making available recordings that otherwise would have languished in corporate vaults, he was actually creating new audiences for this music, which ultimately benefited the larger labels.

Asch's opinions about the larger record companies and their disregard for the value of the recordings they had made were colored by his experiences in World War II. Shellac, a key ingredient in the making of records, was scarce because its primary source in Asia was cut off by the war. Record drives were held where a large number of old records were destroyed. Record collectors such as Asch and Harry Smith were appalled by the cavalier attitude the companies took toward these precious recordings:

> [Records] were smashed into smithereens during the so-called "Record Drive" of World War II. . . . I mean, somebody comes across a really good King Oliver record that somebody had, Bam! A friend of mine [came] across a pretty good King Oliver during the thing that had been broken in half . . . [which] may be worth as much as a hundred dollars.

While the major labels offered to buy back unsold records from their dealers for a few pennies per disc, the dealers reasoned they were better off simply remaindering them themselves, setting up tables where they offered 78s for 15–20 cents each. Unsold inventory—particularly in big-city dealers' stores—tended to be the more offbeat blues, country, and other material that didn't sell in as great quantity as pop hits. For record collectors such as Smith and Asch, it was a bonanza. Asch recalled that electronics and record dealers in New York had stacks and stacks of unwanted inventory laid out on tables, ripe for the picking. Asch estimates that during the 1930s he purchased around ten thousand 78s, educating himself in jazz, blues, and folk music:

Letter from RCA Victor to Woody Guthrie declining to reissue his *Dust Bowl Ballads* set. Guthrie and Asch used this letter as a release for their reissuing the material on Folkways.

> I wasn't really acquainted with the real blues until the black label [popular] records were available, because—at that time—they started to dump, Columbia and Victor, records to get rid of them . . . so I was buying this type of records at 19 and 20 cents. And that's where I started my collection. Harry Smith tells me, just about that time, he starting collecting in that same fashion. Except Harry, like other aficionados, knew where the thing was done, who [the] musicians [were] . . . I didn't give a damn; I heard something, and I knew this was something I wanted to have. This was my base of learning. Not who did it, but how it was done and what was done.

Asch reasoned that if the recording companies did not value this material, he at least could preserve it and make it available for those who cared.

Asch's attitude toward the big labels had crystallized early on when Woody

Postcard 1:
Moe Asch
Folkways
117 W 46th St.
New York
City — U.S.A.

Dear Mr. Asch —
As I financed
Harry Smiths Okla
Trip - - plane tickets
and exspenses, + carried
him 5 months last
year, it would be

Postcard 2:
Moe Asch
Folkways
117 W 46th St.
New York City
U.S.A.

2) polite for me to
use with your
O.K. for the sound
track of my film
a few 100ft. of
tape as it was ostens-
ibly created for this

Postcard 3:
Moe Asch
Folkways
117 W 46th St.
New York
City — U.S.A.

3) purpose. Harry
made me spend
over $6,000 last
year on him. And
he gave nothing
in return. If necessary
I will have
my lawyers Javitts + Javitts

Conrad Rooks wrote this amusing series of five postcards to Moses Asch regarding his underwriting of Harry Smith's peyote ritual recordings. Not expecting to collect from either Smith or Asch, Rooks simply requests permission to use a small portion of the recording as an accompaniment to a documentary film he is making.

Guthrie complained to him that RCA had withdrawn his *Dust Bowl Ballads* album due to poor sales (see Chapter 3). Even though the label was no longer selling the recordings, it insisted it still held the rights and would neither issue the records nor give the rights back to Guthrie. Asch simply took the matter into his own hands, reissuing the recordings himself, challenging Victor to respond.

Victor eventually responded, when the folk revival suddenly made reissuing Guthrie's original recordings commercially viable. In 1964, Victor wrote to Asch challenging his reissue of the *Dust Bowl Ballads* 78s, which Asch had recently converted from the original 10-inch album (issued with Guthrie's blessings in 1950) to a full-size LP. Typically, Asch replied to Victor that he had every right to issue the material, having Guthrie's approval—in fact, Guthrie had pleaded with him to make the recordings available. Further, he had bought the original records on the open market and—once RCA declared them out of print—felt that they were fair game for reissue. Asch notes that Guthrie had approached RCA twice, in 1948 and 1950, and the label had declined to reissue the recordings on both occasions. Asch closed his letter explaining his belief that

cultural property belongs to all and is limited to individual ownership only in so far as the copyright of the material is subjected to and limited to. Since records do not carry this copyright and since Folkways is in a unique position regarding the above, I cannot see what RCA can do about this, except to make a nuisance of it. I have patience and fortitude.

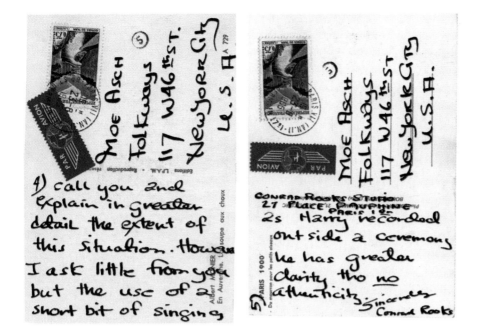

The handwritten postcards read:

(left card, addressed to:) Moe Asch / Folkways / 117 W 46th St. / New York City / U.S.A.

(left card message:) 1) call you and explain in greater detail the extent of this situation. However I ask little from you but the use of a short bit of singing

(right card, addressed to:) Moe Asch / Folkways / 117 W 46th St. / New York City / U.S.A.

(right card message:) Conrad Rooks Studio / 27 Place Dauphine / Paris 1e / as Harry recorded outside a ceremony he has greater clarity tho no authenticity. Sincerely / Conrad Rooks

Indeed, Asch did have "patience and fortitude." Rather than fight with him, RCA simply reissued the *Dust Bowl Ballads* on its own label, adding two previously unissued masters to its LP. Asch could hardly complain.

For Asch the right of the people to have access to recordings such as Guthrie's was greater than corporate ownership rights. During the early 1950s, when he reissued Guthrie, the *Jazz* series, and the *Anthology*, the major labels showed little or no interest in their back catalogs. Soon, specialty labels including Riverside (originally started to reissue early jazz recordings), Origin Jazz Library and Yazoo (blues reissues), and County (old-time country music) would rise to carry forward this mission.

Asch was correct that federal copyright law did not cover sound recordings made before February 15, 1972; technically all records made before that date were in the public domain. However, Asch went further than merely citing copyright law, basing his philosophy on the Constitution, where he found that the people were given a "right to know" that superseded copyright:

> The Constitution of the United States was to me a very basic document. When World War II began there was a shortage of metals, copper and shellac, so the big companies broke up the masters . . . of Bessie Smith and all the other early recordings. They all disappeared. . . .
>
> I started to realize here the Constitution was saying "dissemination"—the right to know is a right of the people, and there the record company wasn't caring whether people have that right or not. They were destroying prop-

erty which they claimed was their own. I always claimed what they were destroying was the culture, so I started to reissue some of the records which I thought ought to be preserved.

In fact, many of his early releases drew on both American and foreign commercial recordings that were either extremely rare or simply unavailable to American listeners.

In the late 1950s, Asch again became interested in reissuing blues and jazz materials, probably due to the influence of Samuel Charters. To protect Folkways against possible lawsuits, Asch formed a new label, RBF (which stood for Record, Book, and Film). The label's first LP, *The Country Blues*, was produced to accompany Sam Charters' book of the same name. Again, there were rumblings of discontent from the major labels, and Charters recalled that Asch had a unique way of dealing with those who questioned his right to reissue this material: "[When] copyright holders demand[ed] royalties . . . I've seen him drive them out the door, waving an 8-by–10-inch American flag and yelling about his rights as a creative artist." Eventually, when the new copyright law went into effect in 1978, Asch agreed to pay an ongoing royalty to Columbia Records for his use of its material.

Equally, when people claimed copyright on material that Asch knew was traditional, he treated them with the (lack of) respect he felt they deserved. Ralph Rinzler tells a story of how Asch reacted when the manager for the British folk star Nancy Whiskey turned up at his office. Whiskey had learned Elizabeth Cotten's "Freight Train" from Peggy Seeger, and then had the nerve to copyright it as her own. Her recording was a hit in England, and apparently her manager came to Folkways looking for other material he could "steal" from folk artists:

Nancy Whiskey's manager [went] up to see Moe . . . saying, "I'm the guy who copyrighted 'Freight Train' in England. And I've heard that your music is wonderful, and I've always wanted to get Folkways Records. Can I give you a list and come back and get them this afternoon." And Moe said, "Sure, sure, give me a list, that would be fine. You're the guy who took that money. . . . Yeah, come back this afternoon, and I'll have all the records ready and break each one of them over your head!" He could do that and roar at the end of the sentence so the guy would just flee.

Another battle over copyright pitted Asch against a man who was at times his collaborator and at others his rival: folklorist Alan Lomax. On his return to the United States in 1959 after nearly a decade in England, sitting out the

McCarthy period, Lomax wrote a letter to one of his oldest friends, Pete Seeger, claiming that Seeger had infringed on his copyright by recording songs that appeared in his and his father's collections on the *American Favorite Ballads* series of records (see Chapter 3). The folk revival was just beginning, and Lomax simply may have been trying to establish precedent, but nonetheless it was odd that he would target Seeger, whom he had championed as a model folk-singer. Asch was galled that Lomax claimed ownership of material that he knew was traditional; further, he didn't feel that Lomax could prove that Seeger or any other artist directly learned a particular song from the Lomax collections. In most cases, the songs were passed around among singers, and no one source could claim ownership.

In an interview a decade later, Asch still seethed at Lomax's claims of ownership, again asserting the constitutional right of singers to perform tra-ditional songs: "Alan Lomax with his father copyrighted songs—and started suing everybody. I went back to the Constitution. A record has no copyright protection. Here is Alan saying it all belongs to me—I'm the father!" Recalling Asch's troubled relationship with his own father, it is interesting that he chose to describe Lomax as a tyrannical father trying to keep his children—including Pete Seeger—from performing "his" material.

The "Look" of the "Listen"

Margaret Asch and Joan Greer

The cover art of Folkways Records was an essential component of the complex whole that made up each recording in the Folkways catalog. The art and design work literally provides visibility to the recordings within and reflects the paramount importance Moses Asch placed on what he intended to be "the marriage between the front art and the inside content." The covers complement in stylistic range and thematic focus the breathtaking diversity of this remarkable collection.

The cover designs are unique and distinctive in several ways. The limited color printing, trademark matte black background and edges, uncoated paper, and use of authentic imagery true to the recording differentiated Folkways covers from others. The look and the feel of the albums stood out among the glossy mainstream covers in record stores. These features created a consistent visual identity among Folkways covers yet allowed for visual differentiation of specific music genres within the catalog.

Tight budgets for production and printing played a part in Folkways cover designs. In some covers, the clever use of inexpensive two-color printing yielded a third color through careful overprinting of one color on another. In the interest of economy, images occasionally appeared on more than one cover, and the same mechanical artwork was sometimes printed in different color combinations to create a series of covers. The distinctive Folkways visual identity remained constant over the decades, with later designers for the Smithsonian Folkways label adopting the

Ronald Clyne outside his home, c. 1960.
(© David Gahr)

original "Folkways look." Despite the modest design production, the record label created some of the most innovative and groundbreaking record covers ever.

Key to the success of the Folkways covers was Asch's respect for the artist and the importance he placed on the visual. In his view, the artist's work, like that of the musician, needed to be preserved and disseminated. The visual component of the album cover should both reach out to and be an expression of humanity. Folkways cover art ranges from reproductions of the works of such widely recognized artists as Pablo Picasso and Marc Chagall to the works of artists closely associated with Moses Asch, such as Ben Shahn and David Stone Martin, whose work reflected his aesthetic sensibilities and social conscience. Many other covers make reference to and use of numerous vernacular pictorial traditions— including preindustrial and non-Western artistic techniques, such as woodcut prints, cutout art, and other kinds of folk handwork.

Although numerous graphic designers worked for Folkways over the decades, the designs of David Stone Martin, Irwin Rosenhouse, and especially Ronald Clyne dominate the body of work. Many of the more than five hundred covers designed by Clyne convey a spare, minimalist aesthetic representing avant-garde tendencies in post–World War II graphic design, which contributed significantly to the Folkways look. The carefully considered images, typography, and layout clearly indicate the Folkways design imperative to reflect and complement the sounds on the recording.

THE SOUNDS OF THE OFFICE BY MICHAEL SIEGEL

FOLKWAYS RECORDS FX 6142

A classic cover by Ronald Clyne for the album *The Sounds of the Office*.

Clyne was a master of type design, as this clever cover for Poe's *The Pit and the Pendulum* illustrates.

Just as Folkways Records gave a voice to ordinary people, including the disenfranchised within society, the covers functioned to make visible the invisible and to represent the underrepresented. The photographic covers, in particular, create a unique "portrait gallery," visually commemorating, documenting, and indeed making visible the musicians, communities, and locales heard on the recordings. These covers reflect the diversity of the collection as a whole—from the early work of the well-established New York photographer Walker Evans to David Gahr's groundbreaking photographs of the folk music scene of the 1960s; from the sensitive and wide-ranging works of musician, filmmaker, and photographer John Cohen to those of preeminent Chicago blues and jazz photographer Raeburn Flerlage. A sizable number of covers display photographs taken by nonprofessional, often anonymous photographers—field ethnographers, family members, or others close to the musicians in the pictures.

Folkways Records was a pioneer in presenting unfamiliar sounds on record. The cover art created for Folkways responded in myriad ways to the special challenge of inviting listeners to discover these remarkable albums.

THE WOMEN BLUES OF CHAMPION JACK DUPREE
FOLKWAYS RECORDS FS 3825

Clyne sensitively uses one of David Gahr's photographs to illustrate the concept of women's blues.

LISTEN UP!

Anthology of American Folk Music • SFW40090 • 1997

The Harry Smith Connection • FW40085 • 1998

Kiowa Peyote Meeting • FW04601 • 1964

First Blues: Rags, Ballads and Harmonium Songs
• Allen Ginsberg • FW37560 • 1981

The Country Blues • RBF1 • 1959

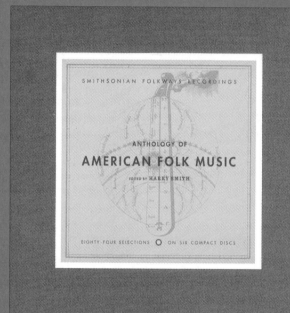

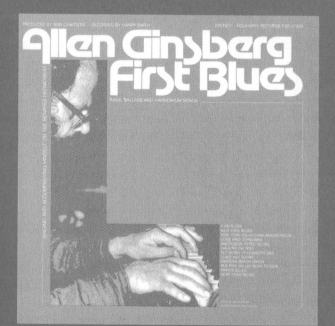

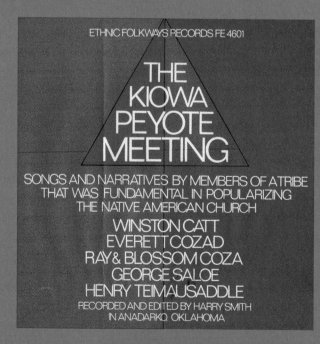

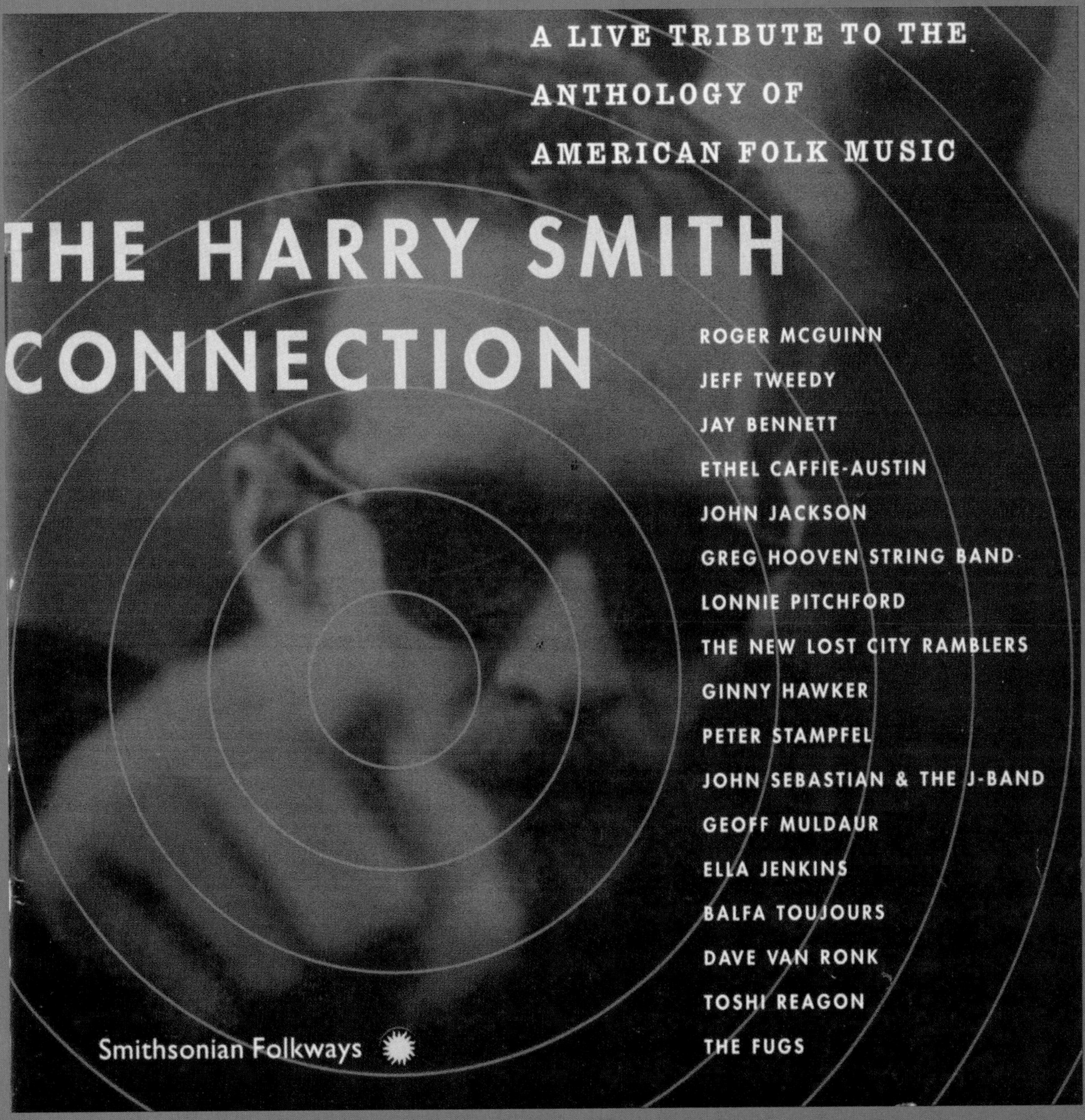
A LIVE TRIBUTE TO THE
ANTHOLOGY OF
AMERICAN FOLK MUSIC
THE HARRY SMITH
CONNECTION
ROGER MCGUINN
JEFF TWEEDY
JAY BENNETT
ETHEL CAFFIE-AUSTIN
JOHN JACKSON
GREG HOOVEN STRING BAND
LONNIE PITCHFORD
THE NEW LOST CITY RAMBLERS
GINNY HAWKER
PETER STAMPFEL
JOHN SEBASTIAN & THE J-BAND
GEOFF MULDAUR
ELLA JENKINS
BALFA TOUJOURS
DAVE VAN RONK
TOSHI REAGON
THE FUGS
Smithsonian Folkways

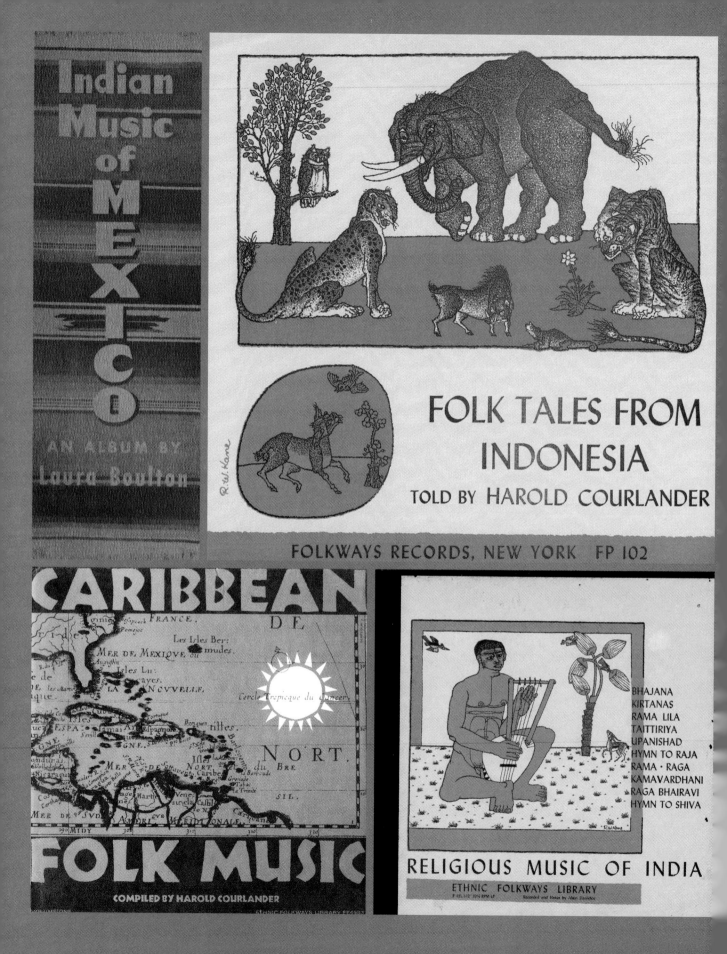

Indian Music of MEXICO

AN ALBUM BY Laura Boulton

FOLK TALES FROM INDONESIA

TOLD BY HAROLD COURLANDER

FOLKWAYS RECORDS, NEW YORK   FP 102

CARIBBEAN FOLK MUSIC

COMPILED BY HAROLD COURLANDER

ETHNIC FOLKWAYS LIBRARY FE4533

BHAJANA
KIRTANAS
RAMA LILA
TAITTIRIYA
UPANISHAD
HYMN TO RAJA
RAMA · RAGA
KAMAVARDHANI
RAGA BHAIRAVI
HYMN TO SHIVA

RELIGIOUS MUSIC OF INDIA

ETHNIC FOLKWAYS LIBRARY
P 431 1-12 33⅓ RPM LP   Recorded and Notes by Alain Daniélou

Chapter 5

MUSIC OF THE WORLD'S PEOPLES

Long before world music became the latest trend, Moses Asch recognized the need for good recordings of musical performances from around the world. He saw folk music as a unifying force among people. As early as 1956, in a paper given to the Music Librarians' Association, Asch noted, "The differences in a people's cultural symbols should not dim our awareness that their response to some stage of the life cycle is essentially very much like our own."

HAROLD COURLANDER AND THE ETHNIC FOLKWAYS LIBRARY

Asch was fortunate to meet a man who could carry forward the vision of creating a library of the world's music: Harold Courlander (1908–1996). Courlander was the son of a painter, and early on showed unusual talents as a writer. He also showed an early interest in Haitian folklore and music and would become an expert on the island's culture. A man of multiple enthusiasms, Courlander divided his time between writing nonfiction accounts of his field work and fictional novels based on traditional folklore.

Courlander came to Asch—as most of his collaborators did—through a personal connection. The folksinger Richard Dyer-Bennet, who was popular in the 1940s and 1950s for his high-art renditions of traditional ballads and songs, was Courlander's friend. When Courlander returned to New York from a Haitian field trip in the mid-1940s, he played some discs for Dyer-Bennet. As Courlander recalled decades later to Gary Kenton:

> I don't think [Dyer-Bennet] was particularly interested in the records themselves, but he said, "Well maybe this is something Moe Asch would be interested in," and he took me down to meet Moe Asch. . . . So I played some of this stuff for Moe, and Dick said, "Well, would you be interested in putting out some of this on your label?" And Moe said, "I'd be crazy not to."

Harold Courlander (right) with an Ethiopian boy photographed during a field trip to Africa in the early 1950s.

Asch had previously issued some foreign recordings—primarily obtained from Eastern European and Russian sources—and was interested in expanding this line. In Courlander he found an ideal partner: someone who had traveled the world, knew other anthropologists interested in music (the term *ethnomusicologist* was yet to be introduced), and also was aware of commercial recordings that could be used to document other cultures. Courlander originally oversaw world music 78 albums released on Asch's Disc label in 1946–47; when the label folded, these first releases were transferred to Folkways. Courlander and Asch decided to name the series the Ethnic Folkways Library, to mark them as distinct from Folkways' other releases. The original albums were issued with plain red covers, with a small sticker on the front indicating the contents. The simple packaging reinforced the idea of these being archival materials, and Asch undoubtedly intended to sell the recordings primarily to librarians.

Courlander was not only the series' editor but also one of its key contributors. During World War II, he had worked for the Voice of America and had accumulated recordings made for broadcast use that would form the basis of several Folkways anthologies. Courlander also was a pioneering field worker,

particularly in Haiti, beginning in the 1930s, where he first recorded folktales and stories, songs, rituals, and other folk expressions. His sympathy for native cultures comes through in his sensitive documentation of the music that he heard.

Like most of Moe's collaborators then—and for decades to come—Courlander didn't expect Folkways to be able to support his work, even though he was committed to supplying the firm with his recordings:

> My work with Folkways never supported my field work; it sort of supplemented it. Moe always wanted the records that I made. But we never had any problems about it. I would get some kind of nominal advance plus promise of royalties. I wouldn't say that Moe was so faithful to those royalty practices, and some of those contracts weren't worth their weight in feathers.

Moses Asch and Harold Courlander in the Folkways offices in the late 1950s. (© David Gahr)

Recording Haitian Music

Harold Courlander

This article was written by Courlander circa 1946 as a part of a press release for the original 78 album of his Haitian recordings.

Cover of Courlander's collection of *Creole Songs*, issued by the Disc Ethnic Series, the predecessor of the Ethnic Folkways Library. (Drawing by David Stone Martin)

I went for the first time [to Haiti] in 1932. . . . I first started by writing down the texts by hand, and then having the singers sing while I worked at the musical notations. . . . [I had] the singers go over and over the songs, and sometimes had considerable difficulty with the melodies . . . until [I] discovered that there was no exact way of singing them. Each singer interpreted a song in his own way, and possibly would sing it differently at different time[s]. . . . I came to the conclusion that only recordings would do full justice to Haitian music. . . . In 1939 I borrowed a recording machine from another folksong collector. . . .

A large part of the collection was taken right in Port-au-Prince, the capital city. In retrospect, the scene is somewhat bizarre. I was staying at the Grand Hotel Oloffson, up the hill on the edge of the city. . . . Often I went back into the hills to do my collecting. But in the course of a half-dozen expeditions to Haiti I had discovered that among the 25 or so hotel employees were some of the best singers and drummers of the South. They were mostly country people who had come to the city in search of work. Two of them were sons of houngans, or Vodoun priests. Virtually all of them had belonged to Congo or Dahomey cults in their own community.

I took a room off the open air kitchen of the hotel and converted it into a studio. Then, every afternoon singers and drummers from over the hill would come down with their drums and other instruments. At the sound of the first drum beat, service throughout the hotel came to a standstill. All the houseboys,

cooks, gardeners, and laundresses converged on the studio and crowded in. And then, for the next 2 hours, I simply cut one recording after another, while the various performers vied with one another to demonstrate the beauties of songs they had learned in their own villages. Often the regular habitués of the afternoon sessions would bring friends with them who had something new to contribute.

The playing of drums in the city day after day was rather unusual and invited comment. In the first place, the playing of drums except on special permit was prohibited in the Port-au-Prince zone. I had made arrangements with the police department, which normally issued the permits, and had received a carte blanche. . . . [However,] people began to whisper that Vodoun cult services were being held [in the hotel].

Although they had no overall plan—and no funds to send people out to record—Courlander and Asch began with what they could find either on existing recordings or from Courlander and his acquaintances. Over time, they encountered more and more field workers, and soon they were inundated with tapes, some very good, some not so good, but all documenting some type of unique musical expression. Although the releases jumped around from region to region, the general idea of trying to fill gaps whenever possible guided them in making their selections, along with concerns for quality and documentation. As Courlander told Kenton:

Courlander's Almanac cover.

> If we knew an anthropologist who was going to the Congo or the Pacific Islands or the Greek Islands . . . who happened to be interested in recording as one of his activities, we sort of got acquainted. And [I] said, "Maybe we could put some of this stuff out, once you came back." There was too much stuff, a lot of it wasn't that good. And even a lot of the stuff we put out, but it was the only thing of its kind available at the moment.

They were also hampered by the technology available at the time. Courlander recalled using a wind-up machine that had a tendency to run down in the middle of a performance; he often would have to keep turning the handle in a regular rhythm to try to maintain the proper speed.

Courlander was a tireless promoter of world music. Besides the Folkways LPs, he featured early recordings—both his own and from commercial and archival sources—on his radio program. These shows were designed to appeal to novice listeners, and so they often focused on a single theme. One of these shows formed the basis of a remarkable album, titled *Courlander's Almanac: Familiar Music in Strange Places*, broadcast in 1954 and issued on LP two years later. It was one of the first albums to show the impact of American popular music on seemingly the most remote and "unspoiled" musical cultures. The recording included a Thai chorus singing the "Maine Fight Song" and Tahitians chanting "Little Joe the Wrangler."

In the record's notes, Courlander recognized a trend that would accelerate greatly over the following decades: the melding of musical cultures as radio and recordings brought different musical styles together.

What happens when a popular Disney tune is heard in Malaya or Burma? Or to an American college song heard in China or Thailand? . . . Or to a modern Chinese "pop" tune in the United States? While cultures everywhere are busy protecting their own traditions, they are eagerly "borrowing" from one another in a fashion that would have been unthinkable 20 or 30 years ago.

The initial sales for most of the Ethnic Folkways Library releases must have been tiny. Syndicated reviewer Bert Metcalf, writing in 1947 on the release of *Folk Music of the Central East U.S.S.R.*, described it frankly as "an album with extremely limited appeal and one that in all probability never will be heard on the average radio station"—not an inapt description. Two years later, the *New York Times* gave a positive review to the first two releases in the new Ethnic Folkways Library, but again noted that few would probably be interested in buying these albums. A week later, however, a surprised reporter noted:

[Al]though [our review] was favorable it was not expected that many collectors would have more than a passing curiosity. But this guess was wide of the mark. The public interest was downright extraordinary. People in all parts of the country . . . kept us busy for days with inquiries about the albums. What most people wanted to know was where they could obtain the disks, since their local dealers did not have them, had not heard of them and did not know where to get them.

In "self-defense," the reviewer ran the company's address in his column.

In creating the Ethnic Folkways Library, Asch and Courlander recognized a growing trend among anthropologists and musicologists, who were increasingly focusing on the music of the rest of the world (i.e., non-western). Asch was in attendance at the 1955 meeting of the American Anthropological Association, where the Society for Ethnomusicology was born. Pioneering scholars Bruno Nettl, Alan Merriam, David McAllester, and Willard Rhodes were among the founders, and most would become "producers" of material for the Ethnic Folkways Library over the coming years or had already contributed to it.

The society's members—mostly professors at larger universities—would become a ready market for the recordings. But, more importantly, they would also become the means by which the series would grow. Often supported by grants, they could afford to spend time in the field, recording traditional music as it was being created. Being academics, they were also used to carefully documenting their sources. All Asch had to do was to edit the tapes and new records could be created.

HENRY AND SIDNEY ROBERTSON COWELL: MUSIC OF THE WORLD'S PEOPLE

Just as Folkways had pioneered in creating multivolume introductions to the history of jazz and American folk song, one of Courlander's first major projects was the creation of the five-LP set *Music of the World's People.* To assemble and annotate this material, he hired a close friend, composer and musicologist Henry Cowell (1897–1965). Cowell had long been involved in avant-garde music (a longtime friend and associate of Charles Seeger, he published the journal *New Music* to present scores by his contemporaries) and also had a long-standing interest in world music, drawing on non-Western tonalities and scales in his own compositions. In 1931 he had studied world music with the pioneering ethnomusicologist Erich von Hornbostel in Berlin. So Cowell was a natural choice to put together this series.

Henry Cowell plays a tone cluster. Peter Bartók took this photo while recording Cowell's piano music album for Folkways. (Courtesy of Peter Bartók)

Source material for such an ambitious project would be more difficult to find than the discarded jazz and country 78s that Asch had previously reissued. But, unrestrained by questions of copyright and ownership, Asch, Cowell, and Courlander scoured transcriptions of radio broadcasts, foreign commercial 78s, and anything else they could lay their hands on to put together this series, which was released between 1951 and 1955. The first LP opens with a girls' chorus from Madagascar followed by a medley of Irish reels, setting the stage for a seemingly random, hopscotch journey among different musical cultures and styles. Unlike Frederic Ramsey's historical approach in the *Jazz* set or Harry Smith's mystical organization for the *Anthology,* Cowell chose to let the music speak for itself.

True to Folkways' vision of all music having an equal and legitimate role in world culture, there is no discernible organization by race, ethnicity, style, or social function; the music is to be listened to on its own terms and the interaction among the musical forms to be judged (or not) by the listener. Cowell's notes are informative and—for their time—offer a good introduction to each musical style, but they don't offer an overarching "theory" for understanding the music as a whole. Typical also of Asch's vision, the performers are usually not identified in Cowell's notes; it is not the personality of the singing "star" that is the focus, but rather the song and its heritage. As his wife and longtime collaborator, Sidney Robertson Cowell, recalled to Peter Goldsmith, Cowell wasn't interested in researching the history of individual musical cultures, but rather drew on his personal knowledge of music to write more generally about each recording: "[Henry's] notes were based on the music; he wasn't interested in, and had no sense, or training, in looking up stuff."

Until Cowell's death in the early 1960s, Asch relied on him to supply notes for world recordings that were otherwise undocumented. Because of their long relationship, Cowell was always happy to comply, as his wife recalled: "He said, 'Well you see it's something I really enjoy. You see for many years Moe and I were the only people in the entire city of New York who were interested in this sort of stuff.'"

Robertson Cowell was also an important contributor to Folkways' ethnic and folk music lists. She began her career in folk music as an assistant to Charles Seeger in the mid-1930s, when Seeger was employed by the Rural Resettlement Program of the WPA in Washington. She made several trips during this period, initially working side by side with John Lomax and then on her own. Her recordings of musicians from the Ozarks, the Wolf River region of the upper Midwest, and California were all important early documents of folk song and instrumental music. In the 1950s, she continued her work in Wolf River, and also traveled several times to the Aran Islands and Cape Breton to record traditional singers there.

"There is no better way to know a people than to enter with them into their musical life."

—Henry Cowell

One of her first releases for Folkways was a record of shape note singing, released in 1951. Robertson Cowell was hired by Columbia University to put together a concert of southern religious music in 1950, so she traveled to Tennessee to see if she could locate a traditional shape note group. She recalled this expedition forty-two years later:

> I went down into Tennessee with an introduction . . . to a small town school teacher named Sally Adams [who] had uncles and cousins and brothers who were singing school masters. And they all got together and Sam [Eskin] sat on the floor [and] made the recording.
>
> They were wonderful because they sang so wonderfully out of tune. Sally Adams was the lead, the most vociferous of the lot. You know, they sing very loud, with a trotting rhythm, all very intent, and they double up the system. They choose the tune they like the best, so you have everybody singing the bass and everybody singing the descant. They sing so ardently. And Sally would stand in front and yell into the microphone; I had such a time getting her to stand away from the microphone. But if I put her back, she was in behind the singers, and they'd sing off pitch.

Although this material was not intended to be released, when she returned to New York either her husband or Moe suggested it would make a good album.

Robertson Cowell always was careful to make sure that the singers understood that she was not profiting off their music and that if there was any commercial use of it, she would see that they were given their fair share. Like many collectors, then and now, she found it hard to get this point across to some informants, even the ones she knew best; she said, "I could never get it through their heads that I wasn't making any money off of this. I had my expenses paid at a very low rate, and they never really believed that I would do such a thing, go to so much trouble, for nothing."

Of course, Moe didn't pay her much for these albums. Nonetheless, Robertson Cowell managed to see that the singers saw some compensation, as in this lovely story about how she got Moe to pay one of the singers from the Aran Islands:

Singer on the Aran Islands, photographed by Sidney Robertson Cowell during her field work there.

I think I told you about the family from Ireland . . . when their cow died, I wrote Moe and said firmly I wanted $150 for this recording. And Moe immediately sent it to me. The reason for $150 was that was what it cost to heat their house for the year, in peat, there [were] no trees or anything growing on the Aran Islands, it was all rocks . . . I just informed Moe that he owed that to them, and without any argument he just sent it to me. He wouldn't have sent it if I had suggested it was payment for singing, I think.

Sam Gesser: Documenting Canadian Music

D. A. Sonneborn

One summer's day in 1950, a young man named Sam Gesser from Montreal was on vacation in Chicago, visiting local jazz clubs and soaking up the scene. Browsing in a record store, he came across a Lead Belly 10-inch LP. He had heard folk music while babysitting for his uncle's children and remembers being thrilled listening to Lead Belly, John Jacob Niles, and Josh White on 78 rpm records. On the way back home, he read in the album's booklet the list of other Folkways albums. But although he visited several record stores in Montreal, not a single one carried Folkways records.

Gesser jumped on a bus headed south to Manhattan, went over to the Folkways office, and met Moses Asch. Asch told him Folkways needed a Canadian distributor—all he had to do was visit those record stores and take orders. Although he was working as a commercial artist, Gesser had taken his first step into entering the music business, and slowly grew a native Canadian network of Folkways outlets.

During one of his early visits with Asch, Gesser asked why Folkways had only one record of Canadian material. Asch replied, "What are you going to do about it?" Sam's answer was to start recording folksingers, field-recording in the nearby Laurentian Mountains, contacting other folk music collectors who had devoted their lives to recording Canada's audio history, and sending the material to Asch. Between 1951 and 1964, Sam produced or helped along nearly a hundred Folkways albums of Canadian-based traditions: aboriginal, First Nations, French, Anglo (British, Scots, Irish), Caribbean, Spanish, South American, German, Near Eastern, and Ukrainian music, poetry, language instruction, and more. Moe never refused an album Sam offered him. Gesser's verbal contract with Asch was simple: he had to promise a wholesale purchase of one hundred copies of each title pressed.

Artists whom Sam Gesser introduced to the Folkways catalog include Canadian folk giants Alan Mills, Hélène Baillargeon, Jacques Lebrecque, and fiddler extraordinaire Jean Carignan; Marius Barbeau's recordings of Canadian Indians; classical performances by well-known violinist Hyman Bress; Canadian maritime songs; Jewish folk songs; and much more. After Folkways, he put together compilations of Canadian folk music for Mercury Records, later Universal. This alone was a magnificent accomplishment and was an important seedbed for what came to be known as the Canadian folk music revival.

That would be enough to be a legend in some circles, but not long into the distribution business, Gesser recognized that live performances by artists would boost his album sales. He put together a Pete Seeger concert in Montreal, and then in 1954 founded Gesser Enterprises, which led to more than forty years of impresario activity: all across Canada, with many hundreds of folk, classical, pop music, dance, and live theater ensembles in more than six thousand performances, from Leonard Cohen to Janis Joplin, guitarist Julian Bream, pianist Van Cliburn, violinist Isaac Stern, the New York Philharmonic Orchestra, national folkloric dance ensembles from Africa, Asia, and Europe, classical and modern dance companies from Alvin Ailey to the Royal Winnipeg Ballet, musical theater galore, European and Chinese opera, and other performance groups. In the 1960s he programmed jazz and classical music festivals as well as the Canadian pavilion stages at the World's Fairs in Montreal (Expo 1967) and Osaka, Japan (Expo 1970). Not only was Gesser a field recordist and record and concert producer, but after he retired from concert production in the 1990s he wrote movie scripts and plays.

Gesser was friendly, unassuming, and easy to talk with. Occasionally, he questioned how he accomplished all he had, or even why he thought he could do it. "I just did what I really wanted to do, what really interested me," he said, "and it never occurred to me that it was impossible."

"They don't care <u>what</u> Folkways is paying. They won't play after the moon sets."

This 1964 cartoon from the *New Yorker* shows how well Folkways' world music recordings had become known in popular culture. (© The New Yorker Collection 1964 Wilson from cartoonbank.com. All Rights Reserved)

OTHER EARLY COLLECTORS: LAURA BOULTON, BÉLA BARTÓK, AND HENRIETTA YURCHENCO

One of the first contributors to the Ethnic Folkways Library was Native American music specialist Laura Boulton (1899–1980). She first heard traditional Navajo singers at the American Indian Village, a part of the Chicago Century of Progress Exposition, held in 1933–34. Along with her colleague George Herzog, she recorded several Navajo singers there. This led to a 1940 field expedition to the southwestern United States, sponsored by the U.S. Bureau of Indian Affairs. Recordings from this trip were used to assemble the first commercial album of Native American music, issued by RCA Victor in 1941. True to form, the major corporation quickly took the 78 album out of print; equally true to form, Moe Asch picked up the entire package, cover art and all, and reissued it.

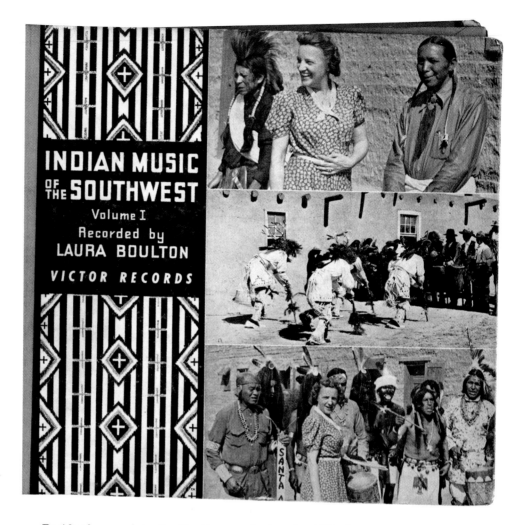

Laura Boulton is shown in the top and bottom panels of the cover of her Victor collection of Native American music. When this collection went out of print, Folkways reissued it—with the same cover.

Besides her work in the Southwest, during the 1950s Boulton also produced for Folkways recordings of Eskimo music from Alaska and the Hudson Bay, along with several albums of Eastern European music. Because her recordings were made by assembling groups of people from across a country in a major city—for example, in Belgrade's state radio station—many felt the performances were not as "authentic" as those collected in the field. Where Boulton lacked expertise about some of the music she recorded, she relied on others to fill in the details. Nonetheless, her early recordings have value as important documents of the musical cultures at that time.

The Demonstration Collection of Erich von Hornbostel

Asch, Courlander, and the Cowells were aware of the history of world music recording, having lived through the development of the field from the turn of the century through World War II. Besides issuing new recordings, they drew on well-known archives and commercial sources to bring into common circulation material that otherwise would have been almost totally inaccessible to students and scholars. True to Asch's vision, the sound quality of some of these early recordings was less significant than their importance in documenting a musical culture that was disappearing (if not already gone).

One of the key sources in world music study was the "demonstration collection" of cylinder recordings housed in the Berlin Phonogramm-Archiv and gathered by pioneering German musicologist Erich von Hornbostel and his colleagues. This collection of 112 musical examples was in many ways the first world music "anthology," and von Hornbostel used it to teach about musical cultures at the University of Berlin through the 1930s. One of his students was Henry Cowell, who brought a copy-set of the recordings back to America to form the basis of (probably) the first course on world music taught in this country, at New York's New School. Cowell's set—along with a second purchased by George Herzog while he was studying in Germany—formed the basis of the release of this material in a two-LP boxed set by Folkways in 1963.

The range of material in the collection is truly extraordinary. Although the first recordings—of a Thai orchestra

that was visiting Berlin in 1900—were made in Germany, it is noteworthy that many were true field recordings. Cylinder machines employed fairly simple technology and portable models were readily available, so anthropologists were easily able to set up in the field. Although playback was limited and the sound quality not ideal, many musicologists used the cylinders only to make transcriptions and didn't really care about the fidelity. It wasn't until the 1930s and the coming of battery-operated disc recorders that the cylinder was finally replaced as the field recording machine of choice.

Henrietta Yurchenco (far right) and her students and members of the Hunter family on John's Island, South Carolina, 1970.

A key early field worker whose collecting would have a great impact on his own compositions—and thus directly on twentieth-century classical music—was Hungarian composer Béla Bartók. Beginning in 1903, Bartók made several recording trips into small towns and villages in his homeland, documenting the tonalities, scales, and rhythms that characterize Eastern European music. He would go on to record widely throughout Eastern Europe and into Turkey. In 1939, he oversaw his last major recordings of traditional music; in what his son Peter described as a "reverse expedition," performers were brought into Budapest to be recorded in the professional studios of the Hungarian Broadcasting Company. Peter recalled: "It was a great event for these people who had never before seen the city. At the end of each performance each person would announce his name, age, where he came from and occupation. A whistle at the end of a side was used . . . in order to check the speed of the recording." (Coincidentally, Peter Bartók became a recording engineer himself, and worked for Asch through the 1950s; see Chapter 11.)

In 1950, Asch issued two albums from Bartók's collections: *Folk Music of Rumania* drew on commercial 78s that Bartók had collected and transcribed, and *Folk Music of Hungary* drew on the 1939 studio recordings that he had supervised. Each was a major collection important in the study of Bartók's music as well as in understanding world music and culture.

Henrietta Yurchenco (1916–2007) was an important field worker who was a key player in the New York City folk revival of the late 1940s and early 1950s (see Chapter 9). In the mid-1930s, she pioneered field recording in Mexico, bringing to the West knowledge of dozens of native tribes and traditions that previously had been unknown. Using donkeys to haul hundreds of pounds of disc-recording equipment into the mountains, she was able to go where no white Westerner had been before. After World War II, Yurchenco started a radio show on New York's public station, WNYC, which would continue through the 1950s and early 1960s. Among her early guests were Woody Guthrie, and about a decade later Bob Dylan. She also taught for many years at Hunter College, and continued her field work in Mexico, in Puerto Rico, and also in Morocco, where she documented the music and culture of the Sephardic Jewish population.

In 1970, Yurchenco took a class of students to John's Island, off the coast of South Carolina. She recalled, "We were housed in modest quarters in . . . a community facility which included a gym, and a grocery store. My students talked with many people, went to church with them, visited their homes and played with their children. On John's Island they came to understand the importance and the meaning of music in a folk community." Thanks to this total immersion, the students became particularly close to one family, the Hunters, including Jane Hunter and her thirteen children, fifty-four grandchildren, and three great-grandchildren. The students were able to compare stories and songs of several generations of the same family. In 1973, the results appeared on Folkways.

COLIN TURNBULL AND THE ITURI PYGMIES

Colin Turnbull's work stands out among the important releases in Folkways' Ethnic Series in the 1950s. He visited the Ituri rain forest in the Congo over several years in the 1950s to record the music and customs of the Mbuti Pygmies. Two albums of this music were issued in 1957–58, with extensive notes by Turnbull. This in turn led to his landmark book, *The Forest People*, published in 1960.

Turnbull was in many ways an unusual scholar; he became strongly engaged with his subjects and did little to hide his personal likes and dislikes in his writings (he preferred the forest-based Mbuti to the more "civilized" tribes that he encountered). Born in England, Turnbull was educated at Oxford before enlisting in World War II. He completed his studies in India, and then made his first trip to the Congo in 1951. While there, Turnbull met Hollywood producer Sam Spiegel, who was in Africa overseeing the John Huston film *The African Queen*. Turnbull somehow convinced Spiegel to hire him to help build the boat for which the film is titled while he began his studies of the native populations.

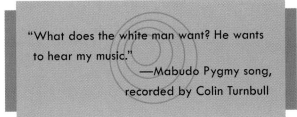

"What does the white man want? He wants to hear my music."
—Mabudo Pygmy song, recorded by Colin Turnbull

Restless after his African sojourn, Turnbull moved to rural Canada to try his luck at gold mining before returning to academic life in Oxford in 1954. Trips to Africa in 1957–58 led to his landmark work with the Mbuti Pygmies, and in

Colin Turnbull recording Mbuti Pygmies, 1953. Turnbull traveled by motorcycle through the area, carrying his recording equipment with him. (Courtesy of the Avery Research Center for African-American History & Culture, College of Charleston)

1959 he settled in New York City to join the staff of the American Museum of Natural History. He would later teach anthropology at Virginia Commonwealth University. He and his lifelong partner, the African American anthropologist Joseph Towles, lived openly as a couple in conservative rural Virginia.

Turnbull was particularly fascinated by the group singing technique that the Mbuti had developed, called *hocketing* by musicologists. Each singer performs only one or two notes; by alternating, a melody is created. This can be used for both vocal and instrumental music. It takes a sophisticated sense of time and musical flow for a group to achieve this effect effortlessly.

Turnbull was concerned by the encroachment of other tribes—notably the Bantu—whose lifestyle was more agrarian and settled than that of the forest-dwelling Mbuti. The Mbuti were being lured to villages and losing their contact with the natural world. Like many other ethnomusicologists of the day, Turnbull was trying to "preserve" the "purest" form of Mbuti music against this encroachment through his photographs, text, and sound recordings.

Turnbull's description of the importance of the elephant hunt in Mbuti society and of the subsequent singing of celebratory songs shows his deep sympathy for the people and their culture.

In [the] elephant-hunting song split sticks are used to mark the time, and only the men and boys around the main fire are singing. They start off with a couple of chords, but then as usual there is a long warming-up period. The solo is taken up by two young hunters, overlapping, taking over from each other the story of the hunt. The chorus, very hesitant and uncertain to begin with, slowly gets under way, using the hocketing technique in which each singer has one or two particular notes, and in this way a harmonic as well as melodic pattern is passed around the circle. As the chorus takes shape the soloist tells his simple story, occasionally breaking off to tell the others that they are putting up a pretty poor show. Then he stands up and begins to dance. The chorus and the split sticks continue without change now, and the soloist dances in the firelight, miming the story of the elephant hunt. He ends his act with a series of yodels of satisfaction.

RUTH STONE AND THE MUSIC OF LIBERIA

Ruth Stone was a college student when she heard *Folk Music of Liberia*, recorded by Packard L. Okie and released in 1954. When Stone was studying African music, it was the only recording available from Liberia (outside of archives, whose recordings were difficult for a student to obtain), and it inspired her to want to study African music further. She enrolled in the graduate music program at Hunter College. As part of her studies, she went to Liberia and made a series of recordings. Knowing that Asch had released the first album, she went to his offices and presented the reels to him, along with the documentation. Typically for a Folkways release, Stone had to type the album's notes herself and her sister contributed the cover art, a sketch based on one of her field photographs. The album was released in 1972, while Stone was still completing her graduate work.

Stone remembers that Asch wanted her to do more recordings, but she was too busy in school to produce further material. She recalls that, not surprisingly, Asch was particularly interested in children's music and specifically asked for that type of material from her field work. She remembers him as "friendly" and "grandfatherly" but somewhat disorganized; when Stone returned to the Folkways offices to retrieve the original tapes, she recalls watching Asch rummage through shelves of tapes, some with their tails hanging out, and wondering whether she'd ever see her original recordings again. He eventually found her reels, much to her relief, with the tags she had placed on each indicating which tracks should be used on the LP.

KEN BILBY AND THE ROOTS OF JAMAICAN MUSIC

Many of the contributors to the Ethnic Series were just beginning their careers, and working with Folkways gave them their first experience putting together their field work into record albums. Ken Bilby was still in college when he recorded two volumes of Jamaican traditional music for Folkways in 1973. Bilby had been visiting Jamaica since he was a child because his grandmother lived there, so early on he became interested in the local music. His inspiration to record Jamaican music on his own came partly from his exposure to it through earlier Folkways albums:

> I became interested in ethnomusicology quite early on. I was still actually just finishing up high school. Part of what got me interested was . . . coming across Folkways Records. I was aware already of a couple of Folkways recordings done in Jamaica. One was called *Jamaican Cult Music*, which was recorded by George Simpson [in 1954], and another one was called *Folk Music of Jamaica* [from 1956], recorded by the future Prime Minister, Edward Seaga.

Bilby enrolled at Bard College to study anthropology. He took a course on world music there taught by avant-garde jazz trombonist Roswell Rudd. At the time, Rudd was working with Alan Lomax, and he encouraged Bilby to try field recording on his next visit to Jamaica. Bilby owned a Sony portable cassette recorder with a built-in stereo mic that he had bought in the late 1960s, and he used it for this field work. When he played Rudd his tapes, Rudd thought the music was fantastic.

Encouraged by Rudd, Bilby made more recordings and then decided to drop in on the Folkways offices to see if they might be interested in releasing his work:

> I was a little scared. I mean, I just showed up, didn't call ahead or anything. And [Moe Asch] was right there, no secretary or anything. He was legendary of course, to me. . . . And I have to say it was a little scary because he was a little gruff, but on the other hand I found it quite amazing that he was encouraging too. So it was very good for me at that stage.
>
> I just said I have some material that I thought [he] might be interested in. And he asked me a little about it, where it was from and all. And I think he became a little bit extra interested when I told him it was from Jamaica and it was from rural areas. . . . I was well aware of the fact that Folkways had done Caribbean stuff . . . so I tried selling it to him by connecting it to reggae. He was aware of reggae as a type of politically charged music . . . that was seen as having this strong rural component. He really perked up when he heard that, and he then strongly encouraged me to send the tapes.

Bilby sent dubs of his rough cassettes, and Asch immediately called and said he wanted to release them—in fact, he thought there was enough good material for two albums. Asch told him he'd have to supply the master tapes and photo-ready notes for the albums. Coincidentally, Bilby had enrolled at a local recording studio for a class in recording techniques, so he was able to get free studio time to make a rough master. He thought that Asch would clean up the tapes before issuing them; instead the albums appeared just as he edited them. "There were some rough beginnings, because I figured he'd have somebody fade in and out, I think I even specified that when I sent in the material. Nothing of the sort, it was just left like that, the tape sort of like switching speed as it got started, or jumping and blurring. But that's on the LPs."

Bilby was thrilled to be working for Folkways and was especially pleased when both albums appeared just a few months after he completed them. He was anxious to have something to show other Jamaican musicians so he could convince them to record. Bilby subsequently spent 1977–78 studying the music of the Maroons of Jamaica, as part of his advanced study in ethnomusicology. So it was natural to gather some of this material together for an album for Folkways, particularly since Asch had expressed interest in having more material from the African-influenced musicians.

Ken Bilby filming an abeng blower in Jamaica, c. 1970s. (Courtesy of Ken Bilby)

Bilby's other work for Folkways also emerged from his undergraduate years. In 1974, he had spent a semester studying in New Mexico on an exchange program, where he heard a local fiddler, Facundo Gonzales, who preserved an older style of solo playing. Bilby loved the music, so he began spending time with the fiddler, eventually recording him in his mountain home. He held the tapes for several years, thinking they would not have enough commercial appeal. But after his experience working with Asch, he decided to mention the tapes to him:

> What's telling to me is that Moe Asch would release this. I mean, talk about something with limited commercial value and also rather limited interest—but of musicological and cultural value. And more sort of academic, although I loved the music, just hearing him play the violin alone. But he was already quite old, and a little bit infirm, and far from the peak of his playing. And it showed to some extent in his playing. But [Asch] released it.
>
> I talked to [Asch] about the value of it, and why I thought it had historical value . . . he was gruff, and just said, "Send me the tape." . . . He probably could tell from my description, I didn't play up the obviously limited commercial interest, but he could obviously tell that. He wasn't all that encouraging, but I sent him the tape, and he said that he wanted to go ahead with it right away.

The album appeared with full notes—just like any other Folkways release—in 1979.

Alhaji Fabala Kanuteh: Master Griot

Samuel Charters

Alhaji Fabala Kanuteh, a Mandingo singer whom I'd been told was one of the two griots who served the president of the Gambia, was an impassive, solidly built man in loose brown robes and a white skullcap. As he came slowly across the packed dirt of his compound in the outskirts of Banjul, the Gambia's capital, he studied me with some misgivings. From my sweaty clothes and my sagging bags filled with a portable tape recorder and all of its equipment he could see that I wasn't anyone who was important. He glanced at the man who had brought me, a young Fula named Musa Camara who had a part-time job with the government's radio station. He turned back to me and spoke in hesitant English. "I would not come except this man ask me." He was to go on to a meeting at the presidential palace, but he was willing to meet me as a "representative of the Mandingo people." He led us to a small stucco building in the center of the compound, with light, brightly patterned curtains swaying in the doorways. A few homemade chairs were pushed back against the walls inside and family photographs mounted in the typical Gambian painted glass frames hung above them. As I set up the recording machine he sat on a mat on the floor and played light figures on the instrument in front of him.

The multi-stringed kora is usually thought of as the instrument of the griots today, but before the kora became popular the traditional instrument was the balafon, the handmade wooden marimba that is played everywhere in West Africa. The instruments played for dancing have as many as fifteen or more wooden keys, but the griots' instrument is smaller, only nine keys, and it can be played with a strap around the neck while the singer is standing. Alhaji Fabala was holding thin wooden mallets, tapping out rhythm patterns and flurries of tones sweeping up and

down the keys. The sound was as dry as the compound's dusty earth, and it created a light counterpoint to the rhythmic thudding the women were making as they pounded millet grain in much-used wooden mortars a few yards away across the compound yard.

The first "song" Alhaji Fabala performer was a long, declamatory telling of the story of Almami Samory Toure, a legendary ruler who fought against the British in the nineteenth century. His grandson, Sekou Toure, was the current president of Guinea. As he told the story, his voice serious and thoughtful, the room slowly filled with a cluster of men from the compound, in ordinary work shirts and rumpled

Alhaji Fabala Kanuteh, 1974. (Photo by Sam Charters)

trousers. There were satisfied murmurs as he finished with a last flourish of notes on the balafon, and he looked up without expression, waiting for me to ask for something else. After some hesitation I asked him if he knew a song about the coming of the Europeans. None of the griot narratives I had recorded over the past weeks had gone back to that early moment. Alhaji Fabala was thoughtful, then he shrugged. "I can tell you the history of everything. Africa, India, China, everything. But you must come when you have time to listen." He played a new figure on the keys. "The Europeans? It is a hard song to do and it goes on for a day and a half. I don't sing it often."

Musa had leaned over to whisper to me the outline of the story of the first song, and he continued to tell me in a low voice what the new story was relating. Now, however, I sensed he was listening more intently, and the men sitting around the walls were also nodding with the words. What I understood, as Musa whispered close to my ear, was that I was hearing something very important. When the song finished, the men stirred and Musa hurriedly got to his feet, saying, "You must have my shilling," and he fumbled in his pocket for a coin as a ceremonial payment for a particularly significant performance. Alhaji Fabala nodded gravely as he shook down the sleeve of his robe, "That was from my father's father, and his father's fathers."

Over the next week, working to translate the words of the song with Musa and his sisters, as well as a school teacher who had introduced me to other griots, Aliu S. Dabo, I understood the excitement I had felt as the song was unfolding in the languid air of the compound. I had been able to make out the words "Portuguese," "America," and "American Negro," and I realized that I had heard a narration of the first meeting with the Portuguese in the sixteenth century and the first sale of slaves. The Portuguese sold the slaves on to Dutch traders, and it was the Dutch who brought them to the Virginia colony in North America. The song ended with his quiet conclusion,

It is because of this
that slaves are plenty in America.
They call them American Negroes.

As I listened to the tape again, following the words on the pieces of paper scattered around me on the bare concrete floor of my room above the Gambia River I felt a shiver of excitement and disbelief. I had recorded so many songs over the years that I'd traveled with my tape recorder, but of all of those songs, this one was the most important.

MUSIC OF INDONESIA

Smithsonian Folkways has undertaken several new initiatives to record the music of the world built on the legacy of the Folkways catalog. A major change in approach was initiated by the label's first director, Tony Seeger (see Chapter 12). He felt that earlier recordings tended to be made by Westerners who were visiting a foreign culture, rather than by the residents of the region being recorded.

One of the first new series, a twenty-CD project to document the traditional music of Indonesia, was designed to address this point. Headed by American ethnomusicologist Philip Yampolsky—who had first been introduced to Indonesian gamelan music while a student in California in the 1970s—the project was largely carried out by groups of local ethnomusicologists. In 1991, the Ford Foundation sponsored a festival of Indonesian music as part of the annual Smithsonian Festival of American Folklife. The foundation soon approached Smithsonian Folkways with the idea of issuing two CDs of Indonesian music, suggesting that Yampolsky serve as editor. Yampolsky was interested, but only

Philip Yampolsky recording in Indonesia. (Photo by Tinuk Yampolsky)

if the idea could be expanded into a multi-CD set to document the many styles of Indonesian music that had not yet been adequately recorded. Ford agreed, and the project got under way.

It was important to Yampolsky and the foundation to find a local partner for the project, so they enlisted the help of the Society for Indonesian Performing Arts (Masyarakat Seni Pertunjukan Indonesia, MSPI). In this way, they were able to enlist local musicologists and anthropologists and their students to aid in the recording, which would eventually cover all of the country's twenty-two provinces. Over the next several years, Yampolsky spent approximately half of his time working with these specialists in locating and recording the music, and then returned to the United States to edit and document the material for release. The project took until 1999 to complete, and included recordings of everything from electric guitar music to bamboo tube orchestras.

One of the challenges was sending people out to areas that had not been previously studied by musicologists. Usually an advance party had to be sent to survey the area for possible material. Jabatin Bangun, one of the young ethnomusicologists enlisted in this work, recalled several areas where "we had practically no information about the place. And there were cases of miscommunication with local people." Getting the local people to understand the mission—and even the process of recording itself—could be difficult. Bangun recalled one incident where a simple hand gesture disrupted the recording:

> One time, we were seated underneath a clump of *lontar* [palm] trees, recording a beautiful song that was hard to get right. We had tried several takes already. Some visitors approached, their footsteps making a racket on the dry *lontar* leaves. Philip put up his hand to halt them. This gesture confused the singers, who stopped abruptly, ruining the take yet again. We had to coax them to sing it one more time, and that one finally went off without a hitch.

Even with twenty CDs, Yampolsky quickly realized that he could not create a complete aural picture of all Indonesian music. Instead, he went for depth over breadth: "The aim was not comprehensiveness, for it was not possible to represent every island or every ethnic group. Rather, it was to make available respectful recordings of the astonishing range of Indonesian musical styles." Rather than offering "one short sample of everything you could possibly hear in one place," Yampolsky was careful to include complete performances so that each performance would have integrity.

Folkways Latino and Latin American Recordings

Daniel Sheehy

Folkways Records' holdings of music from Latin America and Latino communities in the United States closely reflect Moses Asch's vision and method for creating an encyclopedic, worldwide mosaic of sound. From 1950 to 1986, virtually every Latin American country (including Latino USA) came to be represented in more than 120 albums, representing a wide array of music made by Indian, *mestizo*, creole, and people of African descent from throughout the hemisphere. Asch featured some of the principal grassroots Latino communities of the United States, as well—particularly Mexican music from the Southwest (marking the unique traditions of New Mexico and Texas) and Puerto Rican music of New York City and the Caribbean island territory. He rounded off the music collection with recordings of poetry and Spanish Christmas songs and games, and he made Spanish-language music an important thread of his children's catalog.

The first recordings of Latino music joined the Folkways catalog in 1950, long before the terms "Latino" or "Hispanic" were current, with two recordings from Mexico and one from Peru. The 1950 *Mariachi Águilas de Chapala* recording was made by renowned herpetologist Charles M. Bogert and his wife Martha. In the notes, Bogert compared the mariachi in Mexico to the saguaro cactus in the Southwest, noting that the mariachi was more plentiful. Bogert's principal prominence in Folkways history would

be for his 1958 record *Sounds of North American Frogs*. His mariachi recording surely was a byproduct of his frog quest in western Mexico.

Harold Courlander's *Cult Music of Cuba* followed in 1951. *Indian Music of Mexico* (Tzotzil, Yaqui, Huichol, Seri, and Cora) by Henrietta Yurchenco and Gordon F. Ekholm, *Spanish and Mexican Folk Music of New Mexico* by J. D. Robb, and *The Black Caribs of Honduras* (English-speaking Garifuna), produced by Doris Stone, appeared in 1952. In this fashion, early on the Folkways "DNA" was spinning itself out in the Latin American domain, favoring ethnographic recordings submitted by world travelers and "honest" performances by musicians dedicated to grassroots folk music. Building on its famous children's records series, in 1960, Folkways published two volumes of poetry and prose by Octavio Corvalán and an album of children's songs by Jorge Rodríguez, *Niños . . . dejad que os cuente un cuento*. Several more Spanish-language children's albums followed suit over the next quarter century.

The 1960s saw urban folksong movements emerge in Chile, Argentina, and other Latin American countries, first emulating the folk styles of their countries, and later creating the *canción nueva* (new song) with a social message drawing attention to poor, rural, and otherwise disenfranchised populations. Rolando Alarcón's *Traditional Chilean*

Songs (1960) represented the former; political refugee Suni Paz's recordings typified the latter. Suni recounts Asch's interest in having her record children's music for Folkways; she agreed (*From the Sky of My Childhood*, 1979; *Earth and Ocean Songs: Canciones de la Mar y la Tierra*, 1982), only after extracting a commitment to record her *música con conciencia* (music with a conscience) as well: *Entre Hermanas: Between Sisters: Women's Songs in Spanish* (1977).

Following the 1986 album *Lowland Tribes of Ecuador* recorded by David Blair Stiffler, the Folkways Latino catalog passed to the new Smithsonian Folkways Recordings. Folkways Director Tony Seeger added recordings related to the Smithsonian Folklife Festival to the catalog: *Puerto Rican Music in Hawai'i: Kachi-Kachi Sound*, recorded by Ted Solís (1989—the first *música latina* recording on the Smithsonian Folkways label); *Music of New Mexico: Hispanic Traditions* (1992), produced by the Smithsonian's Howard Bass of the National Museum of American History and annotated by New Mexican ethnomusicologist James K. Leger; *Borderlands: From Conjunto to Chicken Scratch* (1993); and *Puerto Rico in Washington* (1996) and *Cuba in Washington* (1997). A collaboration with ethnomusicologist Raúl Romero and the Archives of the Andes at the Universidad Católica in Lima, Peru, yielded the major, eight-volume series *Traditional Music of Peru*, a treasure trove of ethnographic recordings from all of the country's regions (1995–2002).

In late 2000, I succeeded Tony Seeger as Folkways director, bringing with me many longstanding scholarly connections to Latin American and American Latino roots music and over twenty years performing several styles of Mexican regional music, *mariachi* in particular. With the rapidly shifting American demographics in mind—the burgeoning Hispanic population was very much in the news—I launched a new initiative, titled *Tradiciones/Traditions*, a Latino music series. With financial support from the Smithsonian Latino Center, anthropologist Russell Rodríguez surveyed the entire Latino holdings for quality, provenance, strengths, and lacunae. The goal was to expand the Folkways collections with new recordings of signature musics of Latin America (including Latino USA). The first recording of the series was *Heroes and Horses: Corridos from the Arizona-Sonora Borderlands* (2002), produced by James Griffith, former head of the Southwest Folklore Center at the University of Arizona. Recordings of Mexican *mariachi, son jarocho* (Veracruz), *son huasteco* (San Luis Potosí), and *son calenteño* (Michoacán); *seis, bomba,* and *plena* from Puerto Rico; *joropo, marimba de chonta,* and *gaita* music from Colombia; Dominican *merengue típico*; Guatemalan marimba; and much more grew the Latino holdings. By early 2008, twenty recordings had been published, garnering seven Grammy nominations and a Latin Grammy, and recordings of *merengue típico* from the Dominican Republic, regional songs of Chile, *joropo-estribillo* from Venezuela, and Afro-Cuban *rumba* were in production. The *Tradiciones/Traditions* series sparked a larger initiative, called *Nuestra Música: Music in Latino Culture*, that included four years of Smithsonian Folklife Festival programs and a major virtual exhibition, *Música del Pueblo*.

LISTEN UP!

HAROLD COURLANDER

Music of Haiti, Vol. 1: Folk Music of Haiti • FW04407 • 1951

Music of Haiti, Vol. 2: Drums of Haiti • FW04403 • 1950

Music of Haiti, Vol. 3: Folkways Songs and Dances of Haiti • FW04432 • 1952

Creole Songs of Haiti • FW06833 • 1954

Haitian Piano • FW06837 • 1952

Calypso and Meringues • FW06808 • 1953

Harold Courlander's Almanac: Familiar Music in Strange Places • FW03863 • 1956

HENRY COWELL

Music of the World's Peoples, Vol. 1 • FW04504 • 1951

Music of the World's Peoples, Vol. 2 • FW04505 • 1952

Music of the World's Peoples, Vol. 3 • FW04506 • 1955

Music of the World's Peoples, Vol. 4 • FW04507 • 1958

Music of the World's Peoples, Vol. 5 • FW04508 • 1961

SIDNEY ROBERTSON COWELL

Old Harp Singing • FW02356 • 1951

Songs from Cape Breton Island • FW04450 • 1955

Songs of Aran • FW04002 • 1957

SAM GASSER

Classic Canadian Songs • SFW40539 • 2006

Songs and Dances of Quebec • FW06951 • 1956

Folk Songs of Ontario • FW04005 • 1958

6 Montreal Poets • FW09805 • 1957

Folk Music of Nova Scotia • FW04006 • 1956

O' Canada, A History in Song • FW03001 • 1956

LAURA BOULTON

Music of the Sioux and the Navajo • FW04401 • 1949

Navajo Songs • SFW40403 • 1992

Indian Music of Mexico • FW08851 • 1957

Songs and Dances of Yugoslavia • FW06805 • 1951

ERICH VON HORNBOSTEL

The Demonstration Collection of E. M. von Hornbostel and the Berlin Phonogramm-Archiv • FW04175 • 1963

BÉLA BARTÓK

Folk Music of Hungary • FW04000 • 1950

Folk Music of Rumania • FW04419 • 1951

HENRIETTA YURCHENCO

Children's Songs and Games from Ecuador, Mexico, and Puerto Rico • FW07854 • 1977

Indian Music of Mexico • FW04413 • 1952

John's Island, South Carolina: Its People and Songs • FW03840 • 1973

Mexico South: Traditional Songs and Dances from the Isthmus of Tehuantepec • FW04378 • 1976

Music of the Maya-Quiches of Guatemala: The Rabinal Achi and Baile de las Canastas • FW04226 • 1978

ETHNIC FOLKWAYS LIBRARY Volume Two   FOLKWAYS RECORDS FE 4505

MUSIC OF THE WORLD'S PEOPLES

Compiled and with Notes by Henry Cowell

Serbia · Iran · Albania · Congo · China · Finland · French Canada · Ukraine
Chile · Italy · Kashmir · Sioux · Jewish · Australia · Cuba · Azerbaijan

Cover design by Ronald Clyne

Music of the Tarascan Indians of Mexico: Music of Michoacán and Mestizo Country • FW04217 • 1970

COLIN TURNBULL
Mbuti Pygmies of the Ituri Rainforest • SFW40401 • 1992

RUTH STONE
Music of the Kpelle of Liberia • FW04385 • 1972

KEN BILBY
Bongo, Backra and Coolie: Jamaican Roots, Vol. 1 • FW04231 • 1975

Bongo, Backra and Coolie: Jamaican Roots, Vol. 2 • FW04232 • 1975

Drums of Defiance: Maroon Music from the Earliest Free Black Communities of Jamaica • SFW40412 • 1992

Facundo Gonzales: New Mexican Violinista • FW04062 • 1979

PHILIP YAMPOLSKY/ MUSIC OF INDONESIA
Vol. 1: Songs Before Dawn: Gandrung Banyuwangi • SFW40055 • 1991

Vol. 2: Indonesian Popular Music: Kroncong, Dangdut, and Langgam Jawa • SFW40056 • 1991

Vol. 3: Music from the Outskirts of Jakarta: Gambang Kromong • SFW40057 • 1991

Vol. 4: Music of Nias and North Sumatra: Hoho, Gendang Karo, Gondang Toba • SFW40420 • 1992

Vol. 5: Betawi and Sundanese Music of Java • SFW40421 • 1994

Vol. 6: Night Music of West Sumatra • SFW40422 • 1994

Vol. 7: Music from the Forests of Riau and Mentawai • SFW40423 • 1995

Vol. 8: Vocal and Instrumental Music from East and Central Flores • SFW40424 • 1995

Vol. 9: Music from Central and West Flores • SFW40425 • 1995

Vol. 10: Music of Biak, Irian Jaya • SFW40426 • 1996

Vol. 11: Melayu Music of Sumatra and the Riau Islands • SFW40427 • 1996

Vol. 12: Gongs and Vocal Music from Sumatra • SFW40428 • 1996

Vol. 13: Kalimantan Strings • SFW40429 • 1997

Vol. 14: Lombok, Kalimantan, Banyumas: Little-Known Forms of Gamelan and Wayang • SFW40441 • 1997

Vol. 15: South Sulawesi Strings • SFW40442 • 1997

Vol. 16: Music from the Southeast: Sumbawa, Sumba, Timor • SFW40443 • 1998

Vol. 17: Kalimantan: Dayak Ritual and Festival Music • SFW40444 • 1998

Vol. 18: Sulawesi: Festivals, Funerals and Work • SFW40445 • 1999

Vol. 19: Music of Maluku: Halmahera, Buru, Kei • SFW40446 • 1999

Vol. 20: Indonesian Guitars • SFW40447 • 1999

Vol. 21: Discover Indonesia • SFW40484 • 2000

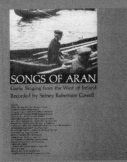

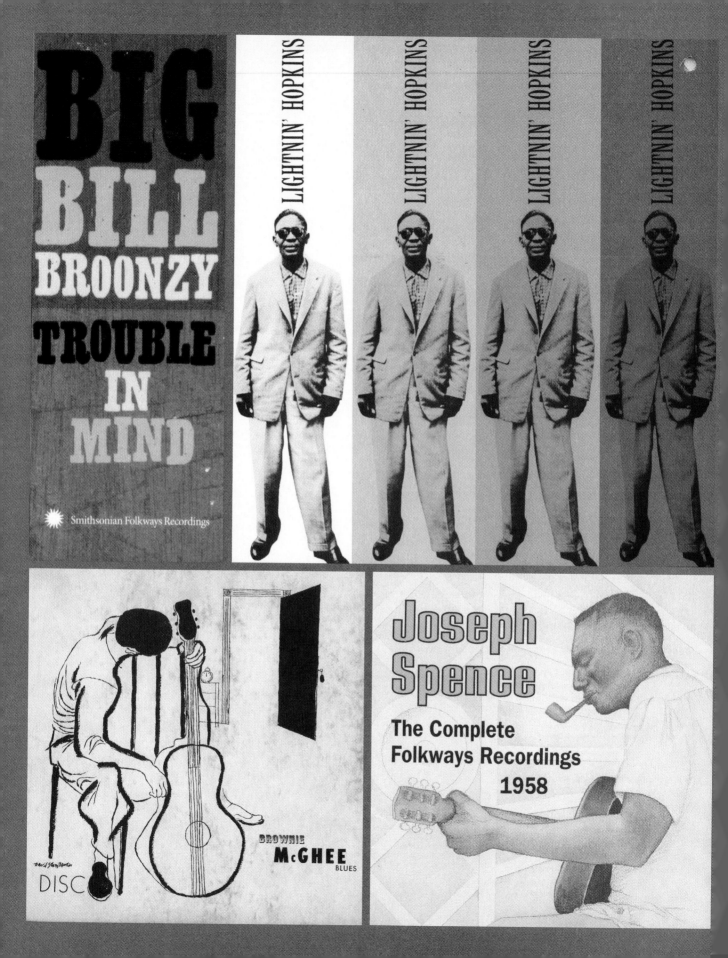

Chapter 6

STRIKING LIGHTNIN'
Folkways and the Blues Revival

When bandleader W. C. Handy published his "Memphis Blues" in 1903, little did he know he was launching a craze for blues music that would last through the twentieth century and beyond. Despite his taking the title of "father of the blues," Handy was not the originator of this style, which probably dates back to the earliest musical interaction between African American slaves and their European American neighbors. Elements of European balladry, hymns, and folk songs combined with African rhythmic and melodic conceptions in an unpredictable mix, and various different forms of the blues began to develop in different regions of the South and Southwest.

However, Handy did much to popularize the blues, particularly through his "St. Louis Blues," the first recorded hit for singer Bessie Smith. Smith began her career in an all-black traveling troupe, the Rabbit Foot Minstrels. Among the cast were comedian-actor "Pa" Rainey and his wife, blues singer "Ma" Rainey. When Ma recorded a blues number in 1920 for tiny Gennett Records, the discs flew off the shelves and the blues recording boom was born. Dozens of others followed in their wake, sparking a craze for the blues in major cities such as New York and Chicago.

Desperate for more blues product, labels combed the South for "authentic" blues performers, and most African Americans who recorded during this period were encouraged to sing the blues. While blues was undoubtedly a part of many of these singers' repertory, they were also repositories of a range of popular music, from the latest pop hits to religious hymns. A street performer—such as Atlanta's Blind Willie McTell, Dallas' Blind Lemon Jefferson, or Chicago's Blind Blake—made his living by catering to his "customers." A kind of living jukebox, he would be called on to perform anything that could attract an audience and— he hoped—open their pockets. Frederic Ramsey Jr. believed that Lead Belly may even have been employed as a "song plugger" by a local music shop, playing the hits of the day to encourage sales of sheet music.

THE BLUES COME NORTH: SONNY TERRY AND BROWNIE MCGHEE, AND REV. GARY DAVIS

Many black performers from the South followed in the footsteps of their brethren seeking more income—and to escape Jim Crow segregation—by moving north. Railroads offered an important route from home to the cities of the North. Mississippi Delta performers—notably Muddy Waters and Howlin' Wolf—traveled by train through the heart of the country to Chicago, where, after World War II, there was a boom in "electric" or urban blues. Others, such as South Carolina's Josh White and Rev. Gary Davis, Louisiana's Lead Belly, and North Carolina's "Sonny Terry," came to New York, where they found work on the streets, in nightclubs, and even in Broadway revues.

Lead Belly's trip from southern prison to northern nightclubs has already been discussed (see Chapter 3). Another talented performer who had worked with a number of guitarists in his native North Carolina was blind harmonica player Saunders Terrell, better known as Sonny Terry. Terry first recorded in the 1930s with guitarist-singer Blind Boy Fuller and came to New York twice in the latter part of the decade, including one trip in 1938 to appear at Carnegie Hall as part of John Hammond's landmark "From Spirituals to Swing" concert. Back in North Carolina, he met a young guitarist-singer named Walter "Brownie" McGhee, and the two came to New York in 1941 after Fuller's death. The matching of Terry's down-home "whooping" vocals and harmonica playing with McGhee's more uptown, smooth-voiced singing was perfect, and the two would record and perform prolifically through the folk revival years.

As friends and accompanists to Lead Belly through the 1940s, McGhee and Terry naturally came into Asch's orbit, who recorded them accompanying the great singer-guitarist and also on their own. Brownie recalled in 1989 that Asch typically advanced money to musicians in need, but eventually expected them to record for him in return:

> Moe Asch was my A–1 man. . . . I met him through Lead [Belly] and we was soon recording. He gave everyone ten bucks. . . . When he was down on 46th Street I would stop by to see Moe, ask him if I could have five or ten bucks. He said "I think I can." But I didn't know that he was putting this money down. . . . He said "Don't you want to clear your sheets with me? All that money I've been giving you all along. Why don't you make me an album?" Then it flashed in my mind that I'd been getting all those five and ten dollar bills from Moe. I thought, well, that's all right.

Asch recognized Terry's remarkable skills as a soloist on the harmonica, issuing his first Folkways album in 1952. The session was arranged by Fred

Brownie McGhee performing in the late 1940s or early 1950s. Sonny Terry is seated to his left.

Ramsey Jr., who brought many jazz and blues acts to Asch's studios in the late 1940s and early 1950s (see Chapter 2).

Terry told Ramsey how he learned to play:

I first played like a kid plays, couldn't play no tune. . . . I just learned a little from [my father], from the rests on up, just tuk it up myself. He could take the harmonica an' hum, in his mouth, an' would put his hand on it, and could play near 'bout like I play now, 'thout puttin' his hand on it. He never didn' use his hand on the harmonica like I did. I think he just learned it, you know, little

David Gahr's iconic image of
Sonny Terry. (© David Gahr)

plantation show used to come through, maybe he caught it from somethin'
like that. [Original spelling and punctuation]

Before the rediscovery of artists such as Mississippi John Hurt and Skip
James, McGhee and Terry were among the most "authentic" rural blues performers that anyone in the folk revival had experienced. Their long experience
as entertainers made them natural hits on the folk and jazz club and festival
circuits. Besides Folkways, they recorded for many other jazz and folk labels,
and by the late 1960s even the major labels. Although the duo stopped performing together in the mid-1970s because of personality conflicts, both continued to
perform until their deaths.

Reverend Gary Davis was perhaps the most recorded of all the blues "discoveries" of the 1950s and 1960s, thanks to his presence in New York beginning
in the mid-1940s. Like Terry, Davis was a protégé of Blind Boy Fuller and first
recorded as his accompanist. An ordained minister, he initially performed only
gospel material (although during the revival years he recorded a good many
party songs and blues as well). A nimble-fingered guitarist, Davis was highly
influential for scores of folk-blues revivalists.

Davis recorded for almost all of the folk and blues labels of the 1950s and

1960s. He made his first recording for Moses Asch in the 1940s, performing his guitar tour de force "Civil War Parade." It is one of Davis' most remarkable guitar showpieces, a reworking of John Philip Sousa's "Stars and Stripes Forever." On the guitar, he imitates the sounds of the soldiers' drill, as well as the firing of the big guns. In 1952, musician John Cohen befriended Davis and recorded him at his home. These recordings went unreleased for over four decades, until Cohen realized that they documented Davis' style before he had been widely exposed to the folk revival. Wonderfully relaxed and informal, these sessions capture Davis as he would have sounded on the streets of Harlem.

Rev. Gary Davis performing on the streets of Harlem in 1953. (© John Cohen)

BLUES IN THE NIGHTCLUBS: JOSH WHITE AND BIG BILL BROONZY

Fellow Carolinian Josh White was another refugee from the South who found considerable success in the folk and jazz revival of the 1950s and 1960s. He began his career working for older performers, including Blind Joe Taggart, whom he accompanied on recordings in 1928, and Blind Boy Arnold. White came to New York in 1932, recording on his own in a modern blues style through the mid-1930s. Suffering an injury to his hand in 1936, he lost the ability to play in his previous, elaborate finger style, and eventually developed a simpler style featuring single-string leads alternating with chords.

Bill Broonzy recording for Folkways in 1956. (© David Gahr)

In the later 1930s, he began appearing with jazz performers such as Billie Holiday and folk/blues singers such as Lead Belly and Pete Seeger. With his hit recording of "One Meat Ball"—which he recorded for Asch in 1944—White made the full transition to club singer. White antagonized many in the folk community when he testified before the House Un-American Activities Committee in the mid-1950s, although he didn't name names but simply recanted his past liberal activities. He became a major star in Europe in the 1950s and worked fancy nightclubs until his death in 1969.

Big Bill Broonzy was another bluesman of the 1930s who found success in the folk revival of

Publicity shot for Josh White taken by George Pickow in the late 1950s or early 1960s. (Courtesy of George Pickow)

the 1950s and 1960s. Born in Mississippi in 1893, Broonzy sought a better life up north, settling in Chicago in the late 1920s, where he recorded prolifically through the 1930s. For many blues fans, Broonzy's early recordings represent his best work, the equal of great performers such as Blind Blake. Like Sonny Terry, Broonzy came to New York to participate in John Hammond's "From Spirituals to Swing" concert in 1938, and Broonzy began shaping his performing to the folk revival audience. He became a major star in Europe in the early 1950s, coauthoring his biography with a Danish jazz fan, Yannick Bruynoghe, in 1955. However, his health began to fail, and just three years later he succumbed to cancer.

"They say everything I sing . . . is the blues. . . . Some people call these folk songs, all the songs that I heard in my life was folk songs. I never heard horses sing none of 'em."
—Big Bill Broonzy

Broonzy was a regular on Studs Terkel's Chicago-based radio show, and several of these performances were included on various Folkways albums. Then, in 1956, jazz scholar Charles Edward Smith brought Broonzy to Moses Asch to record a studio album. Wanting to capture the "pure" sound of Broonzy's music, Asch asked him to perform with just his own guitar accompaniment (also, there probably was no extra money to pay session musicians, as on Broonzy's more commercial releases). These tapes were among Broonzy's last recordings, and were issued after the singer's death in 1958.

BIG CITY BLUES: LONNIE JOHNSON AND VICTORIA SPIVEY

Lonnie Johnson was a guitarist-singer with a long and varied career. He recorded as a traditional blues singer in the 1920s and 1930s, while also playing with jazz great Louis Armstrong and as a partner to white jazz guitarist Eddie Lang. By the mid-1930s, he had settled in Chicago, where he played in a light jazz style for club dates. He switched to electric guitar for his jazz and R&B work and then back to acoustic for folk recordings beginning in the later 1950s. Johnson crossed paths with Moses Asch twice: in 1947, when the singer was working New York clubs, and then again for an extensive session in 1967. Asch heavily promoted Johnson's 1947 release to the jukebox trade, but the disc failed to chart; ironically, just a year later, Johnson had a major hit for Cincinnati's King label. When Johnson recorded for Asch again, it was at the tail end of the folk-blues revival. Asch's business problems in the later 1960s resulted in the tapes being filed away, only to be rediscovered in 1982 when blues scholar Sam Charters prepared them for release. The guitarist died in 1970.

Advertisement for Disc's Lonnie Johnson release in 1947 that ran in *Billboard*. Pianist Blind John Davis is pictured next to Johnson.

One of the few female urban blues singers of the 1920s to reemerge during the 1960s blues revival was Victoria Spivey, who had recorded with Johnson in the 1930s and would work with him again in the early 1960s. Spivey was among the most prolific recording artists of the early blues, as well as a talented songwriter and bandleader. She appeared in King Vidor's landmark 1929 all-black musical film, *Hallelujah*, and also various versions of *Hellzapoppin'* in the later 1930s. After World War II, she retired until the late 1950s, when blues-jazz scholar Chris Albertson interviewed her about her early blues days and encouraged her to return to performing. She appeared at New York's Gerde's Folk City in 1961, where she met young Bob Dylan, whom she hired to accompany Big Joe Williams on harmonica for her label.

The Folkways sessions were held in 1962 and overseen by jazz scholar Leonard Kunstadt. Although a fine pianist, Spivey primarily accompanies herself on ukulele, giving the tracks a somewhat odd ambiance. The songs, all her own compositions, combine standard 1920s blues themes with hokum and party themes. (Titles such as "Good Sissages Blues" and "Six Foot Daddy" need no further explanation.) Perhaps because of the unusual accompaniment, the tapes languished at Folkways for fourteen years before they were finally issued on LP.

WINDY CITY BLUES: MEMPHIS SLIM, ROOSEVELT SYKES, AND BIG JOE WILLIAMS

Another blues pianist, Memphis Slim (born Peter Chatman), found a second career when he began recording for Folkways—again through scholar Charles Edward Smith—in 1959. Although born in Memphis, he was best known as a Chicago-based pianist from the time he came to the city in 1939. By the mid-1950s he had become closely associated with Big Bill Broonzy, who encouraged him to develop his own style. Initially, he recorded in a rollicking 1950s R&B style—in fact, he completed a pop session for VeeJay records just a few weeks before recording for Asch. But the R&B world was moving in more modern directions, and the folk audience was hungry for older-style performers. Slim was able to adapt to these demands, recording a solo album of grace and power, and going on to record several more for Asch through the early 1960s, often accompanied by master Chicago blues bassist and songwriter Willie Dixon. Whenever they came to New York, Dixon says, they would record for whoever would pay for a session, sometimes recording on the same day for Folkways and Prestige, even duplicating some songs.

Memphis Slim at the piano, 1960. (© David Gahr)

The Folkways connection gave Slim a new audience in folk clubs and eventually led to a successful career in Europe. Slim and Dixon were even paired with Pete Seeger at New York's Village Gate nightclub in 1960. Moe sent recording engineer Peter Bartók to record the proceedings. Typically, he made full use of all the material that was recorded on those nights; as Bartók recalled:

> [Moe] told me, "Just go and record every night for a few days [and] put something together for me to publish." I thought he was going to make one record [from the tapes]. . . . Every night the program was almost the same, but there were variations. And I gave it to Moe. I didn't hear from him in a long time.

But finally, he edited the tapes and brought me a record. Well, it wasn't what I put together. . . . A year later, he [came] back with another [album] . . . he used all the tapes I made, in different configurations and in different programs. So what I thought would make one nice LP, he made 3 or 4 albums out of it.

During the later 1960s, Slim recorded for larger labels, but he returned from time to time to Folkways, cutting his last album for Asch in 1973.

Slim apparently also brought Roosevelt Sykes (aka "the Honeydripper") to Folkways. Another barrelhouse-style pianist, Sykes was born in Helena, Arkansas, in 1906. He was already a talented pianist by his early teens, when so many girls flocked around him that "the boys said the girls was buzzing round me like bees or something and so I must be dripping honey!" He made his first recordings at age twenty-three in 1929. He went on to a five-decade career as both an accompanist and a solo artist, and he toured widely both with small combos and on his own. He took under his wing the young Memphis Slim, whom he met while playing in Slim's hometown, Memphis. When Slim moved to Chicago, Sykes helped land him his first recording sessions. Sykes' Folkways album came from a 1961 session that Slim supervised, and the two trade licks on "Memphis Slim Rock," a highlight of the release. Sykes passed away in 1983.

Big Joe Williams came to Asch via another Chicago connection, record store and Delmark label owner Bob Koester, a blues enthusiast. Williams played a nine-string guitar that he created himself by doubling the first, second, and fourth strings, and his playing and singing harked back to traditional Mississippi Delta styles. Born in 1903 in Crawford, Mississippi, Williams was living in the Kansas City area in the mid-1930s when he was "discovered" by producer Lester Melrose, who oversaw his first commercial recordings. Although he recorded for various labels aimed at the black market from 1935 to 1955, his style was increasingly becoming old fashioned for contemporary black tastes. Koester introduced him to a new audience, the folk-blues revival, through a series of albums released primarily on his small Delmark label.

In 1961, Koester also recorded Williams for Folkways. Noted blues scholar Pete Welding describes the value of these recordings:

The superior sonic properties of the[se] recordings, clear and transparent, [bring] Williams' music to vivid, exciting life, capturing with perfect clarity and a real sense of "presence" the full dynamic range of his singing and playing, from the quietest, almost whisper-like quality of his guitar passages, as on "Whistling Pines," . . . to the loudest of his declamatory shouts, and everything in between—the "string buzz" as his fingers slide along the guitar's neck, and even on occasion the sound of his breathing . . . [This is] Big Joe at

Big Joe Williams' hands.
(© David Gahr)

his best, recorded in his prime, full of unrestrained enthusiasm, singing lustily and playing with real fire. It's Big Joe in 1961, at the beginning of the blues revival, all revved up and raring to go, bursting with creativity and eager to strut his stuff.

Williams became a favorite on the blues revival circuit in the 1960s and 1970s, particularly in Europe. As he became older and his health deteriorated, his playing became less adept. Used to playing in barrooms and on street corners, Williams could take a while to warm up, and his performances could be uneven. During the folk revival years, he was often presented in less-than-ideal circumstances; at one Greenwich Village performance in 1965, he was sandwiched between two blues-rock revival bands. Marc Miller describes the scene in his book *Unsung Heroes of the Blues*:

Big Joe Williams . . . looked terrible. . . . He was equipped with a beat up old acoustic guitar which . . . had nine strings and sundry homemade attachments and a wire hanger contraption around his neck fashioned to hold a kazoo . . . . After three or four songs the unseen announcer came on the P.A. system and said, "Lets have a big hand for Big Joe Williams, ladies and gentlemen; thank you, Big Joe."

But Big Joe wasn't finished. He hadn't given up on the audience and he ignored the announcer. He continued his set and after each song the announcer came over the P.A. and tried to politely but firmly get Big Joe off the stage. . . .

Long about the sixth or seventh song he got into his groove and started to wail with raggedy slide guitar riffs, powerful voice, as well as intense percussion on the guitar and its various accoutrements. By the end of the set he had that audience of jaded 1960s rockers on their feet cheering and applauding vociferously. Our initial pity for him was replaced by wondrous respect.

In the mid-1960s, Williams sometimes toured with his own discovery, a young guitarist named John Wesley "Short Stuff" Macon. An informal tape made after a 1964 college appearance was released three years later on Folkways and is Williams' only other appearance on the label. He passed away in 1982.

Elizabeth Cotten: Freight Train

A standout among the many blues performers on Folkways is Elizabeth Cotten. Cotten came from North Carolina but then relocated to the Washington, D.C., area, where through a chance meeting she became a nanny/maid for the Charles Seeger family. It didn't take long for the children—including Peggy and Mike—to discover that Cotten was a fine finger-style guitarist and a capable songwriter. Her "Freight Train" became a major hit of the folk revival, thanks to Peggy taking it to England in the later 1950s, where it was recorded by skiffle artist Nancy Whiskey, and two British songwriters took authorship credit for what they supposed was a traditional song (see Chapter 4). Eventually, Cotten's credit was restored, and thanks to dozens of recordings she earned enough royalty income to live comfortably.

Mike Seeger recorded and produced Cotten's first album, originally titled *Negro Folk Songs and Tunes*, in 1958. (Asch retitled it *Freight Train and Other North Carolina Folk Songs and Tunes* after the song became a hit.) Cotten's playing and singing became more adventuresome and assured as she began touring folk clubs and college campuses, often accompanied by Mike Seeger. Her 1967 album, *Shake Sugaree*, shows her at the height of her powers. Cotten continued to perform well into the 1980s. She died in 1987.

A charming snapshot of Mike Seeger, Elizabeth Cotten, and Alice Gerrard, taken at Seeger and Gerrard's wedding. (Photo by Ralph Rinzler, courtesy of the Ralph Rinzler Archives, Smithsonian Institution)

CHASIN' THE BLUES:
FURRY LEWIS AND LIGHTNIN' HOPKINS

Probably the most important blues producer for Folkways was Samuel Charters, who began his career recording early jazz and jazz-flavored bands in New Orleans (see Chapter 2). In the late 1950s and early 1960s, Charters produced a steady stream of blues recordings for Folkways. Charters searched high and low for many of his subjects, and his palpable excitement when he was able to make a major find—such as convincing Lightnin' Hopkins to record—is reflected in his often riveting liner notes.

Charters' work was initially introduced to Moses Asch by his longtime friend Frederic Ramsey Jr. After working through Ramsey on one album, Charters directly approached Asch, this time with the idea of producing an album documenting his hunt for the legendary gravel-voiced gospel-blues guitarist Blind Willie Johnson. Charters interviewed various members of Johnson's family, but the guitarist himself had already passed away. The album was made up of 78s from the 1920s along with the oral histories that Charters assembled. He recalled to Peter Goldsmith how he put the material together to submit to Folkways:

> I was in New Orleans and drove up in November 1956 with a cardboard box full of tapes. And I was going to meet Moe [for the first time]. So I sat up all night and, using a pair of scissors and a microphone, I put together that Blind Willie Johnson record, my search for Willie Johnson. It was just totally off the top of my head. I brought [it] up to Moe, left the box there, and the next day Moe said "I'll put them out." So from then on, for the next 30 years, Moe "put them out."

What makes Charters' recordings particularly valuable is his you-are-there notes that bring alive the circumstances under which the albums were created. His 1959 Furry Lewis album even features the date of its recording—October 3—right on the cover. Lewis was one of many Memphis musicians who recorded in the late 1920s when the city was teeming with singers and string musicians. Charters was not particularly looking for Lewis, but discovered him after first finding the members of the Original Memphis Jug Band:

The Memphis Jug Band in front of New York's Folklore Center, 1965. Left to right: Will Shade, Gus Cannon, Furry Lewis. (Photo by Ann Charters)

> I drove to Memphis. I was told on Beale Street there was a man named Yancey [who managed several musicians]. So I walked up . . . to this very shabby office, and said "I'm looking for . . . the Memphis Jug Band." And he said, "When do you want them to play?!" And so, right then, I recorded the Memphis Jug Band, Gus Cannon, and all that stuff that came out on Folkways.

A casual conversation with Will Shade, another member of the Memphis Jug Band, led to the rediscovery of Furry Lewis:

> Will and I were sitting in his room . . . talking about the older blues sing-
> ers. I looked out the window, over the roofs toward Beale Street, and said
> to him . . . "I certainly would like to have heard some of the old singers, Jim
> Jackson, Furry Lewis, John Estes, Frank Stokes . . ."
>
> Will leaned out of his chair and called to his wife, Jennie Mae, who was
> working in the kitchen. "Jennie Mae, when was the last time you saw that fel-
> low they call Furry?"
>
> "Furry Lewis, you mean? I saw him just last week."
>
> She said that Furry was working for the city . . . in the evening I found
> someone who could take me to where he was living. . . . When we came in,
> he was sitting in bed writing letters . . . He seemed withdrawn at first, but
> his reserve soon gave way . . . He no longer had a guitar and he hadn't played
> much in twenty years, but when I asked him if he could still sing and play he
> straightened and said, "I'm better now than I ever was." . . .
>
> The next afternoon I rented a guitar, a big Epiphone . . . and took it over to
> Furry's room. He had gotten off work early and was sitting on the porch wait-
> ing for me. He carried the guitar inside, sat down and strummed the strings
> to make sure it was in tune, then looked up and asked me, "What would you
> like to hear?"
>
> I was surprised that he didn't want to try the guitar a little first, but I
> managed to think of "John Henry," one of his finest early recordings. Without
> a moment's hesitation Furry reached in his pocket for his pocket knife, put it
> between the third and fourth fingers of his left hand to slide along the strings,
> and sang "John Henry" almost as he had recorded it thirty years before.
> His fingers weren't as fast as they had been, but there was a new emotional
> subtlety and assurance in his singing. At 58 years old he was still as exciting
> as he had been when he was 28 years old. When he finished he leaned back,
> looked at me, and said "How was that?"

After this first encounter, Charters returned several months later to Furry's home and recorded him playing and singing all in one afternoon. Like many others of Charters' Folkways releases, this album introduced the older player to a new audience, and eventually Lewis toured and played on the folk-blues circuit, and even opened for the Rolling Stones. He died in Memphis in 1981.

Lightnin' Hopkins was probably Charters' most important—and elusive—discovery. Charters himself said bluntly, "I had been looking for Lightnin' Hopkins, off and on, for about five years." Charters had been intrigued by this

Houston, Texas
Jan.16, 1959

Marian,

I've found and recorded the legendary Lightning Hopkins. It's been a hell of a struggle, but I got an l.p out of him.

When I told Moe there was a chance that I'd find Lightning but that he'd probably take money Moe said go ahead; so I have. He's used to the kind of recording fees the major outfits have paid him in the past - he's recorded on Gold Star, Alladin, Herald, and Score - and we had a long weary afternoon. I was able to get him for $300. It took nearly every cent I had, but it was nothing compared to what he used to get from Gold Star and Alladin.

There were other singers Moe and I talked about, but Lightning is the only important one. He's got this sudden reputation among the folk singers, which the Score l.p. has helped, even though it's the old Alladin material. He's the best, without much question; so I'm not going to record anyone else. If anyone's interested in managing him; let me know. There's money here.

I'll be able to talk to Blind Lemon's family and get back to New Orleans, but at that point I'll be completely without money. I'll need the $300. I don't know how this catches you. There was no/time for me to call.

How quickly do you want the tapes? I think you should get this out as quickly as possible. No matter what has to be delayed. He's pretty hot at this moment, and after we listned to the play-back we both agreed he'd never sung better. I can get the notes to you within a few days.

Tell Ed Badeaux that I'm staying with Mack McCormick in Houston. They're old friends.

The General Delivery address is about the best I can do, but it should be alright.

Regards,

Sam Charters

Sam Charters
c/o General Delivery
New Orleans, La.

Sam Charters' letter to Marian Distler, Moses Asch's assistant, relating his excitement at discovering Hopkins.

musician ever since hearing his recording of "Contrary Mary" on a jukebox in New Orleans in 1954. Although a contemporary artist, Lightnin' sounded as though he'd been born decades earlier, and his unusual sense of timing and phrasing made him legendary among blues record collectors. Yet, despite the fact that he was still recording, no one among the jazz-blues revivalists seemed to know where to find him. A distant cousin of the singer told Charters that Hopkins' hometown was Houston, Texas, but that was where the thread of his life seemed to disappear.

Lightnin' Hopkins on the day that Sam Charters first recorded him, 1959. (Photo by Sam Charters)

Through Ramsey, Charters met a fellow blues enthusiast named Mack McCormick who lived in Houston and had also been on Hopkins' trail. The two combined forces, driving around the city, finding many leads unaware or unwilling to help. As Charters recalled:

> After one look at us they decided we were either police or collection agents and they were vague about things as simple as the weather. Mack finally had an idea. Pawnshops. The first one [we] tried had Lightnin's address.

"Sam Hopkins. Electric guitar. He's in and out of here all the time. . . ."

It is probably just as well that the pawn broker had never tried to get in touch with Lightnin' at the address on the pawn card. It was a weathered building in a littered yard in a tenement section of Dowling. After much knocking a little boy came to one of the doors.

"Lightnin' don't stay here."

Lightnin's sister was living across the street. . . . [She was] carefully evasive.

"What you want him for?"

She was a tall, thin woman, her face hard. Finally she said to try a house with a red chair on the porch two blocks away. At the house a heavy, gray-haired woman looked nervously out of a dark living room with a television set flickering in the corner. She said that Lightnin' stayed in a room in her house and she'd take a message for him.

The next morning, when Charters was waiting at a red light on Dowling Street, another car pulled up beside him. "You lookin' for me?" the driver asked, who turned out to be none other than Lightnin' Hopkins. They returned to Hopkins' room in the boardinghouse. Charters held the microphone in his hand, angling it toward the guitar for solos and up toward Hopkins' mouth when he sang. The guitarist performed all afternoon for Charters.

Right after the sessions, Charters wrote excitedly to Marian Distler, Moe's right-hand woman:

> I've found and recorded the legendary Lightnin' Hopkins. It's been a hell of a struggle, but I got an LP out of him.
>
> When I told Moe there was a chance that I'd find Lightning but that he'd probably take money Moe said go ahead; so I have. He's used to the kind of recording fees the major outfits have paid him in the past . . . and we had a long weary afternoon. I was able to get him for $300. It took nearly every cent I had, but it was nothing compared to what he used to get. . . .
>
> I think you should get this out as quickly as possible. No matter what has to be delayed. He's pretty hot at this moment, . . .

Recorded in one afternoon in January 1959, the album was released before year's end. It was an immediate hit among blues revivalists and helped launch Hopkins' new career in America and Europe. Despite having received $300 for recording from Charters, Hopkins wrote several angry letters to Asch demanding royalties, which eventually were paid. The bluesman passed away in 1982, one of the last legendary players of his generation.

"That Only Makes It More Ethnic"

Like many field workers before him, Charters sometimes appears on his field tapes as a participant in the music making as well as a recordist. Early on in his work, he was interested in recording traditional washboard and jug bands. In Houston in 1955, he met Virgil Perkins, a rub-board player and singer. The two spent one night at Perkins' home, recording his music. In order to ease Perkins' fear of recording, Charters suggested that he have a drink, and then Perkins insisted that Charters drink with him. The result was somewhat surprising to the folklorist, as he recalled in an article in the *New York Times* in 1959:

> When I edited the tapes a month or two later I was startled to hear someone playing a 12-string guitar with Perkins . . . I'm still a little hazy . . . but I had a guitar in the car and I have a dim memory of carefully going up and down the porch steps with it. . . .
>
> I used the name "Jack Sims" [on the record notes] for the guitarist with Perkins. . . . I [later] confessed [to Moses Asch] that I was the guitar player. He laughed.
>
> "That only makes it more ethnic."

Charters repeated this story to me nearly five decades later, still laughing about it.

Sam Charters recording Sleepy John Estes, 1962. (Photo by Ann Charters)

DOWN IN NEW ORLEANS: SNOOKS EAGLIN

Talented musicians have a remarkable capability to play what their listeners want to hear, even if it's not their primary style. New Orleans R&B player Snooks Eaglin was first heard at the beginning of the folk-blues revival by local folklorist Harry Oster. Eaglin usually performed modern R&B songs with a full band, but Oster—a university professor—was uninterested in recording this popular material. Instead, he encouraged Eaglin to use an acoustic guitar to record an album of folk and blues songs (although Eaglin also played some of his favorite contemporary numbers in acoustic settings).

Eaglin's guitar style was remarkably developed for someone in his early twenties, which was when he made these recordings. He combined a jazzy chord style with astonishingly difficult single-note runs, marrying calypso rhythms to traditional songs such as "Careless Love." It's impossible to say how much of the material on his Folkways album was part of his normal repertory, although it's clear he was trying to please Oster by selecting more traditional songs. Nonetheless, the energy of the vocals and outstanding guitar work make this album one of the most riveting of the early blues "discoveries."

Eaglin finally got his wish to record with a full band in a modern R&B setting when he partnered with famed New Orleans producer Dave Bartholomew in the early 1960s. (Bartholomew had previously produced Fats Domino.) Never really achieving popular success, Eaglin has made several comebacks, in the 1970s and then again in the 1990s, and remains a favorite of contemporary blues fans.

DAVE VAN RONK AND THE BLUES REVIVAL

The 1960s blues revival was marked by a new generation of blues performers, mostly white, who reinterpreted the original music for a new audience. Among the first of these talented interpreters was Dave Van Ronk. Van Ronk was the kind of larger-than-life figure that all movements need. A gadfly who loved to mock the pretensions of his fellow revivalists, he could also be warm and supportive of new talent, including the young Bob Dylan. A masterly interpreter of the blues, Van Ronk did not slavishly copy earlier recordings, but often created his own unique versions of songs, combining different influences in remarkable ways.

As the folk revival began to heat up in the later 1950s, Van Ronk was restless because he had yet to land a recording deal. In his frank and colorful memoir, *The Mayor of MacDougal Street*, he tells how he begged folklorist Ken Goldstein—then perhaps the most connected person among the various labels in the folk world (see Chapter 9)—to get him a deal with Folkways. Goldstein finally relented and recorded the singer's first album in his basement. Van Ronk's brief,

Dave Van Ronk performing at the Newport Folk Festival in 1963. (© John Byrne Cooke)

sensitive, and somewhat tongue-in-cheek introduction to the liner notes are remarkably prescient in touching on issues of authenticity and interpretation that would become issues for all blues revivalists:

Not infrequently I am taken to task for the manner in which I approach my material. Being of Northern white origin and stressing Southern Negro songs as I do, is, in a way, difficult to justify. I first came into contact with Negro traditional songs through a chance encounter with a recording of "Stackolee" made by Furry Lewis. . . . Taking it to be a form of jazz, in which I was primarily interested and involved, I made some further investigations and discovered a whole field of music which I had not previously known existed. At this point I don't think I had ever heard a white person sing a Negro song . . . and so, having only such singers as Furry Lewis, King Solomon Hill, and Lead Belly for models, when I tried to sing these songs I naturally imitated what I heard, and if I couldn't understand a word here and there I just slurred right along with the singer. At the time, nobody listened to me anyway.

Since then I have learned that the term "folk music" encompasses more than just "Blue Tail Fly" and "On Top of Old Smoky" and that there are quite a few white singers who sing the same material that I do with a very different approach from my own. Although I can appreciate the "white approach" to Negro folksongs and enjoy the work of many of its adherents, I still reserve the right to sing these songs in the style to which I am accustomed, partly because of habit, and partly, I confess, because I feel that my way is the "right way."

Van Ronk would record one more album for Folkways, released in 1961, and then move to larger labels. He enjoyed his greatest success in the mid-1960s, when he lent his raspy voice and strong guitar stylings to both blues and new material; he was among the first to discover and champion the work of Joni Mitchell. Although Van Ronk was slightly embarrassed by his Folkways recordings, particularly by his first album, which he felt did not reflect his mature style, Asch recognized their popularity and reissued them several times in different packages through the 1960s.

Like many Folkways artists, Van Ronk felt he was shorted on royalties on his albums. He told several times an amusing story of going up to Folkways in a ragged coat to demand payment, claiming he couldn't afford a winter coat. Instead of producing a check, Asch brought out a heavy woolen coat from the back room of his office and gave it to the singer. Van Ronk was particularly annoyed when Asch licensed tapes to MGM/Verve for release just as Van Ronk was issuing his first major-label recording on Mercury. Van Ronk sued MGM for unpaid royalties; soon after, he ran into Moe in a New York club. Van Ronk was afraid he would be berated by the famously irascible record producer for his lawsuit, but instead Asch said to him with a twinkle in his eye, "So you finally wised up."

LISTEN UP!

SONNY TERRY AND BROWNIE MCGHEE

Blues • Big Bill Broonzy, Sonny Terry, and Brownie McGhee • FW03817 • 1959

Brownie McGhee Blues • Brownie McGhee • FW02030 • 1955

Brownie McGhee Sings the Blues • Brownie McGhee • FW03557 • 1959

The Folkways Years, 1945–1959 • Brownie McGhee • SFW40034 • 1991

Traditional Blues, Vol. 1 • Brownie McGhee • FW02421 • 1951

Traditional Blues, Vol. 2 • Brownie McGhee • FW02422 • 1960

Pete Seeger and Sonny Terry at Carnegie Hall • Pete Seeger and Sonny Terry • FW02412 • 1958

Washboard Band • Pete Seeger, Sonny Terry, and Brownie McGhee • FW02201 • 1956

The Folkways Years, 1944–1963 • Sonny Terry • SFW40033 • 1991

Preachin' the Blues • Sonny Terry and Brownie McGhee • FW31024 • 1968

Brownie McGhee and Sonny Terry Sing • Sonny Terry and Brownie McGhee • SFW40011 • 1990

Get on Board: Negro Folksongs by the Folkmasters • Sonny Terry, Brownie McGhee, and Coyal McMahan • FW02028 • 1952

On the Road • Sonny Terry, J.C. Burris, and Sticks McGhee • FW02369 • 1959

REV. GARY DAVIS

If I Had My Way: Early Home Recordings • SFW40123 • 2003

Pure Religion and Bad Company • SFW40035 • 1991

JOSH WHITE

Free and Equal Blues • SFW40081 • 1998

BIG BILL BROONZY

Big Bill Broonzy Sings Country Blues • FW31005 • 1968

Big Bill Broonzy Sings Folk Songs • SFW40023 • 1989

Trouble in Mind • SFW40131 • 2000

Blues • Big Bill Broonzy, Sonny Terry, and Brownie McGhee • FW03817 • 1959

LONNIE JOHNSON

The Complete Folkways Recordings • SFW40067 • 1993

VICTORIA SPIVEY

The Blues Is Life • FW03541 • 1976

MEMPHIS SLIM

Chicago Blues: Boogie Woogie and Blues • FW03536 • 1961

Memphis Slim—Favorite Blues Singers • FW02387 • 1973

Memphis Slim and the Honky-Tonk Sound • FW03535 • 1960

Memphis Slim and the Real Boogie-Woogie • FW03524 • 1959

The Folkways Years, 1959–1973 • SFW40128 • 2000

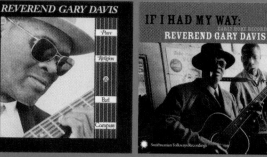

Songs of Memphis Slim and "Wee Willie" Dixon
• Memphis Slim and Willie Dixon • FW02385 • 1960

At the Village Gate • Memphis Slim and Willie Dixon with
Pete Seeger • FW02386 • 1962

Pete Seeger at the Village Gate • Pete Seeger with
Memphis Slim and Willie Dixon • FW02450 • 1960

ROOSEVELT SYKES
Blues by Roosevelt "The Honeydripper" Sykes
• SFW40051 • 1995

BIG JOE WILLIAMS
Mississippi's Big Joe Williams and His Nine-String Guitar
• SFW40052 • 1995

Hell Bound and Heaven Sent Blues Big Joe Williams and
Short Stuff Macon • FW31004 • 968

ELIZABETH COTTEN
Freight Train and Other North Carolina Folk Songs and
Tunes • SFW40009 • 1989

Shake Sugaree • SFW40147 • 2004

When I'm Gone • FW03537 • 1979

FURRY LEWIS
Furry Lewis • FW03823 • 1960

LIGHTNIN' HOPKINS
Lightnin' Hopkins • SFW40019 • 1990

SNOOKS EAGLIN
New Orleans Street Singer • SFW40165 • 2005

DAVE VAN RONK
Ballads, Blues, and a Spiritual • FW03818 • 1959

Dave Van Ronk Sings • FW02383 • 1961

The Folkways Years, 1959–1961 • SFW40041 • 1991

And the Tin Pan Bended and the Story Ended . . .
• SFW40156 • 2004

Chapter 7

"MY CHILDREN'S RECORDS ARE *NOT* KIDDIE RECORDS"

Discovering the Children's Market

Moses Asch's declaration that he didn't produce "kiddie" records but rather records for children showed that he recognized how records could be used to educate as well as to amuse. "Kiddie" music was as heavily produced as mainstream pop; much of it was recorded in Hollywood and featured the same lush orchestrations and smooth vocals that could be heard on the soundtracks of Disney films. Asch's children's records, on the other hand, sounded much like his other folk records. Recorded in the same bare-bones manner in his tiny studio, they featured just the singer accompanied by his or her own guitar.

But Asch had a strong philosophy behind the children's series, as he told Izzy Young:

> I won't do just any children's record; it has to fit my concept of what a children's record is. First of all, we treat children as people, and the content has to be something that a child would communicate with: Would tell him something, would teach, or would motivate for dance or rhythm or writing or seeing things. Like I issued with Langston Hughes, *Rhythms of the World*, he shows the child the waves, the black sheep, and so forth, all have rhythm, and they themselves are a part of rhythm. . . . But they have to treat the child as a child. Like, I would not issue an animal album in which the animals speak, because I can't conceive of a child thinking that an animal *is* a human being.

Some of Asch's literal-mindedness comes through in this philosophy; the fact that he couldn't imagine children conceiving of animals as having human traits, such as speech, is indicative of his own belief that records should reflect the "real" world and not some imaginary playland.

Cover for the Disc album *The City Sings for Michael*, c 1947, one of many albums of children's music that Asch produced from his earliest years.

George Mendelssohn, who founded Vox Records and was an early close friend of Asch, believes it was the birth of Asch's son, Michael, that inspired him to begin his search for children's records that would be intelligent and educational. Mendelssohn recalled to interviewer Gary Kenton: "At that time, his son was maybe 2 or 3. He issued a number of children's records, which he wanted his son to have. One of them was 'Little Brown Cow.' And it was always angled—'brown skin, yellow skin, but they all give milk'—it was always with a message." Even Asch's children's records had to teach equality.

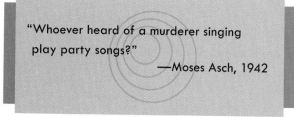

"Whoever heard of a murderer singing play party songs?"

—Moses Asch, 1942

Among Asch's first children's albums was a set by ex-convict Lead Belly—a daring move (see Chapter 3). Seeing Lead Belly perform for children, Asch was amazed by the singer's rapport with the kids, and suggested that he record some of these children's songs for an album. As Charles Edward Smith recalled: "When he first recorded [Lead Belly] Moe wanted to put the singer and the human being first, let the rest sort itself out (with a few nudges), and began with an album that included songs for children. 'Whoever heard of a murderer singing play party songs?' he asked wryly."

SONGS TO GROW ON BY WOODY GUTHRIE

After his initial success with Lead Belly, Asch sought a partner who could help him develop more children's recordings. Asch found the perfect person in a school music teacher and established authority on children's music, Beatrice Landeck. It was probably Landeck who came up with the idea of producing a series of albums to be called *Songs to Grow On*. And although the series was originally designed to feature various singers performing songs selected by Landeck, it is Woody Guthrie's recordings that are best remembered and identified with this series.

Woody Guthrie was prolific as both a songwriter and a father, so it was natural for him to turn to writing songs for his own children once he settled in Brooklyn in the postwar years. Happily married to dancer Marjorie Mazia, Guthrie was at the height of his creative powers, prolifically writing columns for the *Daily Worker*, dashing off lengthy letters to friends and foes, and turning out a seemingly endless stream of children's songs. Unfortunately, this period was short-lived—the first signs of Huntington's disease were already appearing, and Guthrie would soon lose his ability to maintain a normal family life.

An advertisement for Lead Belly's children's recordings run by Asch.

FROM THE REVIEWS:

PM . . .

"Huddie Ledbetter, better known as 'Lead Belly,' is one of America's greatest song spinners."

★

JOHN and ALAN LOMAX . . .

"Lead Belly—master of country dances and songs."

★

WNYC . . .

"Inimitable singer of America's own songs...A real troubador, a real modern troubador."

Children's Songs by Woody Guthrie

Guthrie wrote these charming notes for the original 78 album of his children's songs, *Songs to Grow on for Mother and Child.*

Cathy Ann, we used to call her Miss Stackabones, heard every one of these songs before Moe Asch melted them down onto his records. And so did Tannehill Faulk, who is 1½, and so do Little Annie Lomax. (She's 22 months.) They heard the Lomaxes, the Faulks, and us Guthries sing them in the car and out at the big house on the apple farm in the Pocono Mountains. . . .

I really did try to slant these songs at all of you citizens from four to six, but I spilled over a little on every side, because all of us sang and danced these songs and all of us got about the same kick out of them.

Stackabones liked her songs and stories best of all when her mommy and poppy sing, talk, listen and dance with her. She joins in lots quicker, and louder, and freer when all of us lay down our books, papers, our knitting, twitting, and our heavy spirits, and all get going together on our story, our song, or dance.

We beat on books, boxes, on tin cans and floors. We rattle shakers, spoons, and bells, and we jump all around in a long trot, a rig a jig jig, a crazy lope, gallop, or wild jump. We settle down then and tell some real quiet story in a whisper. We make up some new story if we forget our old ones. She gets more fun out of this at school and at home than most any other thing she does. . . .

As for me, my own self, I don't want to see you use my songs to divide nor split your school nor your family all apart. I mean, don't just buy this record and take it home so your kids can listen to it while you go off and do something else. (Of course, that's one things records are really good for, but that's not the best thing.)

I want to see you join right in, do what your kids do. Let your kids teach you how to play and how to act these songs out . . .

Please, please, please, don't read nor sing my songs like no lesson book, like no text for today. But, let them be a little key to sort of unlock and let down all of your old bars. . . .

Watch the kids. Do like they do. Act like they act. Yell like they yell. Dance the ways you see them dance. Sing like they sing. Work and rest the ways the kids do.

You'll be healthier. You'll feel wealthier. You'll talk wiser. You'll go higher, do better, and live longer here amongst us if you'll just only jump in here and swim around in these songs and do like the kids do.

I don't want the kids to be grownup. I want to see the grown folks be kids.

Woody Guthrie's copy of *Songs to Grow On: Work Songs.*

Woody Guthrie's original booklet illustration for *Songs to Grow On: Work Songs.* (Copyright Woody Guthrie Publications, Inc. Used by permission)

Of all of the recordings that Guthrie made during his lifetime, the children's albums were by far the most commercially successful. As early as 1950, Asch noted that the recordings had become "famous"; even allowing for commercial hype, they were from the start the backbone of the Folkways catalog. The same year, Landeck assembled a book also called *Songs to Grow On*, which furthered the popularity of the series.

QUALITY CHILDREN'S MUSIC: PETE SEEGER

The postwar baby boom fed the need for children's music. While Gene Autry and Roy Rogers cashed in on the kiddie market, Asch quietly cornered the "quality" children's recording sales. Progressive parents who had grown up singing along with the Weavers now had record albums by familiar artists that they could buy for their children. As early as 1955, the *New York Times* was applauding Asch for his "adult" approach to children's records; under the headline "No 'Talking Down': Folkways Records for Young People Are Authentic and Entertaining," Herbert Mitgang wrote:

> Folkways . . . products have the ring of reality. Their children's series has the double virtue of taking from and giving to youngsters. Not only do they introduce old English and American ballads and folksongs but they also descend into the street to record the voices of children at play. It adds up to adult children's listening that, incidentally, infiltrates the young mind with musical Americana.

Pete Seeger was particularly interested in children's music. During the 1950s, when he was blacklisted from appearing in major concert halls, Seeger largely supported himself by playing school concerts, stringing together tours with a $5 show here and a $10 show there. Among his first recordings made for Folkways in the late 1940s were children's records. Asch aggressively marketed these to elementary schools and was able to report back to the singer about song choice and even the correct speed for singing to different age groups. After hearing that younger children had trouble singing along with Seeger's initial releases, Asch asked him to record the songs again, but this time at a slower pace that five- or six-year-olds could follow. Seeger was surprised, because his youngest audiences were mostly eight to ten years old and liked his rapid pace. But he recorded the same songs again, more slowly, so younger listeners could follow them.

As the father of a growing family, Seeger was intimately aware of the need for educational stories and songs. Besides choosing folk songs that would appeal to children, Seeger created his own unique blend of story-songs. He took an old Uncle Dave Macon recording, "Cumberland Mountain Deer Hunt," and transformed it

This poster promoting Pete Seeger, by an unknown artist, brilliantly captures his rapport with young audiences.

into the wonderful story-song "Cumberland Mountain Bear Hunt," including imitating the sound of the guns, dogs, and retreating bears in his recording. His original story-song "The Foolish Frog" is a classic "new" folk tale that also cleverly uses the banjo accompaniment to illustrate key moments in the story.

Perhaps Seeger's most notable accomplishment in the story-song style was "Abiyoyo." Using a fragment of a traditional African song as the chorus, Seeger created a memorable story of an evil giant named Abiyoyo who terrorized a small town. Meanwhile, a magician and his son—a ukulele-playing singer—were scorned by the townsfolk, who didn't appreciate their art. The boy comes up with a scheme to charm the giant by writing a little song to sing to him. The giant starts to dance, and falls to the ground exhausted. Then the boy's father takes his magic wand and—zoop zoop!—makes the giant disappear. Relieved of their troubles, the townsfolk invite the father-and-son duo to rejoin them in a celebration.

The "Abiyoyo" story has special resonance in light of Seeger's own problems at the time with the House Un-American Activities Committee. While he saw music as a unifying force that would heal social ills, the committee accused him of preaching Communism and effectively kept him from performing outside of schools, children's camps, and college campuses from the mid-1950s through the early 1960s. The fact that the song society initially shuns the musician but then comes to see his value may have been a little bit of wishful thinking on Seeger's part at a time when he was very much a commercial outcast.

ADVENTURES IN RHYTHM: ELLA JENKINS

Ella Jenkins was probably the most important discovery in the children's market for Asch. She would record dozens of albums for him, which would outsell most of Folkways' adult catalog. It's no exaggeration to say that Jenkins' recordings helped keep Folkways in business during many lean years when the rest of the catalog was barely selling. Despite this success, Jenkins was not treated much differently by Asch than any of his other artists.

Jenkins was born in 1924 in St. Louis to a musical family; her uncle played harmonica, and she was particularly moved by the sounds and rhythms of gospel music at the family church. After studying education at San Francisco State College, she moved to Chicago, where she became a director of youth programs at a local YMCA. She also hosted a local children's radio show, where she presented local up-and-coming folk performers including Odetta. At a folk club, she happened to meet folklorist Ken Goldstein, and asked his advice as to how she could build on her success leading children's workshops. Goldstein recommended that she make a demonstration tape, mentioning Folkways to her because of its strong catalog of children's records.

Like many who submitted material for consideration to Folkways, Jenkins was at first discouraged by Asch's promotion (or, more precisely, lack of promotion) of the disc. When her first 10-inch LP was released by Folkways in 1957, simply titled *Call and Response*, Jenkins had to do most of the marketing of the record herself. Luckily, she was already working hard promoting her services as a children's performer and educator, so the LP became just another part of her arsenal in spreading her message of music and movement. She often offered to give a free workshop for a school or organization that would agree to buy just one copy of the record for its library.

Jenkins was influenced by her own childhood experiences and her natural love of rhythm. She was exposed to a wide variety of rhythms and musical styles through her teen years, thanks to a household that was apparently teeming with music. As she told interviewer Rosemary D. Reninger in 2000:

> When I was growing up . . . I was always attracted to rhythm instruments like hand drums. Sometimes, I'd start playing with oatmeal boxes, wastebaskets, or pots that my mother had in the kitchen. Then somebody finally gave me Chinese tom-toms, and I started playing rhythms on them.
>
> In addition to my uncle playing the harmonica, I used to like going to watch tap dancing. I listened to a lot of call and response—like Cab Calloway—at music theaters. I became very interested in Latin music before it became popular, and I liked Mexican music. Then, I met someone from Cuba and fell in love with Afro-Cuban music. I liked to imitate some of its rhythms.

This early interest in the musics of many cultures would serve Jenkins well as she worked with the diverse children of Chicago's inner-city neighborhoods.

From her first LP, Jenkins included international material—in this instance an African chant—recognizing the importance of African American "roots" long before the black consciousness movement developed. One of her best-selling records, *You'll Sing a Song and I'll Sing a Song,* features songs and rhythms from around the world, with the intention of showing children that music is a global phenomenon and a means for different cultures to share their experiences. These records had a great impact both in classrooms across the country, where they provided teachers with models for how to incorporate world culture into the curriculum, and on parents at home. While the ideas behind these records may have been radical, offering them in the garb of "children's records" made the one-world message much easier to digest.

Jenkins' interest in world cultures led naturally to a respect for differences among children, and to respect each child's individuality. She told Reninger:

Ella Jenkins performing at the 1998 fiftieth-anniversary concert for Folkways Records. (Photo by Jeff Tinsley)

Whether a teacher has five children or twenty-five, each one is an individual with a unique personality . . . To connect with them, teachers need imagination. They have to try to weave themselves into the child's world, the child's feeling, and the child's thinking. . . .

Even though you direct children toward what you want them to learn, you have to respect them. . . . You have to approach them in many different ways, but each child demands respect. I try to get that across to children before leaving them—respect yourself first, understand yourself, and then go out and respect other people.

Jenkins' career in children's music has spanned more than five decades. Hillary Clinton called her the "first lady of children's music," an apt title that reflects her extraordinary influence on generations of teachers and children. In 2004, she was honored with a Lifetime Achievement Award from the National Academy of Recording Arts and Sciences at the annual Grammy ceremonies. Inspired by this award, a group of children's artists recorded a tribute album to Jenkins, which itself won a Grammy the following year.

FOLLOW THE SUNSET: CHARITY BAILEY

Another key children's star in the early Folkways years was Charity Bailey. Bailey taught at New York's famous progressive elementary school, the Little Red School House (among its graduates are Toshi Seeger, Pete Seeger's wife, Nora Guthrie, daughter of Woody, and Michael Asch, Moe's son). Born in 1904 in Providence, Rhode Island, Bailey's parents were active members of the African American community and strong believers in education as a means of "uplifting the race" (as it was put in the day). Bailey earned an education degree in 1927 but was unable to find work teaching in the North. She worked for a while in Atlanta for the Spelman College Laboratory School, then settled in Harlem. A gifted guitarist and pianist, Bailey studied advanced piano at Juilliard and also Dalcroze Eurhythmics—a method of teaching young children music through movement. She was the first African American to graduate from the Dalcroze School.

After teaching in the Village at the Henry Street Settlement House—a well-known school for young children that attracted many progressive teachers—Bailey took a job at the Little Red School House in 1943. She first recorded for Asch in 1946, participating in the second *Songs to Grow On* album. In 1951, she recorded her first Folkways album, and three years later began hosting a local children's TV show, *Sing a Song with Charity Bailey*. It was the first integrated children's show on television.

Langston Hughes' Children's Records

A somewhat unlikely contributor to Folkways' children's series was African American poet Langston Hughes. Hughes was very much interested in educating young children about the roots of their culture. He produced three innovative children's discs for Folkways, *Rhythms of the World* and *The Story of Jazz*, both in 1954, and *The Glory of Negro History* a year later. *Rhythms of the World* drew from the Folkways sound collection, featuring Hughes introducing recordings of everything from rainfall to children's footsteps, ocean waves, frogs croaking, explosions, and the human heartbeat. Designed for children, Hughes' narrative traces a kind of arc, from morning to night, a day on earth in sound. The recording is an early exploration of how something original can be created through simple tape editing. Typical of Folkways' enlightened philosophy, the message of the recording is that we are all part of this world of rhythm, each sharing in and adding to the vital heartbeat of world expression.

The Glory of Negro History was more of a straightforward narrative than *Rhythms of the World*, but it too made extensive use of recordings from the Folkways library, including sound effects (such as the crashing of the ocean waves against the slave ships) to songs ("Oh Freedom!" sung by Leon Bibb and "Battle Hymn of the Republic" recorded in a bluesy version by Brownie McGhee). *The Story of Jazz* is based on Fred Ramsey's eleven-volume *Jazz* history series, which itself was drawn from 1920s and 1930s recordings for the major labels. In both records, Hughes has created narratives that appeal to children without "talking down" to them.

The Story of Jazz

narrated by LANGSTON HUGHES

with Documentary Recordings

WRITTEN BY LANGSTON HUGHES, AUTHOR OF "THE FIRST BOOK OF JAZZ" PUBLISHED BY FRANKLIN WATTS, INC.

FC 7312 FOLKWAYS RECORDS & SERVICE CORP., N.Y.

MUSIC TIME

A teaching record with CHARITY BAILEY

In collaboration with EUNICE HOLSAERT

BRASS WAGON—a learning song
BRASS WAGON—an activity song
DORMI, MON ENFANT—listening to a quiet song
MISSIE MOUSE—clapping a song
TOODALA—a make-up song

FOLKWAYS RECORDS & SERVICE CORP., N. Y.   FP 7

Charity Bailey shown on the cover of one of her first Folkways releases, *Music Time*.

Bailey took the lessons of eurhythmics—that children learn best when movement is incorporated into the lesson—and wed that with her deep knowledge of folk and world music. She was among the first children's educators to stress multiculturalism in her selection of materials as well as in her use of movements based on traditional dance styles. Her albums were activity records; rather than passively listening, children and parents were expected to participate as they listened. This could include singing along, responding to cues, playing instruments, and moving.

Asch also recorded music for "creative movement," designed to encourage children to improvise their own dances, with some suggestions by the group leader. Just after World War II ended, Woody Guthrie married a dancer-turned-teacher named Marjorie Mazia. (One of Woody's children with Mazia was son Arlo, who followed in his father's footsteps as a singer-songwriter; another, Nora, followed her mother in becoming a dancer.) Mazia had been trained by

Original cover of *Camp Songs*,
released c. 1950 on Folkways.

Martha Graham and performed in her company, and then opened her own
studio in Brooklyn. Knowing that others were teaching creative movement and
needed good music for its accompaniment, Mazia suggested the idea of a record
to Asch. The result was *Dance-a-Long*, released in 1950.

Recognizing a good thing, Asch had many of his artists record children's
records, even those not normally associated with kids, such as the New Lost
City Ramblers. Their *Old Timey Songs for Children* was among their first releases.
The group drew on its repertory of old-time string band songs, choosing those
that would appeal to kids, rather than "singing down" to children. As Tom Paley
comments in the liner notes, "The songs on this record are not just children's
songs, but they are songs that children will enjoy. Who says that children can't
love and understand adult things anyway?"

It is not surprising that well-known folksinger Jean Ritchie's first Folkways
album was devoted to children's music. *Children's Songs and Games from the*

Children's music brochure from the 1960s.

Southern Mountains was released in 1957. Many of the songs were drawn from the Ritchie family repertory. Like many other Folkways children's records, it helped introduce an important artist and a traditional repertory to a wider audience; teachers and parents who might not otherwise hear traditional singing were drawn in by the charm of this and other children's albums.

SPEAKING FOR THEMSELVES: CHILDREN AS CHILDREN'S PERFORMERS

Besides adults performing children's music, Asch pioneered in featuring recordings of children performing music for their own amusement. Tony Schwartz produced a pioneering recording of children's playground games, *1, 2, 3 and a Zing Zing Zing* in 1953, the first in a series of LPs that the innovative sound recorder would release on Folkways (see Chapter 11). Schwartz organized it by the type of activity, carefully stating where each performance was made, and also emphasized the multicultural mix that was typical of New York's inner-city playgrounds. Asch released this album as part of his children's record series, showing that he recognized that it was not only a sound document of urban children's culture but also an entertaining album for children (and their parents) to listen to as a performance.

Another unusual urban documentary appeared in 1959, with the rather clinical title of *Street and Gangland Rhythms: Beats and Improvisations by Six Boys in Trouble*. Its producer—E. Richard Sorenson—characterized these boys as "in trouble" because they all had been ordered by juvenile court to attend a residential training school, where he made his recordings. This fascinating collection of improvised rhythms, chants, and songs shows one of the strands that led to the formation of rap and hip-hop culture more than a decade later. Sorenson gives no indication as to why he made these recordings, although he goes to great lengths to emphasize that the performances are "spontaneous" and that the boys had no "special musical instruction or previous training performance prior to the recordings." According to Sorenson, they were motivated merely by the "prospect of having their efforts recorded on tape." While the recording was not aimed at children particularly as listeners, the fact that Asch valued the performances of these most marginalized of children was typical of his interest in all authentic expressions that reflected individual experience.

As recording tape developed, particularly portable recording equipment, children's singers moved out into the real world of schools and camps, and Folkways issued these recordings just as it had the anthropological recordings of Africans or Native Americans. Asch released dozens of children's records to complement his world music catalog, including children's songs from Kenya,

France, Germany, Israel, Japan, the Dominican Republic, and just about every other country you could imagine. Song lyrics were printed in English and the original language, making it easy to sing along (and for teachers to learn and teach the songs). Long before multicultural education was a buzzword, Folkways was promoting multiculturalism through releases that complemented the more mainstream children's material on the label.

Once he began working with ethnomusicologists recording in the field, Asch urged them not to ignore children's culture. In 1983, he told an NPR interviewer how he always "demanded" that field workers focus on the children as well as the adults:

> Whenever I know some information and I know people are going [to a place outside of the United States to record] I tell them "This is what I want." They never understand that the children are most important to be documented. They refuse. They go into a ceremony with a lot of widows and drunks [laughter] and they don't record the children. I demand that whenever anybody goes down they bring me a record of children. . . .
>
> The children have a culture of their own. It dies out when they become teens. But from very early until they become teens they bring their own games, songs, dances and expressions. That goes from child to child not from mother to child, but from child to child and then it's lost. When they become teens they become more involved with popular things. These are baby things. The more I can document what children do, the closer I will be to what culture, what people are.

DEL CIELO DE MI NIÑEZ: SUNI PAZ

Suni Paz is an artist who combines strong political content with children's issues. Even the name she has taken signifies a part of her mission. As her official biography states:

> She chose her name, Suni which means "ever-lasting," from the Quechua language, so as to be able to disseminate the rich indigenous cultures of the Americas in lyrics, rhythms, and instruments such as the charango, caja, and bombo. Paz is a last name that is found in every Latin American country. Its meaning is peace. To find inner peace and share it with others is Suni's quest in life. To sing and play rhythms, creating a bridge between cultures, has been her trademark.

Paz was born in Buenos Aires, Argentina, and was raised in a musical environment. Her grandfather was a violinist, and her parents encouraged their children to play and sing songs. After her marriage, she moved to Chile in 1960, but left the country with her two children five years later as the political situation deteriorated. Influenced by the *nueva canción* movement, Paz began writing songs in folk styles with lyrics that addressed the poverty and inequality in Latin America. Her first album was released in 1973 on Paredon Records, a label founded by Irwin Silber and Barbara Dane to present social-protest music. In the 1970s, she recorded a groundbreaking record, *Entre Hermanas: Between Sisters—Women's Songs Sung in Spanish,* widening the implications of the women's movement beyond middle- and upper-class Americans. *Bandera Mia: Songs of Argentina* is her latest collection, issued by Smithsonian Folkways records in 2006.

Suni Paz at about the time when she first recorded for Folkways.

Paz's children's music is an extension of her concerns in the adult world. She believes that children can learn all subjects better through music and movement. Learning about their own culture and the cultures of others is important, as it gives children a deeper understanding of themselves and those who share the planet with them. Her children's recordings draw on her native folk traditions and her own personal songs to encourage movement and "active listening"—just as earlier Folkways performers such as Charity Bailey and Ella Jenkins had done in their work. *Music from the Sky of My Childhood (Del Cielo de Mi Niñez)* combines her love of Latin American folk song with her concerns of transmitting cultural awareness to a new generation and is a classic of contemporary children's recordings.

Folk Music: Communism's "New Secret Weapon"

The 1950s were a period of deep distrust in American society. The flowering of liberal culture under Roosevelt was a thing of the past, and those associated with the social movements of the 1930s and 1940s—including folksingers—were open to suspicion as, at the very least, sympathetic to the Communist cause. As late as September 1963, New York senator Kenneth B. Keating was moved to make a passionate denunciation of folk music on the Senate floor, beginning his tirade with "Mr. President, it will come as a shock to many Senators . . . [that] the Communists have developed a new secret weapon to ensnare and capture youthful minds in America—folk music."

Many folksingers suffered at the hands of the House Un-American Activities Committee (HUAC) during this period. Associations with known left-leaning organizations were enough for a summons; many capitulated under the pressure rather than lose their livelihoods. Josh White recanted his past liberal associations, while Burl Ives actually "named names." While the folk community forgave White to some extent—he had to make a living, after all, and was at a double disadvantage being both African American and a folk musician—few forgave Ives, who was enjoying a successful movie career. While most who refused to name names took the Fifth Amendment (against self-incrimination), Pete Seeger insisted that his rights were protected by the First Amendment (freedom of speech and association)—leading to his citation for contempt of Congress in 1957 (see Chapter 3).

Many have wondered over the years why Folkways was not equally vulnerable to attack. The label occasionally drew attention from the FBI—a flurry of activity occurred in 1955 when it was discovered that Folkways had issued an album of songs from "Communist Poland," but the investigation was dropped for lack of any further "derogatory information." Still, it must have been unnerving to have FBI agents show up at the Folkways offices and question Marian Distler, the label's owner of record. The agents found no

> reason to question either the integrity or loyalty of MISS DISTLER and that [portion redacted] she was engaged in a solely legitimate enterprise and [name removed] does not believe that she has any intention of propagandizing the Communist form of government from the music manufactured by her corporation.

More amusingly, in 1961 the Los Angeles field office of the FBI reported on John Greenway's Folkways album *Talking Blues*:

> The subject matter of these ballads ranges from the alleged problems of the downtrodden, suppressed negro in the south to the exploited coal-miner in Illinois. One song is critical of EISENHOWER, his Cabinet, and his administration. Another song opposed the use of the atom bomb. The record has strong overtones of the reported oppression of the "worker" by big business and Government.

This appears to have been an informational report, because no further action seems to have been taken by the New York or national office. Nonetheless, Folkways again came under FBI surveillance in 1962 for issuing recordings from Cuba, and in 1964 for recording Lee Harvey Oswald's mother. Other than this, Moses Asch's work with Folkways seems to have gone unnoticed.

Asch argued that he was never targeted by the HUAC or other government agencies because he was merely a "documenter," and that because he was the owner of his own company there was little the government could do to deprive him of his livelihood. However, Irwin Silber points out that another record company owner, Horace Grenell of

Page of FBI file on Folkways Records. (Courtesy of Gary Kenton)

Young People's Records, was called before the committee and subsequently lost most of his business due to a boycott by public libraries of his product. Young People's Records produced children's music performed by folksingers—like Folkways—and the fact that it was vulnerable should have made Asch nervous.

Silber believes that Asch escaped scrutiny thanks to his ability to never allow himself to be too closely associated with any particular leftist group. Asch had seen the devastating impact on his own family of how political, religious, or social ties could lead to "guilt through association" (see Chapter 1). Asch's own beliefs remained elusive, and so

Silber believed "there was nothing to get Moe on. . . . You could ask Moe why he would produce the records of Pete Seeger and Woody Guthrie, but he could say, 'Well, I'm a documenter.' And he could prove with the sales figures that he had a right to put them out."

For whatever reason, Folkways escaped direct persecution from its longtime association with folk music and the American left. Whether it was Asch's canny ability to present this material without seemingly advocating revolutionary change or another unknown reason, we will never be sure. But, thankfully, the mission of documenting the world of sound went on with little interference from outside forces.

LISTEN UP!

LEAD BELLY
Lead Belly Sings for Children • SFW45047 • 1999

WOODY GUTHRIE
Songs to Grow on for Mother and Child
   • SFW45035 • 1991

PETE SEEGER
Abiyoyo and Other Story Songs for Children
   • SFW45001 • 1991

American Folk Songs for Children • SFW45020 • 1990

American Folk, Game and Activity Songs
   • SFW45056 • 2000

Birds, Beasts, Bugs and Fishes (Little and Big)
   • SFW45039 • 1998

Folk Songs for Young People • SFW45024 • 1990

Song and Play Time • SFW45023 • 1990

PETE SEEGER WITH OTHERS
Songs to Grow On, Vol. 2: School Days
   • FW07020 • 1951

Songs to Grow On, Vol. 3: American Work Songs
   • W07027 • 1951

LANGSTON HUGHES
Rhythms of the World • FW07340 • 1955

The Story of Jazz • FW07312 • 1954

The Glory of Negro History • FW07752 • 1955

ELLA JENKINS (SELECTED RECORDINGS)
Adventures in Rhythm • SFW45007 • 1989

And One and Two • SFW45016 • 1990

Call and Response • SFW45030 • 1990

Counting Games and Rhythms for the Little Ones
   • SFW45029 • 1990

Growing Up with Ella Jenkins: Rhythms, Songs, and
   Rhymes • SFW45032 • 1990

Jambo and Other Call and Response Songs and Chants
   • SFW45017 • 1996

Little Johnny Brown with Ella Jenkins and Girls and Boys
   from "Uptown" (Chicago) • SFW45026 • 1991

Multi-Cultural Children's Songs • SFW45045 • 1995

My Street Begins at My House • SFW45005 • 1989

Nursery Rhymes • SFW45019 • 1990

Play Your Instruments and Make a Pretty Sound
   • SFW45018 • 1994

Rhythm and Game Songs for the Little Ones
   • SFW45027 • 1991

Rhythms of Childhood • SFW45008 • 1989

Song Rhythms and Chants for the Dance
   • SFW45004 2000

Songs and Rhythms from Near and Far
   • SFW45033 • 1997

This Is Rhythm • SFW45028 • 1994

This-a-Way, That-a-Way • SFW45002 • 1989

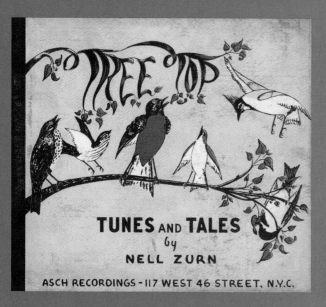

You'll Sing a Song and I'll Sing a Song
• SFW45010 • 1989

cELLAbration: A Tribute to Ella Jenkins
• SFW45059 • 2004

CHARITY BAILEY

Follow the Sunset • FW07406 • 1953

More Music Time and Stories • FW07528 • 1970

Music Time with Charity Bailey • FW07307 • 1952

MARJORIE MAZIA

Dance-a-Long • FW07651 • 1950

NEW LOST CITY RAMBLERS

Old Timey Songs for Children • FW07064 • 1959

JEAN RITCHIE

Children's Songs and Games from the Southern Mountains
• FW07054 • 1957

Marching Across the Green Grass and Other American
Children's Game Songs • FW07702 • 1968

TONY SCHWARTZ

1, 2, 3 and a Zing Zing Zing • FW07003 • 1953

E. RICHARD SORENSON, PRODUCER

Street and Gangland Rhythms, Beats and Improvisations
by Six Boys in Trouble • FW05589 • 1959

SUNI PAZ

Alerta Sings and Songs for the Playground/Canciones
Para el Recreo • SFW45055 • 2000

Canciones Para el Recreo: Children's Songs for the
Playground • SFW45013 • 1989

From the Sky of My Childhood • FW08875 • 1979

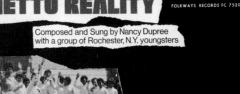

Chapter 8

FROM THE HILLS AND HOLLERS TO THE SUBWAYS AND SKYSCRAPERS

The Old-Time and Bluegrass Music Revivals

Little did Harry Smith or Moses Asch realize that the *Anthology of American Folk Music* would become a touchstone and inspiration for a revival of interest in old-time country music and bluegrass. Among the early listeners to this seminal set were three young, would-be musician-scholars: Ralph Rinzler, Mike Seeger, and John Cohen. Seeger and Cohen would play key roles as both performers and collectors in establishing Folkways as the home of the most important rediscovered old-time musicians of the late 1950s through the mid-1960s; Seeger would also help familiarize the folk-revival audience with a new musical style, bluegrass; and Rinzler would "discover" Doc Watson and revive the career of Bill Monroe, as well as play a key role, decades later, in bringing the Folkways collection to the Smithsonian in 1987.

Cohen and Seeger's importance to the old-time revival went beyond their roles as musicians in the New Lost City Ramblers. Both conducted extensive field work, recording both rediscovered musicians from the 1920s and 1930s and newly discovered performers. Mike Seeger's major find was the rediscovery of banjo player Dock Boggs, who had made a few records in the late 1920s and then faded into obscurity. Boggs' unusual blues-tinged repertory and two-finger banjo style set him apart from many other traditional musicians. Cohen's major discovery was banjo player and vocalist Roscoe Holcomb, who had never previously recorded. Holcomb's intense, high tenor voice, driving banjo work, and unique adaptations of traditional songs made him one of the most influential figures in the old-time revival.

The New Lost City Ramblers: Old-Time Revivalists

In the early 1950s at Yale University, a mathematician and banjo player named Tom Paley began performing, sometimes joined by a painter/banjo and guitar player named John Cohen. After graduation, Paley settled near Baltimore, Maryland, where he met Mike Seeger, and they began to play together locally; Cohen moved to New York's Greenwich Village. When Cohen came to visit his old college friend in 1957, the two landed a local radio gig; Paley brought along Seeger, and the trio clicked.

Cohen first met Moses Asch when he accompanied Guy Carawan on his first album. He told him how excited he was playing with Paley and Seeger, and Asch quickly agreed to record the trio:

> I remember clearly telling him how moved I was [by his 1940s-era recordings], the ones that had Woody Guthrie and Cisco Houston. Those were some of the most lively, live recordings that I ever heard, different from the[ir] commercial ones. . . .

Less then 5 months later, after I first played . . . with Tom and Mike, I came up to Moe and said . . . "I get the same feeling out of this group that I got out of those recordings, and no where else have I ever had that."

He says, "Who are the other characters?"

And I said, "A guy named Tom Paley and a guy named Mike Seeger."

"OK, I will record 'em."

It was that kind of acceptance, no questions asked.

All three musicians approached performing with a keen knowledge of the problems—and possibilities—that the folk revival had created. They understood that they were urban-bred performers who didn't come from a traditional background. They disdained the commercialism of groups such as the Kingston Trio, whose top pop hit, "Tom Dooley," a heavily reworked version of a classic old-time banjo

Peter Bartók recording Mike Seeger of the New Lost City Ramblers at the Westport Public Library.

Poster for a concert by the New Lost City Ramblers with guest Cousin Emmy. (Courtesy of the BenCar Archives)

song, was universally applauded as "American folk music." In forming their own group, Paley, Cohen, and Seeger envisioned a kind of anti–Kingston Trio, which would take as its guiding light an attempt to authentically re-create the original string band recordings of the 1920s. Even their name—the New Lost City Ramblers—was an homage to groups such as Charlie Poole and the North Carolina Ramblers, and a pun on the idea of New York City as being also a home to the "lost city" of traditional music.

By the time Folkways released *The New Lost City Ramblers, Volume 2* (actually the group's fourth release) in 1959, Cohen was amazed by how the band had taken off:

The New Lost City Ramblers, c. 1958. Left to right: Tom Paley, John Cohen, Mike Seeger. (Courtesy of Photosound Associates)

When we set out to make our first record—there was no question in our mind but that we had to make such music—yet some uncertainty as to where such music might stand and to what it might lead.

In the last two years, we have been singing in concerts and at colleges and clubs all over, and seem to be finding friends where we never knew we had them. In many colleges—small country string bands have been springing up and have taken a real place in the general field of folk music.

The Ramblers were never meant to be a rigidly dog-matic band; Cohen himself noted as early as 1960 that "city boys . . . playing music full of old traditions" had to go beyond "rigid styles" of copying traditional old-time recordings and discover the "excitement of finding never-ending possibilities." The Ramblers would adapt over the years, particularly after Paley left the group in 1962 and was replaced by Tracy Schwarz. And by the early 1970s a new generation of old-time "revivalists" would extend their performances well beyond the original sources.

Roscoe Holcomb in 1961, taken on his first visit to New York City. (© John Cohen)

THE HIGH LONESOME SOUND:
ROSCOE HOLCOMB AND DOCK BOGGS

Roscoe Holcomb was a uniquely talented singer, banjo player, and guitarist. He sang in an intense, high-pitched voice, as if he were clenching for air. When I met Roscoe (when I was fourteen years old), he proudly said to me, "If you cut my head off at the neck, I'd go on singing." More than a falsetto, Roscoe's voice embodied the bluesy sound that John Cohen aptly described as "the high, lonesome sound." Roscoe was also a unique banjo player, playing neither chords nor melody as accompaniment, but a kind of intense, rhythmically pulsing pattern that perfectly complemented his vocals. His guitar playing was equally unusual; some said he played the guitar as if it were a banjo (although you could easily say the opposite, that he played the banjo as if it were a guitar). Truly, Roscoe defied categories in his life and music.

However, Holcomb was in many ways a tragic figure. His family did not encourage or even recognize his unique talents, and few local people encouraged him to play or perform. Thanks to Cohen, he was able to travel the folk festival and club circuit in the 1960s and early 1970s, before his health—he had long suffered from lung problems and injuries from working in the mines and performing roadwork—limited him to his home. Roscoe's intense sense of isolation is strongly apparent in his performances and selection of songs; even his "upbeat" songs have a strong bluesy undertone.

The rediscovery of Dock Boggs came about through a series of happy

Dock Boggs performing in Boston (right) with guitar accompaniment by Mike Seeger. (© John Cooke Photography)

accidents. Seeger admired Boggs' recording on the *Anthology of American Folk Music* and wondered what had happened to him. As far as he could tell, no one had seen or heard the singer since the early 1930s. Still, it seemed to be worth a try to find him again. In Seeger's words:

In February 1963 Guthrie Meade [told me that he] met a relative of Dock Boggs who placed his whereabouts about the Mayking, Kentucky area. . . . On [the] way back from California [that June] . . . I decided to try to find Dock Boggs . . . and [I] set off over into Kentucky from Kingsport, Tennessee, on a numbered highway which soon became a rutted mountain dirt road. Just over the mountain was Eolia, Kentucky . . . where [I] stopped at the post office and asked about Dock Boggs. [I was] mildly shocked to be told . . . that he was to be found around Hemphill. . . . On [the] way to Hemphill . . . [I] stopped in Neon and asked directions from some men standing at the main intersection. They all knew Dock Boggs (or knew of him) and we discussed his style of music. . . .

They gave directions which took [me] to Pound, Virginia, and eventually on to Norton where [I] easily found his name in the phone book. After a call, [I] went up to visit him and his wife at their home. . . . Our meeting was one of mutual disbelief; [I] couldn't believe that this was the Dock Boggs and he, though he was pleased that someone remembered his records, was not certain what I was up to. We talked awhile and . . . later that evening . . . he recorded about eight songs. . . .

Two weeks later [Boggs] was on the American Folk Festival [stage] in Asheville, North Carolina.

Boggs was an exceptional singer-performer with a wide repertory of material and unique vocal and banjo-playing styles. Although his original professional career had been relatively short—he recorded and performed from 1927 until the early years of the 1930s, when the Depression hit the South hard—he became a major star on the folk revival circuit of festivals and clubs. Many of Boggs' versions of traditional songs became standards for fledgling revivalists.

> "Our meeting was one of mutual disbelief; [I] couldn't believe that this was the Dock Boggs and he. . . . was not certain what I was up to."
>
> —Mike Seeger

Seeger produced many other albums from his field recordings during the 1950s and 1960s. Some of his recordings were of musicians who had never recorded before, such as master autoharp player Kilby Snow and guitarist Elizabeth Cotten (see Chapter 6). Others were major country stars in their day, most notably the talented brother team of Sam and Kirk McGee, whom Seeger recorded with Fiddlin' Arthur Smith. The McGees had a long pedigree in old-time music; Sam had worked as a sideman for Uncle Dave Macon, and the trio of the McGees and Arthur Smith performed as the popular Dixie Liners in the 1930s. Sam McGee was still performing at the Grand Ole Opry when Seeger recorded the trio's first album, which was released by Folkways in 1964; a second album followed in 1968. Seeger's interests ranged from the most rough-hewn backcountry sounds to the highly polished commercial string band music of groups such as the McGees, helping to deepen the Folkways catalog and the growing urban revival's interest in old-time music.

OLD-TIME MUSIC AT CLARENCE ASHLEY'S

Ralph Rinzler—who would later play a key role in the Smithsonian's 1987 purchase of Folkways (see Chapter 12)—was a professional mandolin player with the successful city-grass group the Greenbriar Boys in the early 1960s, as well as a fledgling folklorist. Like Seeger and Cohen, he was greatly influenced by the *Anthology of American Folk Music* and was on the lookout for the legendary performers who appeared on the set. In 1960, Rinzler competed at the famous Union Grove (Virginia) Old Time Fiddlers' Convention, where he was surprised to meet one of the stars of the *Anthology*, banjo player Clarence "Tom" Ashley, one of the most prolific of the old-time recording artists. Ashley had been a member of the Carolina Tar Heels as well as a solo artist, but no one at the time realized he was still alive, let alone involved with music, until Rinzler rediscovered him. Ashley was performing as a comedian—not a musician—with a group

From left, Tom Ashley, Gaither Carlton, Doc Watson, and Rosalie Watson, his wife, at Ashley's home at the time of their "discovery." (Photo by Eugene Earle, used by permission)

of younger musicians, including fiddler Clint Howard, guitarist Fred Price, and a blind guitarist named Arthel "Doc" Watson. At the time, Watson was playing in a local bar band, playing electric guitar and covering recent rockabilly hits by stars like Carl Perkins. This music didn't interest Rinzler at all:

> On arrival at Ashley's home, [I was] introduced to Doc Watson. Ashley had not taken up the banjo again. Instead he asked Doc to join him and agreed to sing to Doc's electric guitar accompaniment. . . . In response to my expressed concern about recording Tom Ashley with an electric guitar . . . Doc . . . made it clear that he had his own professional standards. He owned no acoustic guitar, and if he were to borrow one, he wouldn't be accustomed to it.

Discouraged, Rinzler abandoned the recording session. However, the next day, when Watson casually mentioned that he played the banjo, Rinzler's interest was piqued:

On the way to [Ashley's] daughter's house where Tom had arranged for us to do the recording, I rode in the back of an open bed pick-up playing old time hoedowns on a five-string banjo . . . Doc hopped in back saying, "Let me see that banjo, son." I handed it over. To my amazement, he deftly played and sang.

It turned out that Watson played both guitar and banjo in old-time styles, had a fine voice and a vast repertory of songs, and came from a musical family, including his father-in-law, fiddler Gaither Carlton. Watson would become a major star of the folk revival, with Rinzler initially managing his career.

The albums that came out of these encounters included two volumes titled *Old Time Music at Clarence Ashley's* and another LP titled *The Watson Family*. To say that these were influential recordings is a vast understatement. The powerful music, ranging from old-time dance tunes to Appalachian ballads, play party songs, country hits of the 1920s and 1930s, and Regular Baptist hymns, was performed in a spirit of joyful camaraderie that is rarely captured on record. The documentation of each album was thorough; the performances were fresh, energetic, and endlessly listenable. Although Watson would go on to make many more studio albums, these albums show him discovering a new performing voice and triumphantly announcing it to the world.

On his return to New York, Rinzler tried to interest one of the major folk labels in the tapes, but none was interested, so it was natural for him to turn to Folkways. A few months after the records appeared, Ashley and crew were brought to New York City for the second concert in a series produced by a group calling itself the Friends of Old Time Music. In fact, the producers were none other than Rinzler and two stalwarts of the New York City old-time music revival, John Cohen and Folklore Center owner Izzy Young. The Friends of Old Time Music would bring many important early blues and country figures to New York, spurring the growth of the urban renewal. Ashley and company's concerts received rave reviews from the *New York Times* and led to a tour in small clubs and colleges through the country. The response also encouraged Rinzler to begin managing and promoting Watson.

Of the entire group of performers, Watson was the youngest and most interested in developing a career, so Rinzler decided to help him get started. Ashley had been a professional performer and had developed a slick stage persona, telling (often corny) jokes and ably managing the other performers. Watson was more of a natural and, Rinzler felt, the most talented of the crew; he waited for an opportunity to give Watson the limelight. One night, Ashley developed laryngitis before the group was scheduled to open at Los Angeles' Ash Grove folk club in April 1962. As Rinzler recalled to Peter Goldsmith in 1991:

Gaither Carlton and Doc Watson performing at the Newport Folk Festival in the early 1960s. (Photo by Diana Davies, courtesy of the Ralph Rinzler Folklife Archives and Collections, Smithsonian Institution)

When Ashley lost his voice when we were out in Los Angeles, I said, "Doc here's what we're going to do." And Doc said—he was kind of shaken up by it—he said "Well, you know I don't do that. I don't tell all the jokes and I don't do all the talking on the show." I said, "Just talk the way you are; talk the way you did on the back of the truck when we first met. . . . It would be a hell of a lot more interesting then someone telling canned jokes. . . ." He said, "Well I could do *that*."

So Doc just took over and he was just wonderful instantly. And when Ashley came back, he wasn't ready for that. He told a canned joke, and Doc made an aside comment that occurred to him was a lot funnier than the joke . . . and Ashley walked off the stage. He said, "You got it; now, take it!" Said he wasn't going to go back up: "If you don't walk down, I ain't never going to go back." Doc was left up there and he just went right on with it, and after a moment's embarrassment [Ashley returned]. . . .

As soon as that thing happened with Ashley's laryngitis, all of a sudden you heard a different ensemble, where Doc would make all kinds of jokes in the middle of songs. Clint would sing the line of the "Crawdad Song," and Doc would come back with little comments that occurred to him. And it was very lively. And he played a lot more innovatively. And, of course, the audience loved it because it was musically better.

Doc soon had a major career in the folk world, which expanded into mainstream country, bluegrass, and even country-rock when he was featured on the

1971 set *Will the Circle Be Unbroken,* put together by folk-rockers the Nitty Gritty Dirt Band.

FROM INDIANA TO GEORGIA: ART ROSENBAUM

Besides Seeger, Cohen, and Rinzler, it seemed as though anyone who could get his hands on a tape recorder was venturing out to rediscover earlier recording stars. Ed Kahn and Art Rosenbaum were just teenagers growing up in Indianapolis when they were bitten by the banjo bug. They had heard Library of Congress recordings made by Alan Lomax of a banjo player named Pete Steele. In the summer of 1957, they found Steele still living in his family home, where Lomax had recorded him, and the result was a Folkways album.

"Last Payday at Coal Creek" is perhaps Steele's best-known song. Played in the up-picking style, the song tells of a coal mine explosion that, according to Steele, occurred in 1911. Coal Creek, Tennessee, had long been a center of labor unrest. Angered by the use of convict labor, there had been a worker uprising in 1891, and mine explosions occurred in both 1902 and 1911. Steele played two pieces related to Coal Creek, this song and an instrumental known as "The Coal Creek March," perhaps associated with the 1891 unrest. Steele is one of the only sources for the piece and may have "assembled" it himself from bits of traditional blues and songs. He first recorded it for Alan Lomax for the Library of Congress in 1938.

Rosenbaum would go on to have a distinguished career as a folklorist, banjo player, and artist. His second project for Folkways Records was a wonderful anthology of traditional music from his home state of Indiana called *Fine Times at Our House,* put together with the help of another longtime musician friend, Pat Dunford. Rosenbaum played the tapes for John Cohen, who arranged for the album's release by Folkways in 1964.

It would be about fifteen years before Rosenbaum again worked for Folkways. In the early 1980s, he was teaching art at the University of Georgia and conducting regular field recording trips. He documented a wide range of musicians, from Gordon Tanner, the fiddling son of James Gideon "Gid" Tanner, the leader of the celebrated string band the Skillet Lickers, to the black "shouters" of McIntosh County, Georgia. The first project he produced for Folkways in the 1980s was a string band record with Gordon Tanner, Smokey Joe Miller, and Uncle John Patterson. Typically, it took Asch a while to respond after Art sent him the demo tape:

> We first decided we'd do some kind of stringband record. We didn't have a company singled out, we just decided to do something. We went to a little studio here in Athens with Gordon Tanner and Joe Miller, and I played the banjo, and we recorded a few things. And then I met Uncle John Patterson . . . and

Smokey Joe Miller and Gordon Tanner. (© Margo Rosenbaum)

I said, "It would really be much more appropriate for him to be playing banjo than me," because he was from their culture and their era. So I recorded it on my Pioneer [cassette] deck . . . in Gordon Tanner's chicken coop/music room. Originally we were going to pitch it to Davis Unlimited, but . . . his company was kind of going under . . . So I said, "Well, I'll send it off to Folkways." And then I didn't hear anything for a year. And Joe Miller, who is always pessimistic, said, "Oh they don't like our music, we're old fashioned. . . ."

So one time I was in the city, I called Moe, said, "Hey, that Gordon Tanner stuff, what's up with that?" He said, "Tell you the truth, I haven't listened to it. I will listen to it tonight." So I called him the next day and he said, "These men are *professionals*, so I'll put it out." He was very decisive at that moment. And after that, it was kind of interesting, Joe Miller and Newman Young went directly to Folkways, and they put out I think 2 different albums with . . . mandolin-guitar harmony singing music.

Rosenbaum's other 1980s-era output included a two-LP set of traditional music from Georgia, along with a solo album by visionary artist Howard Finster.

Collecting Old-Time Music in Grayson and Carroll Counties, Virginia, in the 1960s

Eric H. Davidson

In 1956–57, Wade Ward was visited by folklorists Mike Seeger and Eric Davidson, respectively, and his second career in the folk revival was launched. Through the early 1970s, Davidson produced for Folkways several albums of Ward's music along with his contemporaries and neighbors.

I got the idea of recording the traditional music of Southwest Virginia at its source shortly after I went to college at the University of Pennsylvania. I was trying to play some of that music myself, having become acquainted with it from a girlfriend whose Washington family had a connection with the marvelous Library of Congress collection of recordings. I remember thinking there was a kind of limp, silly, beach-party quality to the "folk music" I heard in Philadelphia cafés that left me burning to hit the road and find the real thing. So about 1957, I obtained a list of Library of Congress recordings, took a Texaco roadmap, and began to stick pins into it for the place name on each and every recording. There was an amazing concentration of pins around the Galax, Virginia area, on west from there, and right across the border in North Carolina. It wasn't that far away, and it wasn't that long after many of the Library of Congress' recordings were made, and so that's where I went. And then went back again, and again, and again. . . .

From 1957 until his death in 1971, Uncle Wade Ward—the finest clawhammer banjo picker I ever heard—was my friend, and an invaluable source as to who had been a famous "musicianer" in the region in earlier days who might still be interesting to listen to. Uncle Wade was a lot more than that, too: he kept us at his place on trips, when we would let him. I will forever remember his "Stay with us, now," the way Uncle Wade said "farewell" when the time was up and we had to return to our other lives up North. I say "we," because I always made these expeditions with friends and companions; it was definitely a two-person job to run the recorder and at the same time talk with the person who we were recording; to figure out how lost we actually were while wandering around dirt roads looking for "a dark kind of shack about a couple miles up the branch . . ."; and to make camp. Usually in the 1960s on those trips (we never went in winter), we would camp on a long, hardwood-covered ridge up above Independence where Uncle Wade lived, called Iron Mountain.

Uncle Wade knew everything about old times in Southwest Virginia, and he was a natural local historian and raconteur with a droll wit. He would say about someone who wasn't up to his musical standards "that old boy couldn't carry a tune if he had it in a bucket with a lid on top"; and once warned us about a rough character who later gave us some wonderful music, "You boys better look out for him, he's about as mean as two snakes." He had a wonderful way of describing "fox-hunting." Some folks ride horses hell bent for leather chasing foxes, he said, but the best way he liked was get yourself a jug of whiskey and your dogs, and some friends, and on some nice moonlit night go on up to the top of the mountain and just set there and listen to the dogs chasing after the foxes all night long. . . . But that was earlier in life. When I knew Uncle Wade, he never would touch a drop of any booze, having fought that battle long before.

Uncle Wade was also my occasional instructor in the Virginia clawhammer style, a driving style

From left, Glen Smith, Fields Ward, and Wade Ward, c. 1964. (© Eric Davidson)

of downpicking with both melodic and rhythmic counterpoint that can sound alternately like a fast harpsichord or an African dance tune, not surprisingly, given its very Southern mixture of black and white origins. Unlike some others I ran into in those days and in those parts, Uncle Wade had no discernable problems about race; he once told me the most horrible thing he ever saw was when he was 11 when, looking through his father's legs, he watched a black man hung before the county court house in Independence. He was, in the years I knew him, a natural country gentleman. He helped us over and over again, telling musicians who were suspicious of outsiders, "Let them have your music! You don't think you're going to be able to take it with you, do you?"

I became conscious that the riffs and motifs of the instrumental styles, though terrifically complex and sometimes technically demanding, were for both banjo and its traditional mate, the fiddle, basically canonical. There was a certain way of doing them, just as in the co-extant ballad literature, there was a certain way of describing a beautiful woman (lily white hands, long yellow hair, etc.). And so two musicians who had never played

together could fit perfectly with one another with no lead time or adjustment. One night in 1964, we put Uncle Wade together with a fiddler from the other end of the stretch of country where the pins in my map had been most dense: Glen Smith, from Hillsville, Virginia. They had heard of one another vaguely, but never before played together. It was in the parking lot outside the Galax Fiddle Convention. A lot of that parking lot session, recorded in the dark on a portable machine amongst the old black Fords lined up on that field, was immortalized in Folkways recordings, mainly in *Traditional Music from Grayson and Carroll Counties, Virginia*. Later we continued at Uncle Wade's house in other sessions until each had played all they knew, and further recordings of this wonderful pair were on a record titled *Bluegrass from the Blue Ridge*.

When Uncle Wade died, Jane Rigg and I went one last time to the Peach Bottom Creek house in back of Independence, Va. and we recorded some reminiscences for use in a retrospective album that we made for Folkways, *Uncle Wade, A Memorial to Wade Ward, Old Time Virginia Banjo Picker, 1892–1971*. That was 37 years ago, and in my own reminiscence, the memory of how important Uncle Wade was to me all those years remains as clear as was his farsighted gaze.

Wade Ward, 1963. (© Eric Davidson)

OLD-TIME REVIVALISTS

In the late 1960s and early 1970s, the Chapel Hill/Raleigh-Durham region of North Carolina became a hotbed for old-time bands, producing the Hollow Rock and Fuzzy Mountain string bands, which in turn gave birth to the Red Clay Ramblers. While the Ramblers were still establishing their identity, they recorded their first album with guest fiddler Al McCanless, combining some bluegrass influences with the old-time songs and instrumentals they loved. In his liner notes, singer, banjo player, and bandleader Tommy Thompson traces the genesis of the band to a desire to explore the rich old-time song tradition, and from the first the band was well known for its harmony singing. He shows how earlier old-time revivalists, notably the New Lost City Ramblers, influenced them, but also draws a distinction that would be important for the next genera-tion of re-creators of old-time music: younger bands felt the need to reflect their own musical influences beyond the old-time repertory and had to move beyond the "creative imitation" that had been the focus of the earlier revivalists. He admits that its repertory was still fluid, as the band searched through old-time, blues, jazz, bluegrass, and early-twentieth-century pop music for its identity. Nonetheless, their first album, in 1974, helped establish them as a band that would lead the way to a new level of creativity in the old-time world.

The Red Clay Ramblers would explore many styles of music—and write their own songs, which mixed these wide-ranging influences—over the next decade and a half. The retirement of Tommy Thompson due to increasing symptoms of Alzheimer's, and his subsequent death, ended this period of wide-ranging explo-ration. But the legacy of the band lives on in younger bands such as the Freight Hoppers and the Yonder Mountain String Band.

The old-time revival of the 1970s and 1980s led to scores of new performers recording and performing on the folk club and festival circuit. Most of these performers acknowledged the tension between re-creating classic old-time music—whether it was learned from 78s or living performers such as Wade Ward or Tommy Jarrell—and creating something new. All responded in dif-ferent ways. Bruce Hutton, a multi-instrumentalist based in Washington, D.C., recorded *Old Time Music: It's All Around* in 1978 as part of his work performing in schools, to demonstrate the wide variety of instruments, accompaniments, and song styles that are found in the old-time repertoire. Also in 1978, banjo player Andy Cahan and fiddler Lisa Ornstein produced *Ship in the Clouds*, one of many instrumental collections from the period that drew heavily on the Mount Airy–Round Peak area traditions, notably the playing of Tommy Jarrell and Fred Cockerham. Ken Perlman combined old-time banjo and blues guitar techniques in his arrangements of Celtic dance tunes on the album *Clawhammer Banjo and Finger Style Guitar Solos* from 1983. Banjo player Eric Davidson and

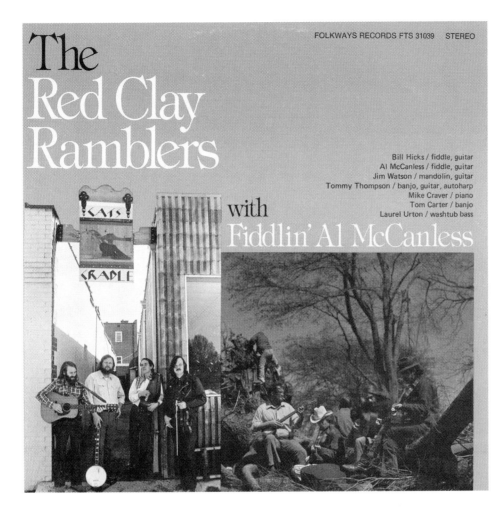

FOLKWAYS RECORDS FTS 31039   STEREO

The Red Clay Ramblers

Bill Hicks / fiddle, guitar
Al McCanless / fiddle, guitar
Jim Watson / mandolin, guitar
Tommy Thompson / banjo, guitar, autoharp
Mike Craver / piano
Tom Carter / banjo
Laurel Urton / washtub bass

with

Fiddlin' Al McCanless

Red Clay Ramblers album cover.

his associates guitarist Paul Newman and fiddler Caleb Finch—who had documented the music of Wade Ward and his compatriots in two northern Virginia counties from the 1950s through the late 1960s—also formed a revival band, the Iron Mountain String Band. They attempted to re-create their source's style and music rather than experiment with it.

While Folkways did not document the entire old-time music revival, the label's output was representative of the wealth of new music that was produced. And certainly in the early years, without Folkways' involvement, the old-time revival would have had much less of an impact.

DOCUMENTING URBAN BLUEGRASS

It took a while for the folk revival to recognize bluegrass music. Many felt that bluegrass was "too modern" and preferred the older styles of string band music. Because bluegrass recordings on the major labels were not marketed much in the North and often appeared only on 45s aimed at the jukebox market, it was hard for urban folk fans to hear them. It's not surprising that it took a while for Folkways to present bluegrass music, and even then Folkways was never primarily known for its bluegrass acts.

Although bluegrass was a "southern" music, it did make itself felt as far north as Baltimore, Washington, D.C., and their neighboring suburbs. By the mid-1950s, dozens of acts, both local and national, could be heard at local parks, and a homegrown bluegrass scene was exploding. Among the enthusiastic followers of this growing scene was Mike Seeger.

A half brother of Pete Seeger, he showed an early interest in bluegrass music—particularly the showy three-finger banjo-picking style of bluegrass legend Earl Scruggs. With Mike's assistance, Pete Seeger updated his influential *How to Play the Five String Banjo* book, adding a chapter on Scruggs' picking in acknowledgment of its growing popularity. Asch certainly was aware of this trend and asked Pete to recommend someone to put together an LP of bluegrass banjo music. As Mike Seeger recalled:

Moe Asch's letter to Mike Seeger inviting him to produce an album of bluegrass banjo music.

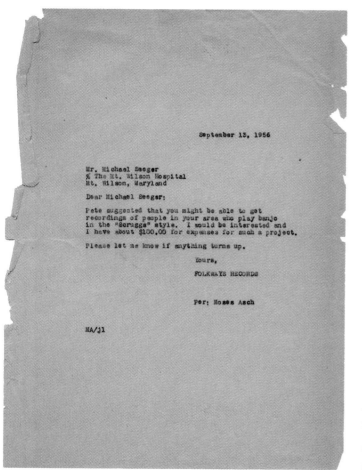

September 13, 1956

Mr. Michael Seeger
% The Mt. Wilson Hospital
Mt. Wilson, Maryland

Dear Michael Seeger:

Pete suggested that you might be able to get recordings of people in your area who play banjo in the "Scruggs" style. I would be interested and I have about $100.00 for expenses for such a project.

Please let me know if anything turns up.

Yours,
FOLKWAYS RECORDS

Per: Moses Asch

MA/jl

In late 1956 Moses Asch of Folkways Records asked me if I would make a record of Scruggs-style banjo picking, and I assumed that he wanted me to record traditional players. This started me on the path of making occasional documentary recordings, mostly for Folkways. . . . All were recorded and produced in my spare time on a budget of about $100 each, in people's homes or any quiet location, often with recording machines of marginal quality. All recording was done with a single microphone. . . . My intent was usually just to make a copy of the sound, not to record for commercial release.

The album that resulted, *American Banjo: Three Finger and Scruggs Style*, became an instant classic, inspiring a new generation of city-based bluegrass pickers.

Seeger next brought to Folkways a new group called the Country Gentlemen, recording their first album (released in 1960). The group came together by accident—in several senses. Following a performance, Buzz Busby's

COUNTRY SONGS, OLD AND NEW
Charley Waller, John Duffey, Eddie Adcock & The

COUNTRY GENTLEMEN

The Country Gentlemen's first Folkways album. Left to right: John Duffey, Eddie Adcock, Charlie Waller.

Bayou Boys were involved in a car crash that temporarily decimated the group's ranks. Anxious to keep their regular gig at a local grill, the group's banjo player, Bill Emerson, called on two others—guitarist Charlie Waller and mandolin player John Duffey—to fill in for the injured band members. In the words of bluegrass scholar Les McIntyre:

> The chemistry between Duffey and Waller was instantly apparent, and they soon decided to form their own group. It was Duffy who would give the band its name. . . . "I looked around at the names of the bluegrass bands back then, and it seemed they were all Mountain Boys; we didn't want to be Mountain Boys, so I said let's be 'Gentlemen.'"

The band's initial lineup—Emerson, Duffey, and Waller—was soon performing in the Washington area. In 1958, Emerson left, replaced first by Pete Kuykendall (who used the stage name Pete Roberts) and then by Eddie Adcock.

Adcock's banjo playing brought together many influences beyond the standard Scruggs licks. The combination of Adcock's banjo and baritone singing with Duffey's energetic mandolin playing and soaring high tenor vocals and Waller's rock-solid guitar and lead vocals—and in 1960 the addition of bass player Tom Gray—created the "classic" Country Gentlemen lineup. As Adcock recalls:

> The thing that made [us] what [we] were and made [our] style was the pull among us from our different musical preferences and our putting it all together—Duffey liked folk music a lot, I liked rock 'n' roll and jazz, and Charlie liked country. It was Charlie pulling against me, and John pulling against Charlie, and John pulling against me. That is how we created the style of the Country Gentlemen.

The group probably would have remained a local phenomenon if it hadn't been for the folk revival. The Kingston Trio's 1958 chart-topping version of "Tom Dooley" inspired—as one of many unintended consequences—a new interest in traditional acts on college campuses and even urban nightclubs. As McIntrye relates:

> The Country Gentlemen were quick to recognize the importance of this new audience and were soon playing concerts at colleges . . . a far cry from the smoke-filled neighborhood bars that had been the normal venue for most bluegrass bands. Then on one Saturday night in September 1961, the Country Gentlemen made history when they appeared at the prestigious Carnegie Hall in New York City as part of a folk "Hootenanny" sponsored by *Sing Out!* magazine. The event was emceed by Pete Seeger . . . John Duffey [recalled,] "We played Carnegie Hall . . . and sold well to the people but not to the critics. The people at Folkways said we were too slick for them. They still want this music in the raw. From the looks of the other performers, (Pete Seeger included) we made a big mistake in dressing and shaving."

Duffey's wry comments about the "authentic" look of the folk performers—clad in jeans and sporting scruffy beards—showed that many bluegrass bands felt alienated from folk audiences. Bluegrass groups always dressed well, sporting matching suits and shined shoes; even their barroom audiences expected them to appear neat and present themselves professionally. It took a while for these groups to let their hair down under the influence of their folk-oriented (and later rock-oriented) fans.

Another group brought to Folkways by Mike Seeger was the Boston-based duo the Lilly Brothers, who recorded with banjo player Don Stover. The Lilly

Brothers' music was firmly rooted in the tradition of brother vocal duets of the 1930s. Everett and "B" Lilly first played regionally in West Virginia, working briefly on the famed WWVA Jamboree out of Wheeling. Mandolin-playing Everett joined Flatt and Scruggs' band in 1951, but then reunited with his brother a year later. Lured by fiddler Tex Logan, who had moved to Boston to study at MIT, the brothers moved north and began playing at a small club called the Hillbilly Ranch, where they remained in residence through 1970. With Stover and Logan, they developed a group style that blended the old-style brother duets with a more modern bluegrass drive.

The group made its first album for Folkways in 1961 under the guidance of Mike Seeger. Dick Spottswood, writing many years later, noted that the label didn't do everything it should have to promote the recording: "Folkways unwisely called it *Folk Songs from the Southern Mountains*, aiming it at the folk audience and implicitly characterizing the Lillys' music as quaint and unsophisticated. Undoubtedly it would have been called something like 'The Lilly Brothers' Greatest Hits' had it been targeted to country buyers, who understandably don't think of their music as folk." Unlike the Country Gentlemen, the Lilly Brothers didn't perform much outside Boston, except occasionally at folk festivals and clubs, and never broke into the bluegrass circuit. This may account for the record's high status among collectors but low overall sales.

NEW YORK GRASS

The New York scene was not as receptive to bluegrass as Washington, but one unique banjo player did arise during the early days of the folk revival: Roger Sprung. Sprung's repertoire was very eclectic—he played everything from bluegrass standards to Broadway show tunes, Sousa marches, Dixieland jazz instrumentals, and pop songs such as "Malaguena." Born in 1930, Sprung was originally a boogie-woogie and jazz fan until his older brother introduced him to folk music. By the late 1950s, he had become a regular at the Sunday afternoon folk gatherings in New York's Washington Square, when he and Mike Cohen—John's brother—formed the Shanty Boys, one of many Kingston Trio–like groups that briefly flourished in clubs, on records, and on the pop charts during this period. The group disbanded in the early 1960s, and Sprung began focusing on his solo banjo work.

Sprung released his first Folkways album in 1963, which included North Carolina guitarist Doc Watson along with several other musicians, including—unusually for the time—a drummer. Subsequent albums featured New York–based bluegrassers such as Jody Stecher and Jon Sholle. A controversial figure in the bluegrass world because of his eclectic taste, Sprung's single-string banjo work and incorporation of jazz harmonies did influence the next generation of New York players.

Truer to the legacy of bluegrass were two groups that emerged in the late 1950s and early 1960s. Washington Square was the breeding ground for the Greenbriar Boys, originally formed by banjo player Bob Yellin, guitarist-vocalist John Herald, and mandolin player Paul Prestopino. After a few changes, Ralph Rinzler took over the mandolin chair; Rinzler would become a leading performer, scholar, and promoter of old-time and bluegrass music in the coming years. The Greenbriar Boys recorded for Vanguard Records, which had a more commercial orientation than Folkways, thanks to the success of its best-selling folk artist Joan Baez. Another group of musicians formed around mandolinist David Grisman, guitarist Jody Stecher, and banjo player Julian "Winnie" Winston. This group eventually became the New York City Ramblers (later, they dropped "City" from their name because of the considerable confusion it caused with the New Lost City Ramblers). The group never recorded officially, but various members of this group accompanied Roger Sprung on his Folkways outings and were also involved in one-off projects for the label, including two important releases: *Bluegrass* by Frank Wakefield and Red Allen and *Who's That Knocking?* with Hazel Dickens and Alice Gerrard. Local producer and promoter Peter Siegel was involved with both projects.

> "Moe gave me $75 to make the record. He gave me $37.50 before I went down to [Washington to] record, and I bought the tape and a bus ticket . . . and then when I got back he gave me another $37.50. I thought it was big time."
>
> —Peter Siegel, on recording Hazel and Alice's first album

The Wakefield-Allen project actually brought together the Washington, D.C., and New York City bluegrassers who had been involved with Folkways. Banjo player Pete Roberts (Pete Kuykendall), who had played with an early Country Gentlemen lineup and produced their second Folkways LP, was featured on and produced the initial sessions. The rest of the album was recorded in New York following an appearance by the band at a 1963 *Sing Out!* benefit. Grisman and Siegel produced the album, which appeared in 1964. Perhaps thanks to its title, which proclaimed proudly that the music on the record *was* bluegrass, it was influential in the growing folk-bluegrass scene. It helped that Wakefield soon replaced Ralph Rinzler in the Greenbriar Boys, so his name was well known on the folk circuit.

Hazel and Alice

Hazel Dickens and Alice Foster (now Alice Gerrard) also came out of the Washington, D.C., bluegrass scene, but were "discovered" and recorded by New Yorker Peter Siegel for two Folkways albums. Hazel Dickens came from the coal fields of West Virginia. Like many of her eleven brothers and sisters, she left home after World War II in search of employment in the Baltimore, Maryland, area. Mike Seeger again comes into this story: while working as a conscientious objector in a Baltimore tuberculosis sanatorium, he met one of Hazel's brothers, who introduced him to the singing family. Hazel was swept into the nascent folk-bluegrass scene around Baltimore and Washington. Sometime around 1955 or 1956, she met Alice, who was born on the West Coast. Gerrard enrolled at Antioch College in 1953, which led to a student cooperative job in Washington, D.C. At Antioch, she met Jeremy Foster, who became her first husband; Foster was a fan of old-time music and "hard-core" bluegrass acts such as Monroe and the Stanley Brothers. After Hazel and Alice met, the two began singing around Washington, D.C.

After a brief return to Ohio so that her husband could complete his college studies, Alice settled in Washington in 1962, where she renewed her friendship with Hazel. It was around that time that visiting New Yorkers David Grisman and Peter Siegel heard them singing at a house party and determined to record them. As Siegel recalled to Alice thirty years later, "I heard you guys sing in the kitchen. I thought you were great singers, and I was totally knocked out." Hazel adds: "I remember sitting on the floor and singing. David and Peter got real interested, and they started talking to us and asked if we'd ever thought of recording. . . . when we knew they were serious we got defensive and said we wouldn't [compromise] our music. We wanted to do the songs the way we wanted to do them. We were fiercely pro-

Smithsonian Folkways' reissue of Hazel Dickens's and Alice Gerrard's two Folkways albums.

tective." A demo tape was made in 1963 in Pete Kuykendall's basement studio and Alice attempted to interest the larger New York folk labels in it, but only Folkways responded.

The sessions for the album were held sometime in 1964, although they were overshadowed by the tragic death of Alice's husband in a car accident. The album appeared on the new Verve/Folkways label in early 1965; Asch had made a distribution agreement with MGM records, who owned Verve, to reach the broader folk-rock market, and this album was among the first launched. However, this also meant that when the deal collapsed about a year and a half later, the album went out of print and did not reappear in the Folkways catalog until years later.

Their second album was a more formal affair. The singers had honed their skills by performing over the year or so after the first record appeared, and their new LP was recorded in a formal studio. For the second album, Bill Monroe gave them a new song he had written called "The One I Love Is Gone." Siegel had begun hanging out at Elektra's recording studios, which were far more modern than anything Folkways usually used, so he decided to record the second album in stereo. This was somewhat off-putting for the singers, as Hazel recalled: "It was the first time that either of us had used headphones. They wanted to separate us and put us on opposite sides of the room, which we had never done. It really threw us off."

Apparently, the tapes were lost in the shuffle during Folkways' breakup with MGM/Verve. Hazel and Alice continued to perform together and established their presence as an acoustic duo singing their own material. This led to an album on Rounder Records released in 1973. The tapes for their second album were quickly resurrected and released by Folkways in light of their newfound status on the folk-revival circuit that same year.

Bill Monroe at the Newport Folk Festival, July 27, 1963. (© Ralph Rinzler)

BILL MONROE ON THE FOLK REVIVAL CIRCUIT

The folk revival of the late 1950s and early 1960s offered new opportunities for bluegrass performers to play in folk clubs and on college campuses. However, it took a while for older players such as Bill Monroe to discover this new audience. Many of Monroe's 1950s recordings were unavailable by the early 1960s, when the new bluegrass audience was developing. Luckily, Monroe was befriended by mandolinist and promoter Ralph Rinzler, who thought his work had been overlooked by the urban revivalists. Rinzler convinced Monroe's label, Decca, to reissue his key recordings on LPs. He also booked Monroe into folk festivals, clubs, and college campuses. Rinzler also introduced Monroe to guitarist-singer Doc Watson. Watson was a fan of Monroe's first recordings made with his brother, Charlie, and the two started to play some of these earlier songs together for fun. This led to a few legendary club engagements, and plans for an album (which never materialized). Years later, Rinzler drew together some of these live recordings to create a CD for Smithsonian Folkways.

PICKIN' IN THE SEVENTIES AND EIGHTIES: RED ALLEN AND MORE

In Asch's last decade, Red Allen and his sons (Harley, Greg, and Ronnie) played a large role in the label's bluegrass catalog. Singer-songwriter Red Allen had been active in the bluegrass world since the 1950s, performing as lead singer for the Osborne Brothers on their first band recordings. He left that group to pair up with Frank Wakefield, and the two toured and recorded as the Kentuckians with various other musicians through 1964. After Wakefield left to join the Greenbriar Boys that year, Allen formed a new band that eventually featured a young David Grisman as its mandolin player. Allen also briefly took Lester Flatt's place in the Flatt and Scruggs band when the older singer was unable to perform due to illness. Red next worked briefly with banjoist J. D. Crowe in another Kentuckians lineup, which was the seedbed for Crowe's progressive bluegrass band, the New South. Allen spent much of the 1970s and early 1980s touring with his sons.

A few other bluegrass groups also appeared on Folkways during its last decade. By the late 1970s, the cost of opening a small recording studio, even with multitrack capabilities, had dropped greatly; many studios (some associated with a label, some not) blossomed to service local musicians. One of these microstudios, named Star Studios, was founded by Marshall Craven of Miller's Creek, North Carolina, who supplied material to several labels.

Craven founded his studio in 1975 to record local musicians. Producer John R. Craig, based in Lenore, North Carolina, who had produced an album by local fiddler Fox Watson for Folkways in 1977, brought Craven into contact with Asch. As Craven recalls, Craig first brought singer Shanna Beth McGee, a student at Appalachian State College in nearby Boone, North Carolina, to record an album of traditional ballads and songs, which appeared in 1980. She was accompanied by fiddler and banjo player David Johnson, who would appear on several Folkways albums along with his father and grandfather. Craven asked Craig who was going to issue the album, and Craig told him he had a relationship with Folkways and could bring him lots of work. This led to a series of albums of local musicians, mostly from family groups, including the Johnson family and the Sage family (who formed the group Sagegrass).

Once Asch became comfortable with Craven, he began working directly with the studio owner. In the early 1980s, Asch even suggested to Craven that he should buy Folkways. Surprised, Craven replied, "No, I ain't got the money." "Oh, don't worry," Asch replied, "you can get it." Craven discussed the offer with Craig, who assured him that Folkways was a valuable property. In the end, though, Craven turned Asch down, telling me, "I didn't want to fool with it."

LISTEN UP!

MIKE SEEGER, PRODUCER

American Banjo: Three-Finger and Scruggs Style
• SFW40037 • 1990

Mountain Music Bluegrass Style • SFW40038 • 1991

Masters of Old-Time Country Autoharp
• SFW40115 • 2006

Berkeley Farms: Oldtime and Country Style Music of
Berkeley • FW02436 • 1972

Close to Home: Old Time Music from Mike Seeger's
Collection, 1952–1967 • SFW40097 • 1997

MIKE SEEGER, PERFORMER

Old Time Country Music • FW02325 • 1962

Tipple, Loom and Rail: Songs of the Industrialization
of the South • FW05273 • 1966

Southern Banjo Sounds • SFW40107 • 1998

True Vine • SFW40136 • 2003

Early Southern Guitar Styles • SFW40157 • 2007

NEW LOST CITY RAMBLERS

New Lost City Ramblers • FW02396 • 1958

New Lost City Ramblers, Vol. 2 • FW02397 • 1960

New Lost City Ramblers, Vol. 3 • FW02398 • 1961

New Lost City Ramblers, Vol. 4 • FW02399 • 1962

New Lost City Ramblers, Vol. 5 • FW02395 • 1963

Old Timey Songs for Children • FW07064 • 1959

Songs from the Depression • FW05264 • 1959

American Moonshine and Prohibition Songs
• FW05263 • 1962

Tom Paley, John Cohen, and Mike Seeger Sing Songs of
the New Lost City Ramblers • FW02494 • 1978

Rural Delivery No. 1 • FW02496 • 1964

String Band Instrumentals
• FW02492 • 1964

Modern Times
• FW31027 • 1968

The Early Years,
1958–1962
• SFW40036 • 1991

Out Standing in Their
Field: Vol. 2, 1963–1973
• SFW40040 • 1993

There Ain't No Way Out • SFW40098 • 1997

Where Did You Come From, Where Did You Go:
50th Anniversary Box Set • SFW40180 • 2008

JOHN COHEN, PRODUCER

Mountain Music of Kentucky • SFW40077 • 1996

Dark Holler: Old Love Songs and Ballads
• SFW40159 • 2005

There Is No Eye: Music for Photographs
• SFW40091 • 2001

Backroads to Cold Mountain • SFW40149 • 2004

DOCK BOGGS

His Folkways Years, 1963–1968 • SFW40108 • 1998

ROSCOE HOLCOMB

Music of Roscoe Holcomb and Wade Ward
• FW02360 • 1962

High Lonesome Sound • SFW40104 • 1998

An Untamed Sense of Control • SFW40144 • 2003

THE MCGEE BROTHERS AND ARTHUR SMITH

Look! Who's Here: Old Timers of the Grand Ole Opry
• FW02379 • 1964

Milk 'Em in the Evening Blues • FW31007 • 1968

CLARENCE "TOM" ASHLEY/ DOC WATSON

Original Recordings, 1960–1962 • SFW40029 • 1994

Clarence Ashley and Tex Isley • FW02350 • 1966

The Doc Watson Family • SFW40012 • 1990

FRIENDS OF OLD TIME MUSIC

The Folk Arrival 1961–1965 • SFW40160 • 2006

PETE STEELE

Banjo Tunes and Songs • FW03828 • 1958

ART ROSENBAUM, PRODUCER

Fine Times at Our House • FW03809 • 1964

Down Yonder: Old Time String Band Music from Georgia
• FW31089 • 1982

Folk Visions and Voices, Vol. 1 • FW34161 • 1984

Folk Visions and Voices, Vol. 2 • FW34162 • 1984

Slave Shout Songs from the Coast of Georgia
• The McIntosh County Shouter • FW04344 • 1984

Man of Many Voices • Howard Finster • FW07471 • 1985

WADE WARD/ERIC DAVIDSON, PRODUCER

Music of Roscoe Holcomb and Wade Ward
• FW02363 • 1962

Traditional Music from Grayson and Carroll Counties,
Virginia • FW03811 • 1962

Ballads and Songs of the Blue Ridge Mountains:
Persistence and Change • FW03831 • 1968

Bluegrass from the Blue Ridge: A Half Century of Change
• FW03832 • 1967

Uncle Wade—A Memorial to Wade Ward: Old Time
Virginia Banjo Picker, 1892–1971 • FW02380 • 1973

IRON MOUNTAIN STRINGBAND

Iron Mountain String Band • FW02473 • 1973

RED CLAY RAMBLERS

Red Clay Ramblers with Fiddlin' Al McCandless
• FW31039 • 1974

URBAN REVIVALISTS

Ship in the Clouds • Andy Cahan, Laura Fishleder, and
Lisa Ornstein • FW31062 • 1978

Clawhammer Banjo and Fingerstyle Guitar Solos
• Ken Perlman • FW31098 • 1983

COUNTRY GENTLEMEN

Country Songs, Old and New • SFW40004 • 1990

Going Back to the Blue Ridge Mountains
• SFW40175 • 2007

On the Road (and More) • SFW40133 • 2001

The Country Gentlemen Sing and Play Folk Songs and
Bluegrass • SFW40022 • 1991

Going Back to the Blue Ridge Mountains, Vol. 4
• FW31031 • 1973

LILLY BROTHERS

Bluegrass at the Roots, 1961 • SFW40158 • 2005

ROGER SPRUNG

Progressive Bluegrass and Other Instrumentals, Vol. 1
• W02370 • 1963

Progressive Bluegrass and Other Instrumentals, Vol. 2
• FW02371 • 1964

Progressive Bluegrass and Other Instrumentals, Vol. 3
• FW 02472 • 1965

HAZEL AND ALICE

Pioneering Women of Bluegrass • SFW40065 • 1996

BILL MONROE

Live Recordings 1956–1969: Off the Record, Vol. 1
• SFW40063 • 1993

Live Recordings 1963–1980: Off the Record, Vol. 2
• Bill Monroe and Doc Watson • SFW40064 • 1993

RED ALLEN

The Folkways Years, 1964–1983 • Red Allen and Frank
Wakefield • SFW40127 • 2001

Dedicated to Lester Flatt • FW31073 • 1980

Live and Let Live • FW31065 • 1979

Red Allen and Friends • FW31088 • 1981

JOHN CRAVEN, PRODUCER

Bluegrass • David and Billie Ray Johnson
• FW31056 • 1983

Old Time North Carolina Mountain Music • David, Bill and
Billie Ray Johnson
• FW31105 • 1985

Clawhammer Banjo
• David Johnson
• FW31094 • 1983

Sagegrass
• FW31106 • 1985

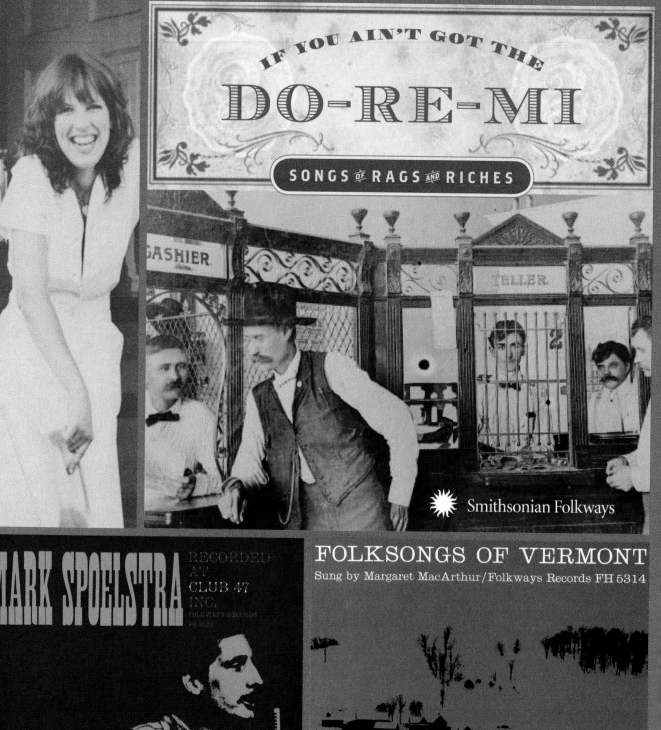

IF YOU AIN'T GOT THE

DO-RE-MI

SONGS OF RAGS AND RICHES

CASHIER. TELLER.

Smithsonian Folkways

MARK SPOELSTRA

RECORDED AT CLUB 47 INC.
FOLKWAYS RECORDS
FU 2971

FOLKSONGS OF VERMONT

Sung by Margaret MacArthur / Folkways Records FH 5314

Chapter 9

"IF I HAD A HAMMER"
The Folk Revival

The twentieth century could aptly be called the century of folk. In 1910, John Lomax published his book *Cowboy Songs*, which established the image of the singing cowboy, and introduced Americans to classic folk songs such as "Home on the Range." In 1928, the Library of Congress established the Archive of American Folk Song. In the mid-1930s, John Lomax took his young son Alan along on a field trip to record southern folk music, focusing primarily on prison populations. Their work led to the discovery of Lead Belly, whom they brought north for performances and lectures. In 1934, the first National Folk Festival was presented in St. Louis, Missouri, and four years later Eleanor Roosevelt helped bring it to Washington, D.C. In its wake, other regional festivals cropped up in the 1930s and 1940s. In 1959, the first Newport Folk Festival was held; it would help launch the careers of the next generation of folk performers.

THE FIRST REVIVAL: NEW YORK IN THE 1930S AND 1940S

The first folk revival began in the late 1930s and was primarily centered in New York City. New York was the epicenter of the arts and mass media, with most major radio networks and recording labels headquartered there. The war effort brought many soldiers through New York, and when they were discharged they often ended up in the city. Woody Guthrie, Pete Seeger, and Cisco Houston all took leaves in New York during the war (during which time they recorded and appeared on radio) and settled there after the war; Lead Belly made New York his performing base beginning in the mid-1930s; Alan Lomax came to the city in the early 1940s to work for national radio and recording labels.

Many of these folksingers were interested in social justice and other left-wing causes. Informal sing-alongs (known as "hootenannies") were held in lofts and apartments, which led to the formation of loose-knit performing and recording groups, most notably the Almanac Singers. The Almanacs included at

American Folksay photo from Disc Records catalog, 1947. Left to right: Pete Seeger, Betty Sanders, Sonny Terry, Lee Hays, Tom Glazer, Brownie McGhee.

one time or another Seeger, Guthrie, songwriter and activist Millard Lampbell, Agnes "Sis" Cunningham, and Bess Lomax Hawes (Alan Lomax's sister) and her husband, Butch Hawes. Their songs reflected the changing face of the left as the war progressed. In early 1941, they recorded *Songs for John Doe*, which promoted pacifism in the face of the growing drumbeat for war. However, once Germany invaded the Soviet Union in mid-1941, American Communists supported the U.S. war effort. The Almanac Singers and others changed their tunes to support the fight against fascism.

The casual atmosphere of these groups and their eternal need for pocket change led many of them to record for Asch. These records were thematic, rather than focused on a single artist; *American Folksay,* for example, was an album illustrating the richness of American folk song, rather than an album promoted as "featuring Pete Seeger." These albums had a freewheeling charac-ter, as Charles Edward Smith recalled:

[The] typical groups that sang ... at Moe's studio ... were most of them young people and most of them sang in the same or slightly different groupings . . . before unions and other much-chronicled occasions. Some groups on records resulted when individuals met at [the] Asch Studio and Moe suggested they sing together. Songs and singers were much as those you might hear, if you were lucky, at a hootenanny. . . . Bess Lomax, Alan's sister, who married singer Butch Hawes in the early 1940s, helped to get some of the musical settings and sessions at Asch organized.

After the war, many of the Almanac Singers joined in supporting the campaign of independent candidate Henry Wallace, who had been a member of Roosevelt's cabinet and positioned himself to the left of the mainstream Democratic Party nominee, Harry S. Truman. Alan Lomax was hired by Wallace to organize music for his campaigns and naturally drew on singers he knew to perform at rallies and fund-raisers. However, soon after the election, in which Wallace failed to win many votes, the Almanac Singers drifted apart. Like many other folksingers who previously had supported progressive causes, they were unable to find steady work.

Two members of this loose collective, Pete Seeger and Lee Hays, still believed in the mission of using music to educate the "workingman," but both

also wanted a more organized setting where the music could be performed more professionally. In 1948, they formed the Weavers (see Chapter 3). At first, the Weavers performed for audiences similar to those the Almanac Singers had played for: union groups, left-leaning organizations, and the like. An engagement at the Village Gate club led to their discovery by producer-arranger Gordon Jenkins, who worked for Decca Records. In 1950 he produced their first major hit, "Goodnight Irene." Suddenly folk music was topping the pop charts.

The Weavers' popularity was short-lived, however. In 1950, the anti-Communist publication *Red Channels* listed Seeger as a Communist sympathizer. By 1952, the Weavers could no longer be booked in major clubs, and the group disbanded. Seeger was called to testify before the House Un-American Activities Committee in 1955 but refused to name names (see Chapter 3). By then McCarthyism was beginning to unravel, and that winter the Weavers triumphantly reunited for a sold-out appearance at New York's Carnegie Hall.

Advertisement for *The Weavers* songbook, c. 1951. (Courtesy of David A. Jasen)

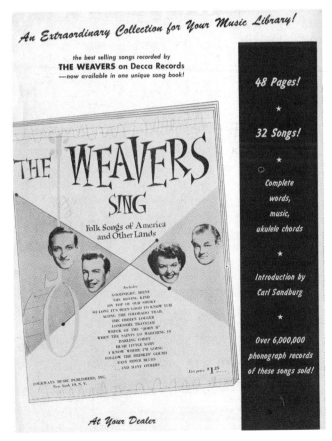

Their recordings would no longer make the top of the pop charts, but the group enjoyed renewed popularity on record and tour.

FOLKSINGER FROM KENTUCKY: JEAN RITCHIE

During the mid-1950s, a new generation of folk revivalists began to emerge, many performing in the small clubs of New York's Greenwich Village. Longtime radio DJ and folk fan Oscar Brand made a name for himself with a series of theme albums, ranging from the political to the risqué. Ed McCurdy became a hit recording star for Elektra thanks to his collections of "bawdy" Renaissance songs. But of all of these early performers, the most grounded and authentic was Jean Ritchie, who came from a singing family from Viper, Kentucky.

From the folk revival point of view, Ritchie was a dream performer: she hailed from a traditional background and also was college-educated. Unlike the more rough-hewn mountain singers of the 1920s and 1930s, she sang in a clear-

Jean Ritchie recording Seamus Ennis on her 1950 field trip to Ireland. (Photo by George Pickow)

throated, lightly ornamented style—a style that would be emulated by younger singers including Joan Baez and Judy Collins. She had a large repertory of ballads and songs, and presented them in a language and style that urban "folks" could understand. And she played the easy-to-learn Appalachian dulcimer, launching the revival of interest in the instrument.

Working with her husband, photographer and folklorist George Pickow, Ritchie made a field trip to England and Ireland in 1950. Before leaving, they tried to interest a number of record companies in helping to support the trip:

> At Decca, Sy Rady gave us a lot of tape and expressed some interest, but he recommended that we go to Moe Asch. So we went over to this rather dingy little office and he took us into this incredible little room . . . piled from floor to ceiling with records and tapes with just enough space for Moe and a small desk. It looked like these piles could cave in on him at any time. . . . And he just sat there; he didn't say anything. We said hello and he said, "So what do you want?" . . . We tried to tell him what we had in mind but after 3 or 4 halting sentences he had the whole thing summed up and he said, "Go on, have a good year, and come see me when you get back. If you've got anything I want, I'll talk to you then. As for giving money in advance, I don't do that." I was sort of shaken when we came out of there. I thought that was the rudest and most unfriendly person I'd ever met in my life. I later found, of course, that this was just his manner. So we went away and said, "The heck with him, we'll never see him again."
>
> So we came back a year later and went back to see Sy Rady who was interested but he wanted to take our Irish singers [and] put orchestras behind them! . . . We tried to tell him that wasn't a good idea. . . . Somehow—this was 1954 or 1955—we got back in touch with Moe. He said in the interim he had found out who I was and what I did, and although he wasn't interested in those tapes, why didn't I do something for him myself. So I started making records for Folkways.

Not surprisingly, Ritchie's first album for Folkways was a children's record, a market Moe knew well. Eventually, in 1959–60, Moe issued two albums of material drawn from their field trip to England and Ireland, including many fine traditional performers. Although Ritchie eventually became friendly with Asch, she remained wary of his moodiness.

Ritchie recorded only a few albums for Folkways. Most notable was a live concert recording made with Doc Watson at the famous Greenwich Village club Gerdes Folk City in 1963. Ritchie and Watson were perfectly paired; both sang in the "relaxed" style of the upper South, both shared a love of traditional songs

Jean Ritchie and Doc Watson performing at New York's Folk City, 1963. (Photo by George Pickow)

and ballads, and both were virtuosos not just on their instruments but also in communicating with the audience. This live album captures them at an important juncture in their careers, with Watson ascending and Ritchie at the height of her powers as a performer.

One of her more unusual releases—at least for Folkways—was the 1962 album *Precious Memories*, a collection of country songs of the 1920s and 1930s, as opposed to the "ancient" ballads with which she was associated. The accompaniment was also broadened to include younger folk revivalists Eric Weissberg, Art Rosenbaum, and Marshall Brickman. Weissberg was a hot-shot bluegrass banjo player active on the New York scene who would become (accidentally) famous when his recording of "Dueling Banjos" was used in the 1973 film *Deliverance* and became a surprise pop hit. Rosenbaum was a more traditional-style banjoist; he recalled that the sessions, typically for Folkways, were "very casual and impromptu . . . There was . . . no one producing it. We went to a little studio and had just rehearsed a few things."

Although the selection of songs was "radical" when compared to folk ballads, numbers such as "Wreck on the Highway" and "Little Rosebud Casket" were hardly different from the traditional material Ritchie had previously recorded and performed. Perhaps anticipating a backlash, she wrote an introduction to the album as a defense of the record:

"What is *Jean Ritchie* doing, singing hillbilly songs?" I can already hear the howls of protest around the countryside from many of my loyal friends—devotees of the Elizabethan ballad and the Kentucky survivals and variants of Scotch-Irish-English folksong with which I have become associated. . . . These friends are, as I have been, anti–hillbilly music, resentful of the "new music" which we in the mountains felt had been thrust in upon us with the coming of the radio.

However, Ritchie makes the point that many of the "newer" songs extended and built on the same issues found in more traditional material. She was simply reflecting the ever-changing definition of "folk music" as the tradition expanded beyond the confines of "ballades and songes."

KENNETH GOLDSTEIN, FOLK PROMOTER

One of the most important producers of folk recordings in the 1950s and 1960s was Kenneth Goldstein, who worked for just about every folk label and helped promote the careers of many artists. After graduating from college in the early 1950s, Goldstein landed a PR job in an office near Union Square. A fan of folk music, he spent his lunch hour going through the record bins at the nearby Stinson record shop. During World War II, when shellac to press records was rationed, Asch made a deal with Stinson for them to release his recordings. Herbert Harris, the label's owner, who had worked with Asch during World War II, had died, and the store passed to his son, Bob. Bob offered Goldstein $5 an album to take old Asch-Stinson 78s and assemble them into LPs. Harris assured Goldstein that he owned the rights to these masters, although Asch claimed differently and for years protested their publication. Goldstein went from putting together albums to suggesting new artists to record.

Gradually Goldstein built a roster of other clients—including Riverside, Tradition, Folkways, and eventually Prestige—enabling him to build a small studio inside his home on Long Island. Goldstein admired Asch because he would issue albums that were far less commercial than those of his competitors, but he was always wary of him. He found Asch to be not terribly reliable, either in paying artists or in following his instructions. However, there was one project that Goldstein felt was a true collaboration between himself and Asch and valued highly: the album *The Unfortunate Rake*. As a folklore-like study, the album presented different versions of the famous ballad (best known in America as "The Streets of Laredo"). Despite its lack of strong commercial appeal—who would want to listen to several versions of the same song?—Asch enthusiastically embraced the idea, opening his recording archives to Goldstein.

KENNETH S. GOLDSTEIN
28 CROWN STREET
HICKSVILLE, NEW YORK
—
OVerbrook 1-2436

Bill To: FOLKWAYS RECORDS
117 West 46th Street
New York, N.Y.
April 28, 1958

For services in producing and editing TALKING BLUES,
sung by JOHN GREENWAY

Editing tapes, 4 hrs, @$5/hr.	$ 20.00
Transcribing texts	15.00
Notes for booklet, 15 songs	75.00

Total $110.00

Ken Goldstein's invoice for producing, recording, editing, and annotating John Greenway's *Talking Blues* record, 1958. Clearly, Goldstein was not getting rich working for Folkways.

However, Goldstein and Asch were both too headstrong to work together for long. When Goldstein made a trip to Scotland in the late 1950s to record traditional singers and musicians, Asch promised a stipend of $25 a week. Not surprisingly, the checks soon stopped arriving, and Goldstein was left high and dry. He delivered just one of a planned series of albums of traditional Scottish music to Folkways and didn't work for the label again. As he later summed it up, "My fights with Moe were almost always money fights—not on aesthetic grounds."

THE FOLK BOOM: 1958–1965

Although the Folkways catalog continued to grow through the 1950s—reaching nearly one thousand albums by the time the firm completed its first decade in business—it would be a new, younger, slicker group that would bring folk music back to the charts. Coming out of California, the Kingston Trio scored an unlikely hit in 1958 with their recording of an old folk ballad, "Tom Dooley." There soon came a wave of similar groups with names vaguely indicating that they were "just working folks," such as the Tarriers and Highwaymen. Meanwhile, Pete Seeger was still barred from appearing on television, and the older revivalists were somewhat miffed by the appearance of these slickly produced, apolitical groups on the pop charts.

With the sudden popularity of folk music—particularly on college campuses—the tiny Folkways offices were flooded with letters and tapes from would-be folk revival groups. Many were from college students who were forming their own trios, some heavily influenced by the folk-pop groups, others more purist in their approach. Dave Laibman—later well known as a ragtime guitarist—formed his own group while attending Antioch College. He sent a sampler tape to Folkways in 1961, along with a letter describing their approach:

We believe that "purism" and "hybridism" are not incompatible, and that it is possible to arrange folk songs for harmony, to create out of the original song a presentational form, and, at the same time, to preserve the spirit and integrity of its ethnic origins.

The Kingston Trio, c. 1959, inscribed to their fans at France's *Song Parade* magazine. (Courtesy of the BenCar Archives)

Laibman freely admitted that the group was only three months old and that the tape they sent was a "first effort" at best.

Asch's reply was typical: "Thank you for sending your tapes for audition. However, I am sorry, but the performances are a little too slick for Folkways use." Anything that smacked of commercialism was taboo for Asch.

Another college student—located in nearby Oberlin, Ohio—formed a strong relationship with Folkways. Joe Hickerson attended Oberlin a little earlier than Laibman was at Antioch, in the late 1950s. He had impressed Pete Seeger when the older folksinger met him while Hickerson was working as a song leader at a summer camp. Hickerson's group, the Folksmiths, spent the summer of 1957 "rambling" from town to town, spreading the folk song word. Before graduating, the group produced an album for Folkways that was a typical combination of traditional American folk with international favorites, including the soon-to-be folk revival standard "Kum Ba Yah." Hickerson also served as a campus representative for Folkways, selling records to his fellow college students and making a small profit that he used to pay for books and supplies.

He moved on to graduate school at Indiana University, where he wrote to Asch proposing a new album recorded on his own:

> Heart (and guitar) in hand, I write to tell you that I wish to record an
> album . . . for Folkways. Requests from friends, wellwishers, and taunts from
> skeptics have driven me to this position, together with a growing desire to
> communicate to a larger audience. . . .

In the late 1940s, informal gatherings to share songs were already called "hootenannies," and the term returned big-time during the folk revival years of the 1960s, particularly after ABC launched a variety program of the same name in 1963. In this advertising piece, Folkways tried to cash in on this trend by promoting several albums originally recorded at benefits for *Sing Out!* magazine.

I am completely confident that sales of this record . . . would justify its production and satisfy the many friends who I have made in Ohio and Indiana and the many audiences I have sung for.

Although the letter has a note from Asch to request a sample, the album apparently was never made. Hickerson worked with Asch on a landmark reissue of Uncle Dave Macon's music that appeared in 1961, and then had a long and distinguished career at the Library of Congress' Archive of American Folk Song. He also continues to record and perform.

Asch had little to do with the popular side of the folk revival. However, one idea that he nurtured over the years would have a great influence on the next generation of singer-songwriters. During the 1940s, he had discussed with Woody Guthrie the idea of issuing records on topical subjects as a kind of "singing newspaper." Although Guthrie never followed through, the idea of the "singing newspaper" continued to interest Asch as well as his star recording artist, Pete Seeger. This led to the release of two albums titled *Gazette* in 1958 and 1961. The first album appeared carrying on its cover a newspaper-like front page, labeled "Volume 1, Number 1," emblazoned with various quotes underscoring the importance of free speech and liberty.

The album notes for both volumes uncharacteristically open with a boxed statement by Moses Asch, as an editor's introduction to the music:

I have always believed that is the duty and privilege of publishers . . . to make available to the general public as great a variety of points of view and opinions as possible—without the heavy hand of censorship or the imposition of the publishers' editorial view. It is with this point of view that Folkways Records and Peter Seeger have collaborated on this new album of contemporary topical and political songs—believing that the complete documentation of American life makes the issuance of such material our public responsibility.

This message was underscored in the full liner notes by Irwin Silber, who as the editor of *Sing Out!* magazine was heavily involved in the promotion of

contemporary folk songs. (Silber also joined the staff of Folkways Records about this time and was a well-known political activist.) He clipped relevant newspaper headlines to complement the songs on the album. Not all of the songs were exactly "contemporary": Woody Guthrie's "Pretty Boy Floyd" told the story of the Depression-era desperado, while "Reuben James" related to a World War II event. Nonetheless, the album also included songs about desegregation, nuclear bomb testing, and UFOs that were certainly fresh.

Moving beyond the original *Gazette* idea, Pete Seeger began working with old friends and political leftists Agnes "Sis" Cunningham and her husband, Gordon Friesen, to revive the idea of a "singing newspaper" that would include both print and recordings. The Friesens set up a tape machine in their apartment and invited young singers over to record their songs so they could be transcribed and printed inexpensively on a mimeograph machine. Their publication/recording was called *Broadside*. Among the singers they first published and recorded were Bob Dylan (who appeared on record as "Blind Boy Grunt") and Phil Ochs.

Agnes Cunningham and Gordon Friesen in their New York City apartment, c. 1960s. (Photo by Diana Davies, courtesy of the Ralph Rinzler Folklife Archives and Collections, Smithsonian Institution)

Birth of a Broadside

Josh Dunson

Broadside's base is a small little room that's got chairs and a sofa with a tape recorder finishing off the bottom wall space. [The] first people Sis Cunningham welcomed in after me was two-thirds of the New World Singers. Gil Turner took out his 12-stringer, borrowed a flat pick, Sis took out the mike for the tape recorder, and out came a talking blues Gil just wrote about the newspaper strike that had us all quietly laughing. We didn't want to laugh louder than quietly because that might get on the tape.

Before the song's over, in walks Bob Dylan. . . . Gil took out his 6-string Gibson, handed it over to Bob Dylan saying how Bob's new song "Masters of War" was a powerful and a great one, one of the best Bob had ever written. I kept on thinking he had written

Bob Dylan and Pete Seeger at Newport, 1963. (© David Gahr)

a lot of good ones, some that had real lyric poetry like "Blowin' in the Wind" and "Hard Rain's Gonna Fall" (which makes you think right away of Lorca), and I waited for the images of rain, and thunder, and lightening to come out in great spectacles. But no, this time there was a different kind of poetry, one of great anger, accusation, just saying what the masters of war are, straight forward and without compromising one inch in its short sharp direct intensity. I got a hunch this is the most difficult Dylan song for others to sing right, 'cause it can so easily be over sung, made a melodrama. But when Bob sings it, it rings honest and true. I hope a record is made of Bob singing this song and that a lot of people will listen to the quiet voice that Bob sings this song in because there is a dignity in the words that comes from when they have been thought about for a long, long time.

And right after that, not waiting for a chance to get two breaths, Bob came along with "Playboys & Playgirls Ain't Gonna Run My World," a group song that like Pete Seeger said later in the evening, "is going to be sung by a million people in the next year." Its tune catches whole crowds easy, and the words come right along from the feeling, Hell man, I was born here and I live here, but I'm not goin' to let rats knock things down where I was born, where I live.

In the meantime, Phil Ochs, his sidekick, and the third third of the New World Singers, Happy Traum, came in. Boy, this room was so jammed packed with people that there was real foot and banjo and guitar shifting necessary to get Phil Ochs close enough to the mike to record his three new songs. Phil Ochs. What a guy! Quiet, soft spoken, but there with his guitar he spun some of the most real verses that's goin' to be written about the death of N.Y. Youth Board worker Linda C. Marsh and the miners striking in Hazard, Kentucky. There was an immediateness about the two songs that Phil did. I got a strong feeling that his song on Hazard is going to be remembered past this strike, and be resung in many strikes to come.

Phil's last song, a fine one of hope with a great group chorus had the last half of it heard by Pete Seeger who later that night was going to sing at the Hazard strikers rally at Community Church. After hearing the tape of the songs, Pete sang through a number of new songs sent to him recently.

We were all *out of* breath without breathing hard, that feeling you get when a lot of good things happen all at once. Pete expressed it, leaning back in his chair, saying slowly in dreamy tones: "You know, in the past five months I haven't heard as many good songs and as much good music as I heard here tonight."

PHIL OCHS ON MACDOUGAL STREET JANUARY 3, 1965

Phil Ochs on MacDougal Street in Greenwich Village, January 3, 1965.(© Fred W. McDarrah)

Dunson's enthusiastic description of Bob Dylan's performance shows how influential Dylan was after arriving in 1962 in New York. Dylan's self-created character—modeled on his idol, Woody Guthrie—found immediate resonance among the old guard, including Pete Seeger and concert promoter Izzy Young, who were anxious to discover the "next Guthrie" to carry forward the revival's social message. An unknown figure when he first arrived, Dylan could easily shape his life story to fit exactly what was desired in a folksinger; Izzy Young's journals that record how Dylan told his "biography" read as though they were cribbed from *Bound for Glory*.

Of course, Dylan had the talent to back up the image, and it was this talent that simply blew away the competition. Some loved him; many were jealous of the attention he received; still others learned to be wary of his ability to pull what he needed from them, only to discard them as he moved further along in his self-development.

Phil Ochs was probably the most prolific contributor to *Broadside*, with sixty-nine of his songs appearing in it between 1962 and his death in 1976. Ochs was

Mark Spoelstra performing at the Newport Folk Festival. (Photo by Diana Davies, courtesy of the Ralph Rinzler Folklife Archives and Collections, Smithsonian Institution)

one of the most talented and troubled of the 1960s social-protest singers. A competent singer with a sharp sense of irony, his songs were often based on specific events, and consequently many have not aged well. Unlike Dylan, who mimicked Woody Guthrie's raspy singing and wrote obliquely poetic lyrics, Ochs had a pleasant tenor voice, and his message was never difficult to understand.

Paul Kaplan recalled how the energetic young singer-songwriter would show up at the Friesens' apartment brimming with ideas. They were always ready to record his songs, which seemed to tumble out by the dozen:

> Almost every week, [Ochs] would arrive at the *Broadside* apartment on West 104 Street in New York City, hungry and with his pockets stuffed with scribblings. After eating, he would sit down before the ancient Revere tape recorder and sing his new songs. One time he has seven of them, all composed within the previous few days. . . . Phil's output was so great that many of his songs were "lost in the shuffle." *Broadside* couldn't fit them all in, and his records didn't have room for all of them. So, many songs were never heard by more than a handful of people.

Ochs' career zigzagged through various phases as he challenged himself and his audience to grow with the times. Although he never gave up purely political songwriting, he did go through a period where his songs were more self-reflective, in the manner of the singer-songwriter movement of the late 1960s and early 1970s. When he returned to pure protest singing in the early 1970s, he found only a small audience interested in this new material. Ochs became increasingly erratic in his behavior, often influenced by alcohol, although he continued to record new material for *Broadside* to publish. Much of these later recordings were issued by Folkways after Ochs' death. While the quality of performance and recording was not always the best, they represented a side of Phil Ochs that was not available then on commercial recordings.

Another folksinger-songwriter who emerged from the pages of *Broadside* was Mark Spoelstra. Spoelstra's music bridged many different elements of the folk revival. Although a contributor to *Broadside*, he was not primarily a social-protest songwriter. Unlike most songwriters, who strummed a six-string guitar, Spoelstra was influenced by Lead Belly to take up the twelve-string guitar, and much of the material on his first Folkways album came from the country blues repertory. As early as 1963, he was writing his own material, which had a more personal edge, forecasting the singer-songwriters of the later 1960s.

Gil Turner's liner notes for Spoelstra's first Folkways album reflect how the revivalists' biographies were molded to fit certain expectations. In Turner's description, the rambling young Spoelstra traveled "somewhat aimlessly" until he "ended up" in New York City; the truth of the matter was that by this time New York had become a magnet for young singer-songwriters who were trying to make it. Nonetheless, Turner sensitively addressed the age-old question of whether a twenty-two-year-old white guitarist from California legitimately can play the blues, a nagging issue when "authenticity" was one of the touchstones of the folk revival:

Portrait of Peter La Farge. (Photo by Diana Davies, courtesy of the Ralph Rinzler Folklife Archives and Collections, Smithsonian Institution)

> Occasionally, the white blues singer is faced with a kind of "crow-Jim" attitude that fails to recognize the possibility of new forms developing from older ones. . . . Yet is this not the process by which virtually all forms of music have evolved? . . . The real challenge to the white blues singer then has nothing to do with his color, but is related to the degree of understanding and creative sensitivity which he applies to his material. It is to ask the question which may rightly be asked of any singer: "Are you doing that which is real and meaningful for yourself, and can you communicate it?"

This emphasis on being "true to yourself" was a hallmark of the folk music movement. Many in the folk community felt that pop songs were not authentic because they were designed to be hits; the moon-June-spoon sentiments of most popular songs were crafted to appeal to the sentimental listening public, not to reflect real-life experiences. However, is it any more real to sing about mules and picking cotton if you were born and raised in post–World War II suburban America? The entire question of what is "real" continues to dog folk performers.

Peter La Farge was a talented singer and songwriter whose life was tragically brief. His best-remembered song is the moving "Ballad of Ira Hayes" (a number three country hit for Johnny Cash), which told the story of the Native American marine who helped hoist the flag at Iwo Jima only to return to America and find little opportunity for success, eventually drinking himself to death.

La Farge came from a complicated family background. He was descended from Native Americans and lived on a reservation outside of Santa Fe, New Mexico, until the age of nine, when he was adopted by left-wing novelist Oliver La Farge. By his teens, he was singing on the radio and performing at local rodeos. During this period, he met Cisco Houston when the folksinger was passing through New Mexico, and the two formed a lasting friendship.

In the early 1950s, La Farge served as a marine in the Korean War, in which he was exposed to racial prejudice and radicalized by what he viewed as a senseless, bloody conflict. He returned to rodeo work after his tour of duty, but that career ended following an accident in 1956. He lived briefly in Chicago before coming to New York's Greenwich Village, where he encountered the burgeoning folk scene and began performing at coffeehouses.

La Farge made an album for Columbia before being dropped due to poor sales, and Moses Asch quickly signed him to Folkways in 1962. Like many other protest singers, La Farge believed the words of his songs were more important than the music or even his performance; singing in a near-monotone, he avoided any attempt to commercialize his sound. Meanwhile, Johnny Cash heard La Farge perform and was inspired to record the concept album *Bitter Tears*, about the plight of Native Americans, which featured half a dozen La Farge originals. Despite the resistance of country DJs who found the song too radical, Cash had a major hit with "Ira Hayes," memorably performing it at the 1964 Newport Folk Festival. La Farge was once again signed to a major label, MGM, this time as a country performer. Unfortunately, he died of an apparent heart attack in 1965, at the age of thirty-four, before recording could begin.

Greenwich Village: The Heart of the Folk Revival

In many ways, Folkways Records could not have grown and thrived if it had been located anywhere else but New York City. As Frederic Ramsey Jr. commented: "I think it's a logical place to have gotten into music from all over the world and from all kinds of ethnic groups. Because there was more knowledge of that to be found in New York than elsewhere." Beyond that, New York was the epicenter of the folk revival from the late 1940s on.

And the most important neighborhood for folk music was Greenwich Village. Long sympathetic to radicals and artists, the Village housed numerous small clubs and coffeehouses where poetry readings, stand-up comedy, and folk music were all regular parts of the bill of fare. Young performers could begin by playing at pass-the-hat clubs, move on to open-mic nights at more established places, then graduate to being opening acts before finally becoming headliners. Even Bob Dylan began by playing harmonica to accompany better-established performers until he could move up to being a solo performer.

A group of folksingers in Washington Square Park, 1964. (© Fred W. McDarrah)

Izzy Young at the Folklore Center, 1962. (© Fred W. McDarrah)

bluegrass musicians, and many groups arose out of these informal jam sessions.

As the crowds grew, city officials began to worry. In March 1961, they decided the folkies were getting out of hand, and imposed a ban on musical performances in the park. The result was weeks of unrest, known locally as the "Washington Square Riots." On one Sunday afternoon, several thousand folk musicians and their supporters pushed past the police barricades in small groups and then assembled around the fountain to sing "This Land Is Your Land." Finally, the city relented in May, and the folksingers returned peacefully.

Greenwich Village was also home to Izzy Young's Folklore Center, among the first stores devoted to folk music in the country. Young put on concerts at his tiny shop (and in larger venues) and was a general gadfly on the New York folk scene. His shop was one of the few places where musicians could buy fifth-string pegs for their banjos, the latest Folkways releases, or a book on how to play the sitar. His prices were always a few dollars more than other dealers; when I questioned him about why he charged $10 for a capo I could buy uptown at Manny's music store for $5, he replied, "That's capitalism for you!" A devoted socialist, Young left New York to move to Sweden in the 1970s.

Other Village shops became unlikely homes to folk music. The Music Inn on West 4th Street was a tiny shop that featured all types of instruments in varying states of repair hanging from the ceiling and walls. For a while, the store's owner charged an admission fee to weed out the freeloaders. Old-time fiddler Alan Block ran a famous hole-in-the-wall shop next door where he sold handmade sandals. Musicians would gather there to play with him through the 1960s, and he was always happy to put down his leather-working tools to play a tune or two.

Informal get-togethers of musicians of all styles and stripes occurred regularly on Sunday afternoons in the warmer months at Washington Square Park. The park had long been the central gathering spot for Village denizens, and informal speakers and performers would appear to entertain or challenge the crowds. The park became particularly important as a gathering spot for old-time and

EWAN MACCOLL AND THE
BRITISH FOLK SONG REVIVAL

In the late 1950s, just as the U.S. folk revival was heating up, so was a similar revival in Great Britain. In 1951, Alan Lomax escaped the U.S. blacklist by relocating to England, and immediately began recording and promoting traditional music in Britain, Ireland, and Scotland. He worked in association with local collectors, including Peter Kennedy in England and Seamus Ennis in Ireland, as well as two key performers who would play a major role in the British folk song revival: A. L. "Bert" Lloyd and Ewan MacColl.

Just as commercial folk groups such as the Kingston Trio hit the pop charts in the late 1950s, the British folk song revival inspired so-called skiffle bands, which combined jazz, blues, and folk influences. Lonnie Donnegan was the major star of the skiffle movement, and his first hit was a cover of Lead Belly's "Rock Island Line." Donnegan's success inspired countless others to begin playing American folk and blues, including a high-school-age guitarist in Liverpool named John Lennon, who formed his own skiffle band, the Quarrymen. Not all welcomed skiffle with open arms. Scottish balladeer Ewan MacColl was particularly appalled by the sudden popularity of American folk music as opposed to native British, Scottish, and Irish styles.

Like many others in the post–World War II British folk song revival, MacColl began his career singing American folk songs, even attempting an American accent. However, he soon realized that "the pseudo-American accent which I acquired by watching gangsters and western gunmen flicker across the threadbare screens of a hundred flea-pits, twisted the songs into mere parodies of themselves." By the mid-1950s, MacColl had returned to performing the "music I grew up with." While he noted that the skiffle movement began as a rebellious reaction against the tame pop music of the era (something akin to the punk movement of the 1970s, some two decades later), it was eventually co-opted by the music industry, and its original fervor was dulled:

> [The mid-1950s was] the short-lived age of skiffle, when the kids of Glasgow, Hull and Manchester discovered the guitar and the tea-chest bass . . . tried to unlearn reading and writing and looked at you with the hyperopic gaze of men whose eyes have grown dim with staring over the eternal deserts of Arizona, Utah, and the Bronx . . . and to stare at you with contemptuous eyes because you hadn't been in a chaingang. . . .
>
> Well, finally [the music industry] made up their minds and took skiffle over, gave it a haircut and a shampoo and sent the results rolling down the conveyor-belt of the pop industry. It didn't last long, just long enough to produce the inevitable reaction. So the kids hocked their cheap guitars and

Ewan MacColl and Peggy Seeger performing in Cuba, 1968.

moved out of the cellars and the upstairs rooms of numberless pubs and looked around for something else that they could identify themselves with. Many of them, moved by the hard instinct found refuge in the "rock" joints, others found their way into the jazz clubs and the rest began to form folksong clubs.

MacColl took a purist approach, insisting that British singers sing British traditional songs, at least in clubs where he was in charge. However, he noted that he loosened the rules when it came to his own performances with his wife, Peggy Seeger:

During the time I have spent working in this field, I have rarely moved outside of my own musical tradition. At the hundreds of concerts and hootenannies where I have sung or acted as chairman, I have made a point of insisting on the rule that singers do not sing anything but the songs of their own native tradition. It is, I think, a good rule and one that has produced extremely good results in Great Britain.

[But] now I am not only singing American songs with Peggy but encouraging her to sing Scots and English songs with me!

Despite his sometimes dogmatic attitude, MacColl was an excellent folk-lorist and songwriter. He created a series of "radio ballads" in the late 1950s for the BBC that combined field recordings of traditional musicians and performers with his own songs, focusing on traditional British occupations, including fishing, coal mining, and farming. Many of these songs have entered into tradition. MacColl also wrote the lovely ballad "The First Time Ever I Saw Your Face" for Peggy Seeger.

MacColl recorded prolifically from the mid-1950s over the next two decades. Through the Seeger connection, MacColl's recordings of both traditional and topical songs began appearing on Folkways in the late 1950s and early 1960s. These albums ranged from scholarly re-creations of sixteenth-century ballads to the latest anti-nuclear-proliferation songs. MacColl was often accompanied on his recordings by Peggy Seeger on banjo and guitar and the sensitive concertina player Alf Edwards.

Peggy Seeger—half sister to Pete and full sister to Mike—has gone through several phases in a long career that began with her marriage to Mac-Coll. New to England, Peggy Seeger was criticized for being too American by some, while others pointed out that since leaving her homeland she was out of touch with the latest American folk styles. In her own defense—and in defense of all "city folksingers," who of necessity are not part of the community where the music originated—Seeger wrote:

Peggy Seeger at the 1959 Newport Folk Festival. (© David Gahr)

> For the city folksinger today, there are two main avenues of contact, of replenishing his repertoire and techniques: (1) community musical activity and (2) resource to original sources, either discs or field singers themselves. At the present, passing through limbo, I find myself in a double crisis: no oral sources from which to draw and no natural community with which to sing (for one can sing American folksongs to a group of non-Americans, but not *with* them, for the communication the musical growth, is one-way).

Nonetheless, Seeger realized that working with MacColl and living in England would inevitably lead her to incorporate some aspect of local folk songs into her performances: "I am not *trying* to sing Scots and English songs—I merely *cannot help* it, living as I do and where I do." Through her own career—which has spanned American and British traditions and her own contemporary songwriting—Seeger has shown that these once rigid and divisive lines have eased, enhancing the growth of traditional music.

Another major figure in the British folk revival made her debut recording for Folkways in 1959, Shirley Collins. Collins had met Alan Lomax during his years in self-imposed exile in Britain, and the two had become involved professionally and romantically. In the notes accompanying her first record, Lomax seemed most concerned with assuring the listener that—despite her youth—Collins belonged in the same pantheon as Texas Gladden or Aunt Molly Jackson, both of whom he had introduced to a wider public. Again, the tension between the city-bred folksinger and her "right" to sing traditional music is underscored; Lomax was particularly attuned to this subject. At the same time he was writing editorials in *Sing Out!* criticizing some younger city singers for their slickness and commercialization. Of course, the fact that Collins was his protégée made it easier for Lomax to forgive her the sin of being born outside the tradition. And Lomax was correct in predicting that Collins would become one of the greatest interpreters of British traditional song of her generation.

AN ERA ENDS

By the mid-1960s, the folk revival was beginning to lose steam, being overwhelmed by rock 'n' roll. Although it roiled the folk world at the time, Dylan's "going electric" at the 1965 Newport Folk Festival was only one symbol of the changing world that would transform popular musical styles. Like many in his generation, Asch did not understand electric folk-rock and felt that it was an attempt to court the popular audience, with all the evils associated with mass marketing and commoditization that folk music stood proudly against. This confusion of presentation with substance led many of the elders in the folk music movement to lose a vital connection with emerging performers.

In a way, however, Asch was smart to resist the lure of commercialization. While folk-rock would be popular for a brief period, its time would pass also, and meanwhile the mission of recording all the world of sound would continue for Folkways. One of his most successful later signings was dulcimer player Kevin Roth. Roth was just a teenager when he first visited Moses Asch, along with his father, who wanted to make sure that his son's interests were protected. A prodigy on the Appalachian dulcimer, Roth would record a series of albums for Folkways from the mid-1970s through the early 1980s, and worked hard to promote them. In the 1990s, Roth became a well-known performer of children's music while maintaining his adult repertory as well.

However, one of Asch's key signings of the 1970s came about nearly by accident. Through a connection with one of his latter-day regulars, topical songwriter Jeff Ampolsk, whose songs appeared regularly in *Broadside*, Asch

Lucinda Williams.
(Photo © David Gahr)

chanced upon Lucinda Williams, a rising singer-songwriter. As Williams later recalled:

> An old friend of mine in New Orleans, who had put out a record on the label called *God, Guts and Guns*, suggested "You should make a record for Folkways too." So I sent them a demo from Arkansas and they send me back this one page contract, "Here's $250—go make a record." So I went to Jackson, Mississippi. A friend of the family knew one of the engineers at Malico Studios, so we went in and recorded it in one afternoon.

Her first Folkways album, *Ramblin' on My Mind*, released in 1978, consisted of covers of traditional country and blues songs. Williams said, "I had a few songs I'd written but I didn't use them. Boy, I was so naive! I was a real purist. I thought Folkways wouldn't want anything contemporary. I thought they'd want nothing but the blues." The second album, 1980's *Happy Woman Blues*, featured a few originals and pointed toward her more mature work. However, as was the case with many latter-day Folkways acts, Asch had little or no contact with Williams, who was simply thrilled to have an outlet for her recordings. It was just a twist of fate that he was able to present this last new folk star while she was rising from her original local base.

LISTEN UP!

JEAN RITCHIE

British Traditional Ballads in the Southern Mountains, Vol. 1 • FW02301 • 1960

British Traditional Ballads in the Southern Mountains, Vol. 2 • FW02302 • 1960

Ballads from Her Appalachian Family Tradition • SFW40145 • 2003

Precious Memories • FW02427 • 1962

Jean Ritchie and Doc Watson at Folk City • SFW40005 • 1990

The Ritchie Family of Kentucky • FW02316 • 1958

Field Trip—England • FW08871 • 1959

As I Roved Out (Field Trip—Ireland) • FW08872 • 1960

KENNETH GOLDSTEIN

The Unfortunate Rake • FW03805 • 1960

BROADSIDE (SELECTED RECORDINGS)

Broadside Ballads, Vol. 1 • FW05301 • 1963

Broadside Ballads, Vol. 2 • Pete Seeger • FW05302   1963

Broadside Ballads, Vol. 3: The Broadside Singers • FW05303 • 1964

Broadside Ballads, Vol. 4: The Time Will Come and Other Songs • FW05306 • 1967

Broadside Ballads, Vol. 5: Time Is Running Out • FW05312 • 1970

Broadside Ballads, Vol. 6: Broadside Reunion • FW05315 • 1972

Broadside Ballads, Vol. 7 • FW05316 • 1973

Broadside Ballads, Vol. 9: Sundown • Sis Cunningham • FW05319 • 1976

The Best of Broadside 1962–1988 • SFW40130 • 2000

PHIL OCHS

Phil Ochs Sings for Broadside • 5320 • 1974

Interviews With Phil Ochs • 5321 • 1976

MARK SPOELSTRA

Recorded at Club 47 • FW03572 • 1963

The Songs of Mark Spoelstra • FW02444 • 1963

PETER LA FARGE (SELECTED RECORDINGS)

As Long as the Grass Shall Grow • FW02532 • 1963

Iron Mountain and Other Songs • FW02531 • 1962

On the Warpath • FW02535 • 1965

EWAN MACCOLL (SELECTED RECORDINGS)

Bothy Ballads of Scotland • FW08759 • 1961

Songs of Robert Burns • FW08758 • 1959

The English and Scottish Popular Ballads, Vol. 1: Child Ballads • FW03509 • 1961

The English and Scottish Popular Ballads, Vol. 2 • FW03510 • 1964

The English and Scottish Popular Ballads, Vol. 3 • FW03511 • 1964

The Singing Streets • Ewan MacColl and Dominic Behan • FW08501 • 1958

EWAN MACCOLL AND PEGGY SEEGER (SELECTED RECORDINGS)

Folkways Record of Contemporary Songs • FW08736 • 1973

New Briton Gazette, Vol. 1 • FW08732 • 1960

New Briton Gazette, Vol. 2 • FW08734 • 1962

Traditional Songs and Ballads • FW08760 • 1964

Two-Way Trip • FW08755 • 1961

PEGGY SEEGER (SELECTED RECORDINGS)

Different Therefore Equal • FW08561 • 1979

Folkways Years, 1955–1992: Songs of Love and Politics • SFW40048 • 1992

Songs of Courting and Complaint • FW02049 • 1955

SHIRLEY COLLINS

False True Lovers • FW03564 • 1959

KEVIN ROTH (SELECTED RECORDINGS)

Don't Wait for Me and Songs of the First Decade • Kevin Roth Sings and Plays Dulcimer • FW02367 • 1975

The Mountain Dulcimer Instrumental Album • FW03570 • 1977

LUCINDA WILLIAMS

Happy Woman Blues • SFW40003 • 1990

Ramblin' • SFW40042 • 1991

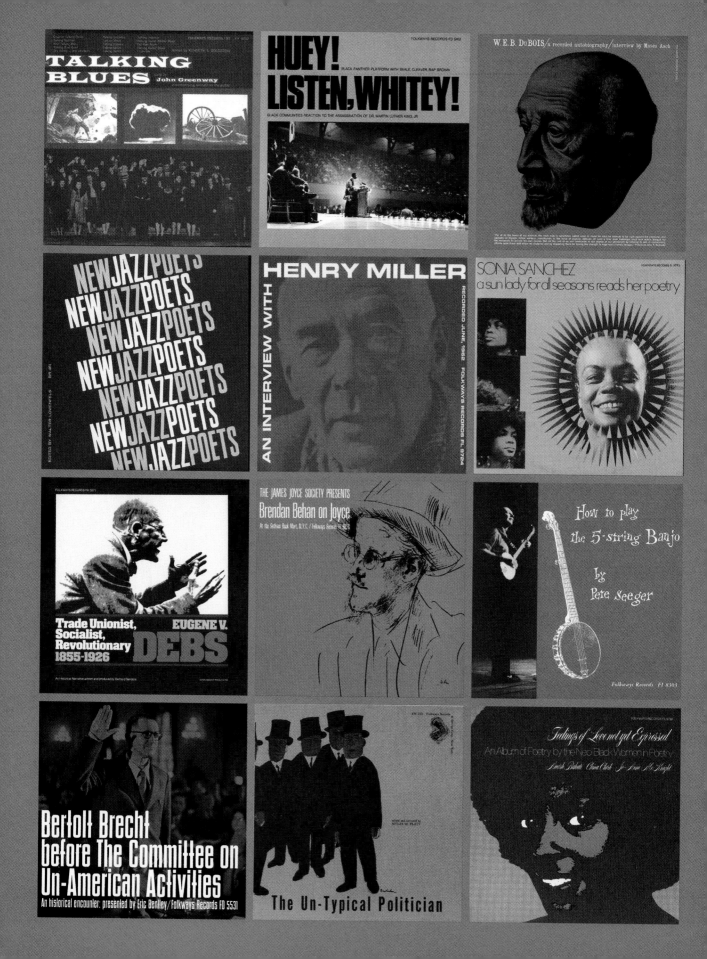

Chapter 10

HISTORY AND SPOKEN WORD

Capturing "Contemporary Expression"

From the start, Moses Asch viewed sound recordings as important documents, preserving not only music but also the entire story of an era. Among his first releases were a series of speeches by Franklin Roosevelt, and he continued to issue spoken word and historical records throughout his career. This expanded to the work of contemporary poets, particularly African American poets such as Langston Hughes. Over the years, Folkways' spoken word and history list grew to include a multitude of voices, from Alfred C. Fuller (of Fuller Brush fame) and Al Capp (creator of *L'il Abner*) to early African American activist W. E. B. Du Bois (Asch personally interviewed him), songwriter W. C. Handy, and poets Kenneth Rexroth, Theodore Roethke, and Allen Ginsberg. It is not surprising that in the 1970s Asch issued several discs taken from the Watergate hearings within months after they occurred. Nor did Asch shy away from more radical voices, issuing recordings by Angela Davis, Huey Newton, and Ishmael Reed.

AFRICAN AMERICAN LITERATURE ON RECORD

Not surprisingly for an admirer of African American culture, Asch's first spoken word recordings beyond political speeches focused primarily on African American poets. Coming toward the end of the Harlem Renaissance, Asch was able to record dozens of important figures of the era, most notably Langston Hughes. Like many of Folkways' recording artists, Langston Hughes was introduced to Asch through a personal connection, the jazz critic and record producer Frederic Ramsey Jr. It took considerable courage—not to mention a willingness to ignore commercial realities—to issue recordings of these poets at the time: the audience for poetry readings was barely developed, and the category of spoken word discs was hardly the most commercial to explore. But this was all part of Asch's mission.

Carrying forward his idea of issuing "anthologies" on key subjects, Asch asked contemporary black poet and critic Arna Bontemps to compile an *Anthology*

Langston Hughes was introduced to the folk revival by Moses Asch and attended several key events, including the first Newport Folk Festival in 1959, where he is shown here (on the right) with Frederic Ramsey Jr. and Barbara Dane. (© David Gahr)

of Negro Poetry in 1954. The recording included six prominent poets: Langston Hughes, Sterling Brown, Claude McKay, Countee Cullen, Margaret Walker, and Gwendolyn Brooks. For many, this was their first appearance on record. While Hughes had become fairly well known since his first book, *The Weary Blues*, was published in 1926, the others in the collection were not very familiar to the general public. Bontemps described Gwendolyn Brooks as primarily a "busy housewife and mother"; Brooks' first book of poetry had appeared only nine years earlier. This recording was issued ten years before the Civil Rights Act, and only a year after *Brown v. Board of Education*. Nonetheless, the collection became a standard in school libraries, particularly with the advent of the civil rights movement.

Of all the poets he recorded, Asch was closest to Hughes, whom he admired as both a poet and as a lover of African American folklore. He collaborated with the poet on various projects, from children's records (see Chapter 7) to spoken word recordings for adults. In 1943, Hughes created an alter ego named Jesse B. Semple (pronounced and often spelled "Simple") for a regular column in the *Chicago Defender*, the leading national African American newspaper. Semple became a means for Hughes to employ the folksy language and old-time "common sense" of his upbringing to address current racial problems. Asch loved this character, sharing with Hughes a fascination with the common language of the "ordinary man." He asked Hughes to select articles for a "best of Simple" album, which was released in 1961.

Another important project that Asch undertook was the recording of key excerpts from Frederick Douglass' autobiography. He employed the well-regarded historian Philip Foner to make the selections, and employed noted black actor Ossie Davis to do the readings. Davis brings real passion to these readings, which were released on two albums in 1966. Foner also oversaw Davis' recording of *The Meaning of July 4 for the Negro*, one of Douglass' key writings. About a decade later, Asch brought Davis back to the studio to record a series of Douglass' speeches. All of these releases included the full texts in the enclosed booklets.

In 1957, Asch hired a new secretary named Marilyn Conklin who would become a key figure in helping him reach out to the African American community. Over the following three decades, Conklin encouraged Asch to record many contemporary writers, including the poet Nikki Giovanni, who made several albums of her poetry for Folkways during the 1970s, and the more radical feminist poets Sonia Sanchez and Sarah Webster Fabio.

RADIO AND STUDS TERKEL

Coming from a background as a radio engineer, Asch early on recognized radio shows as a potential source of records. Most radio programs were broadcast once or twice and then forgotten; Asch, a keen fan of radio who made many recordings directly off the air, knew that much of this material deserved to be preserved and exposed to a wider audience. During the 1950s and into the 1960s many radio shows were locally produced, and the announcer was often the booking agent, producer, and writer. Most stations cared little about what happened to the material once it was broadcast, so many shows could be easily picked up for LP release.

Perhaps the most famous radio personality to contribute to the Folkways catalog was Chicago-based Studs Terkel. Terkel was a well-known on-air personality in Chicago from the mid-1940s through the 1990s and gained fame for his oral histories of the Depression and working-class Americans and for his deep sympathy for the African American experience. Terkel first wrote a fan letter to Asch in the 1940s, addressed simply to "Disc" (Asch's label at the time), pointing out that folk music was drawing as well on his local radio show as more popular styles:

For the past 11 months, I've been riding discs on a 50,000 watt station, WENR, Chicago, an ABC affiliate. The program, WAX MUSEUM, has a hefty following, judging from the mail pull. . . . We've spun records ranging from Dixieland jazz to contemporary pop tunes to operatic arias to folk songs. . . . Now . . . here's our discovery. . . .

For every letter or postcard requesting a Perry Como chant or a Dick Haymes ditty, we receive five hastily scribbled, excited notes asking about a tune they never heard before, about a voice, new to them. . . . We've got a slew of 'em . . . inquiries concerning Leadbelly's "Irene," Ives' "Blue Tail Fly," Woody's "Poor Lazarus" . . . etc. right down the line. During one week, a simple song, "Aunt Nancy," out of your album, "America's Favorite Songs," ran away with the popularity poll. . . .

Here's my point, gentlemen. Folk music, the real stuff, done by real artists, such as those whose stuff you've been waxing, is definitely on the upbeat with the public. If adequately plugged and promoted, it can be as COMMERCIALLY socko as any Hit Parader.

Studs probably wrote this letter in search of promo records, but for whatever reason, Asch stuck it in the files. It would be nearly a decade before Terkel would again contact Asch, this time as a leading promoter of folk and blues performers. On his local radio show, he featured blacklisted performers such as Pete Seeger and hard-to-book bluesmen including Big Bill Broonzy, Sonny Terry, and Brownie McGhee. Asch invited Terkel to submit programs for release as albums in the mid-1950s.

"The program was unplanned. We approached the mike, and let come what did."

—Studs Terkel

One of Terkel's first contributions to Folkways was a 1956 program originally aired on Chicago's WFMT featuring Pete Seeger and Big Bill Broonzy. Like the Asch studios of the 1940s, Terkel's informal show was very much a place where people showed up, the mic was turned on, and Terkel "let come what did." A second album, again featuring Big Bill Broonzy along with Sonny Terry and Brownie McGhee, was recorded as a radio program in 1957 and released in 1959. Again, the recording was unplanned and spontaneous. Terkel recalled:

This was Big Bill's idea.

Sonny Terry and Brownie McGhee were . . . Bill's good friends, two blues artists among the few he considered authentic. "Let's get 'em up to the studio and do a program of blues as three different guys see it.". . .

It was an early July morning, somewhere between midnight and 2 AM. We assembled at the studios of WFMT . . . whose facilities were always available to Bill.

[We] sat informally around one studio microphone and exchanged views and songs . . . with an emphasis on the blues. The entire tape was broadcast the following evening.

545 Aldine, Chicago, Ill.

September 27, 1955

I hereby give my permission to Moe Asch of Folkways Recordings to issue as part of an album the WFMT broadcast in which I participated.

William Broonzy
Big Bill Broonzy

This goes for me, too!
Studs Terkel

Studs Terkel and Bill Broonzy's "contract" giving Folkways permission to issue one of their radio shows.

Somewhat akin to Alan Lomax's famous *Blues in the Mississippi Night* session (which also featured Broonzy), Terkel encouraged the three performers to talk frankly about their experiences as black artists in a white world, the joys and difficulties of a blues life. By this time, Broonzy was a major star in Europe, but nonetheless faced difficulty on the road caused by his skin color, as well as the language gap between himself and his audience. As he told Terkel:

> I've had as high as two and three hundred dollars in my pocket and was in a place I couldn't get food, couldn't get nothin' to eat. Because I didn't know how to ask for it. I was in a neighborhood in France. The people didn't understand me and I didn't understand them. . . .
>
> When I sing of my mule bein' dead, they don't know. They never had no mule die on 'em. Like people in Europe tellin' us about the bomb fallin' on 'em and destroyin' their homes. What do we know about a bomb?

"When I sing of my mule bein' dead, they don't know. They never had no mule die on 'em."

—Big Bill Broonzy

Perhaps here Bill hit on why he was so popular in postwar Europe: his experiences of dispossession and difficulty were mirrored by the devastation and destruction faced by the French, whose own country just recently had been overrun by outside forces intent on destroying their civilization.

HISTORY AS IT HAPPENS

With his motivating idea that recordings are historical documents, it's not surprising that Asch was interested in documenting American history through sound. An admirer of Roosevelt's New Deal, he issued two albums of Roosevelt's

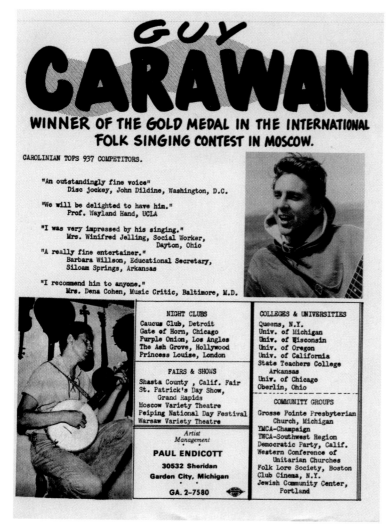

GUY CARAWAN

WINNER OF THE GOLD MEDAL IN THE INTERNATIONAL FOLK SINGING CONTEST IN MOSCOW.

CAROLINIAN TOPS 937 COMPETITORS.

"An outstandingly fine voice"
Disc jockey, John Dildine, Washington, D.C.

"We will be delighted to have him."
Prof. Wayland Hand, UCLA

"I was very impressed by his singing."
Mrs. Winifred Jelling, Social Worker,
Dayton, Ohio

"A really fine entertainer."
Barbara Willson, Educational Secretary,
Siloam Springs, Arkansas

"I recommend him to anyone."
Mrs. Dena Cohen, Music Critic, Baltimore, M.D.

NIGHT CLUBS	COLLEGES & UNIVERSITIES
Caucus Club, Detroit	Queens, N.Y.
Gate of Horn, Chicago	Univ. of Michigan
Purple Onion, Los Angles	Univ. of Wisconsin
The Ash Grove, Hollywood	Univ. of Oregon
Princess Louise, London	Univ. of California
	State Teachers College
FAIRS & SHOWS	Arkansas
Shasta County , Calif. Fair	Univ. of Chicago
St. Patrick's Day Show,	Oberlin, Ohio
Grand Rapids	
Moscow Variety Theatre	COMMUNITY GROUPS
Peiping National Day Festival	Grosse Pointe Presbyterian
Warsaw Variety Theatre	Church, Michigan
	YMCA-Champaign
Artist	YWCA-Southwest Region
Management	Democratic Party, Calif.
	Western Conference of
PAUL ENDICOTT	Unitarian Churches
	Folk Lore Society, Boston
30532 Sheridan	Club Cinema, N.Y.
Garden City, Michigan	Jewish Community Center,
	Portland
GA. 2-7580	

Promo piece for Guy Carawan issued c. 1959–60 when he was still primarily performing as a solo folk singer.

speeches, including the famous "we have nothing to fear but fear itself" first inaugural address. When he began shaping the Folkways catalog in the early 1950s, among his first albums were collections of songs associated with the individual states and songs of the various American wars—a clever marketing ploy for someone who sold to schools.

But history for Asch was not only the past; history as it was occurring was equally important. And the 1950s made history primarily through the insidious growth of McCarthyism. Senator Joe McCarthy's witch hunt aimed at Communists and sympathizers during the 1950s had a chilling effect on the folk music revival, among many other areas of American society (see Chapters 3, 7, and 9).

In 1968, Asch issued a documentary recording on McCarthy produced by noted filmmaker Emile de Antonio, which was a strong indictment of the senator and his tactics. Following over a decade of social change—but still in the midst of the Vietnam War—it was somewhat safe for Asch to issue this recording, although it could do little to endear him with the incoming Nixon administration. Asch had little love for Nixon; in 1979, he issued de Antonio's second LP release, the soundtrack to his satiric documentary *Millhouse: A White Comedy,* which lampooned the Republican politician.

THE CIVIL RIGHTS MOVEMENT

With his keen interest in African American culture, Asch was among the first to recognize the growing civil rights movement and its importance in transforming American social and political life. It was also fortunate that many of his recording artists—notably Pete Seeger and various members of the *Broadside* magazine circle—were early supporters of civil rights and performed at many gatherings both in New York and on marches through the South during the early 1960s.

Much of this material came to Folkways through folksinger Guy Carawan, who had recorded several solo albums for the label in the late 1950s. Carawan was raised in a middle-class family in Los Angeles and began his career performing in folk clubs during the late 1950s, in the early days of the folk boom. As he related in a letter to Moses Asch, "After having a taste of night club folksinging and the atmosphere of trying to make a commercial success at folksinging with all the *folk* being removed from the folksinging," he accepted a job in Tennessee at the Highlander Education and Research Center. Founded in 1932, the center originally focused on labor issues, but in 1953 it expanded to include the growing struggle for racial equality.

The Tennessee and federal governments were not happy with the school's activities and from time to time attempted to shut it down. On one occasion, Carawan was briefly held in a local jail, and—as he sometimes did when he felt his performers were in trouble because of their beliefs—Moses Asch wired him money to pay his bail. Along with the money came a letter urging Carawan to stop making the distinction between "Negro" and "white" folk music, and recognize both as part of "people's" or "American" music. Carawan thoughtfully replied: "Do you want me to refrain from mentioning the difference between Anglo-American traditions and those of the Negro in America? Don't you put out albums of each? And, isn't [it] the role of folklorists to describe different traditions and the way they mix?"

From left, Guy Carawan, Fannie Lou Hamer, Bernice Johnson Reagon, and Len Chandler performing at a Newport Folk Festival workshop, c. 1965. (Photo by Diana Davies, courtesy of the Ralph Rinzler Folklife Archives and Collections, Smithsonian Institution)

Theodore Bikel and Mary Travers listen as the Freedom Singers perform at Newport. (© David Gahr)

One of Carawan's jobs at Highlander was to help train organizers to lead workshops to promote voting rights and equality; as a part of these workshops, songs were used for both education and entertainment. Drawing on the repertoire of traditional hymns and spirituals, the participants also began developing new lyrics and entirely new songs addressing the contemporary struggle for freedom. One of the most famous of these songs is "We Shall Overcome."

"I Will Overcome" was an African American hymn that was sung in many small churches through the South. It entered the contemporary folk world in 1947, when a labor group attending an organizing workshop at the Highlander Center taught the song to the center's music director. It was subsequently reworked by Pete Seeger and, most importantly, Guy Carawan. Carawan reintroduced it to the Highlander repertory, notably teaching the song at a 1960 workshop for a group of college students from Nashville. The song quickly spread and was heard at a sit-in held in North Carolina later that spring, sung by a group of people who would shortly form SNCC (Student Nonviolent Coordinating Committee). It was soon the anthem for the civil rights movement.

In early 1961, a concert was held in New York City to benefit the Highlander school's efforts to train civil rights workers. Two groups of southern singers, one high-school-age from Montgomery, Alabama, and the other college-age from Nashville, were included, along with Carawan, Pete Seeger, and blues performers Memphis Slim and Willie Dixon. Carawan tells the story of how they came to record the landmark *We Shall Overcome* album for Folkways in 1961:

This was both groups' first trip to New York. Their Staten Island Ferry ride to the Statue of Liberty and the view from the top of the Empire State

Building topped off a memorable weekend. After a weekend of sightseeing, shopping, parties, singing, and making many new friends, the girls from Montgomery commented on what a different world this was, especially the freedom of contact with whites which at present is not possible in Montgomery. The morning before they started home . . . Moe Asch phoned and asked them to come up to his studio and make this record. Though they were all tired from the weekend, they still felt like singing, and what you hear . . . is a fairly spontaneous session of impromptu singing and harmonizing that took place that morning.

On this record, "We Shall Overcome" was sung by the Nashville college students, which Carawan noted was "the favorite of all the songs they sang."

Thanks to his ability to release recordings only a few months after the master tapes were complete, Asch could document the civil rights movement as it occurred. He released an album of highlights of the famous March on Washington, which occurred in August 1963, before the end of that year. Asch took advantage of this remarkable speed during other periods of national crisis, notably the Vietnam War and Watergate years.

Bob Dylan, Joan Baez, and Paul Stookey at the Lincoln Memorial on the day of the March on Washington, August 28, 1963. (© Fred W. McDarrah)

Bernice Johnson Reagon

Foremost among the civil rights singers and activists was Bernice Reagon (later, Johnson Reagon). Reagon tells briefly her life story in the liner notes to her first Folkways solo album from 1965:

> I was born in Dougherty County, Georgia, October 4, 1942, seven miles outside of Albany. My father was and is a Baptist minister. I was brought up in the Baptist Church. I was baptized when I was eleven years old.
>
> The strongest thing I remember about home was the emphasis put on getting ahead which meant going to school, getting a degree and becoming a teacher or some similar occupation which was considered respectable for a college graduate. I didn't really get a real love of the church music from home, it seemed that church singing was for the older members and the young people had little part in the church. We were encouraged to sing gospel music or sing in the school chorus. There was very little attempt to instill in us the beauty, or love, or pride for the music that expressed and preserved the history of the Negro.
>
> I finished High School and entered Albany State College on a scholarship. Against the caution lights of my parents, I became involved in the Albany Movement [for civil rights] in 1961. It also brought about my first real decision for myself and I found that I had the capacity to think for myself. I began to wonder who I was, what I was doing here, what really was behind the fear and atrocities suffered by the Negro. I found the answers only after I attended Spelman College in Atlanta and found that the answer lay in the music I had left home in the Baptist church.
>
> My history was wrapped carefully for me by my foreparents in the songs of the church, the work

Bernice Johnson Reagon and Len Chandler performing at Newport, 1969. (Photo by Diana Davies, courtesy of the Ralph Rinzler Folklife Archives and Collections, Smithsonian Institution)

> fields and the blues. Ever since this discovery I've been trying to find myself, using the first music I've ever known as a basic foundation for my search for truth.

In 1962, Reagon became a founding member of SNCC's Freedom Singers, and a year after releasing her first solo album she joined Atlanta's Harambee Singers. In 1973, while working for a theater company in Washington, she formed the first version of what would become the a cappella group Sweet Honey in the Rock, one of the most important feminist/progressive singing groups of the last four decades. (Reagon left the group after thirty years of being its artistic director.) She has also produced numerous radio programs and recordings, as well as books on the civil rights movement. Her daughter, Toshi Reagon, is a well-known singer-songwriter.

GOOD MORNING VIETNAM

Asch's close ties with *Broadside* magazine and social-protest music in general led him to be among the few to issue a wide range of material on Vietnam, going beyond protest songs to include documentaries. Certainly the major labels reflected the antiwar mood in many of their pop recordings, but few if any were willing to issue such diverse material.

In 1966, Folkways issued *Teach In: Vietnam*, recorded at the Berkeley, California, teach-in just months after it occurred. The recording including complete speeches by Dick Gregory, Dr. Benjamin Spock, and other noted antiwar voices early in the conflict. It also included informative notes on the history of the teach-ins and their purpose by the record's editor, Louis Menashe. All in all, it was a radical move considering that the peace movement was just developing and the majority of Americans still supported the war.

Cover, *Good Morning Vietnam*, produced by Claude Joyner, 1972.

The 1968 record *Poems for Peace* was recorded and edited by Ann Charters, who—besides being Samuel Charters' wife and an expert on ragtime piano—is a leading historian and critic of the Beat poets. Charters brought together leading antiwar voices on this record, including Allen Ginsberg, Peter Orlovsky, and Ed Sanders, along with old-time radicals such as Walter Lowenfels. The album was recorded at a live benefit for the New York Center for Nonviolence held at St. Mark's Church. Like many Folkways documentaries, the liner notes simply present the texts of the poems, with no direct comment on the contents; the record speaks for itself.

Good Morning Vietnam is an oral documentary created by photographer and reporter Claude Joyner and issued by Folkways in 1972. It is named after the popular Armed Forces Network radio program that would inspire the 1987 movie featuring Robin Williams. It is a remarkably bleak and frank look at the war and its effects on a civilian population and the young men who were sent to fight it. Joyner opens his liner notes with a description of the sounds that inspired the record:

> It was during the Tet offensive of 1968. In one of the quarters of Cholom, the battle raged, the gunships machine-gunned the market . . . dead . . . wounded . . . houses in flames. And in this world of destruction, from the first

floor of a house that was untouched there came the sound of the scales of the piano, clear and laborious, as if the war did not exist at all. It was easy to imagine the child who was trying to do his best and whose scales resembled the last trace of life on a destroyed planet. . . . [I] never forgot those scales coming from another world which at that moment conjured up that yet other world of war more powerfully than any visual image could have done.

Taking fifty hours of raw taped materials, Joyner assembled a fifty-minute audio documentary with tracks ironically titled "Radio Informs and Entertains You," "The Abstract Universe of War," "Western in Saigon," and so on. On the back half-sleeve Joyner placed a succinct quote: "War is not something you forget like a car crash." Issuing this in 1972 when the war was still very much under way was another example of Asch's ability to present an immediate and alternative vision to the views propagated by mass media.

WOMEN'S AND GAY RIGHTS

Vietnam and the civil rights movement of the 1960s gave way to a wave of further social change in the 1970s and 1980s. It's not surprising that Asch continued to document those on the fringes of society. A year before the famous Attica, New York, prison riots revealed the inhuman conditions of modern prisons, Asch had released *From the Cold Jaws of Prison*, a record of poetry and songs by prisoners from Attica, Riker's Island, and the Tombs. The recording is of a piece with Asch's mission to give voice to the voiceless, those in society too weak to be heard.

The 1970s brought forth the women's and gay rights movements, both of which were documented as they occurred by Folkways. In 1971, Asch released a two-record set titled *But the Women Rose* consisting of historic speeches and documents dating back to pre–Revolutionary War America, revealing the depth of women's involvement in U.S. history. It was an early and important document for the women's studies movement that would blossom over the coming decade. He followed this in 1977 with a second two-LP set of speeches, called *What If I Am A Woman?*, read by Ruby Dee, and focusing on African American women's experiences from slavery to today. Asch had long released recordings by important women in many fields, including Margaret Mead and Angela Davis, as well as works by contemporary women writers, as we've noted.

Asch was similarly open to gay performers, as always emphasizing those who he felt had something important to say. As early as 1973, Folkways released *What Did You Expect?* by songwriter-performer Michael Cohen. In a small white box, appearing like a warning sticker on the record's cover, this simple statement appears: "Songs Sensitively and Honestly Dealing with the Experience of Being

Gay." Five years later, Asch released *Walls to Roses: Songs of Changing Men*, assembled by Willie Cordill, a singer-songwriter who led a collective of seventeen gay performers. In the spirit of the *Broadside* albums of the 1960s, the record was an important anthology highlighting the work of several new songwriters. Again, it was an early and important statement at a time when gay performers had few outlets in mainstream media. In 1980, Asch released *Gay and Straight Together*, a collection of songs gathered by well-known singer-songwriter Ginni Clemmens.

"YOU COULD LEARN SOMETHING FROM A RECORD": MOSES ASCH

From the earliest days of the label, schools and libraries were a major market for Folkways recordings. As Moses Asch told a meeting of the Music Library Association in the mid-1950s, it was up to librarians to be the custodians of today's culture—and the best way to do that was to buy Folkways records.

Luckily for Asch, the 1950s and 1960s were the era of the baby boom, and across the country new schools and libraries were being built with the mission of serving their communities. Sound recording collections were an important part of any library, having the allure of offering patrons material that could be both educational and enjoyable. Libraries were eager collectors of esoteric items such as sound effects recordings, science and nature material, spoken word, and instructional materials—all areas that Asch would explore and exploit.

Ironically, the folk music movement itself inspired a huge market for instructional materials to teach people how to be folk musicians—or at least how to reasonably strum a guitar or pick a banjo. Pete Seeger had mimeographed his own banjo instruction book in the late 1940s to meet this need, and Folkways produced a record to go with it in 1954. He followed it in 1956 with the *Folksingers Guitar Guide*. Seeger's somewhat whimsical notes take the listener step by step through the process of getting started on folk guitar:

You need a phonograph, to play this record. . .
    You need a guitar. . .
    You also need a capo. . .
    Now put the needle in the groove, play the record completely through.
Later on you may spend a whole day mastering some 15-second segment of it,
but now get a general idea of what you have ahead of you.

Although not immediately successful, these instructional recordings would gain great popularity in the late 1950s, when suddenly just about every college student had to have a guitar or banjo stuck under the bed. Buying a cheap instrument (or even just buying the instruction book and record) was a way to

LEARN FOLK GUITAR

HERE'S a simple easy method for those who would like to play rich chord harmonies to their favorite folk, union and freedom songs. Lorrie's wonderful method avoids dull, meaningless exercises, enables you to PLAY RIGHT AWAY even if you don't know a single note now! Absolutely guaranteed. Full refund if this method doesn't teach you!

SPECIAL FREE OFFER! "Lift Every Voice!" The 2nd People's Songbook! Over 75 exciting songs and ballads—Preface by Paul Robeson, songs by Pete Seeger, Woody Guthrie, Earl Robinson and many others. Regular List Price $1.25. Yours absoultely free to encourage you to order your copy of this wonderful method now!

RUSH THIS NO-RISK COUPON

LORRIE 241 West 108 St., New York City 25, N. Y.
I enclose $3.00. Please send my method and my free copy of Lift Every Voice to

Name ....

Address ....

City.................. Zone...... State.......

"Learn Folk Guitar," this 1956 advertisement from *Sing Out!* offers. (Courtesy of the BenCar Archives)

get started, although many never got beyond the first few plunks.

Asch's folk instructional series really took off with the creation of Oak Publications. Founded by Asch along with irascible *Sing Out!* editor Irwin Silber, the company enjoyed enormous success with its first instructional book, *The Folksingers Guitar Guide*, tied to Seeger's 1956 recording. Other record-book combinations followed, including guides to the dulcimer, recorder, blues harp, and different guitar styles.

But Asch's enthusiasm for instruction went further than just teaching folkies how to accompany "Kum Ba Yah." He produced recordings on English pronunciation and speech, foreign language instruction, writing, test preparation, health and self-examination, hypnosis, and just about any other subject you might imagine. As in many of his other areas of interest, he relied on a key group of contributors to develop these series. In the early 1950s, Asch met actor-singer Wallace House, who taught at Columbia and New York University and was a specialist on speech and pronunciation. House recorded several albums for Folkways of traditional English and American songs, accompanying himself with guitar or lute, in the manner of early folk song stylists such as Richard Dyer-Bennet and John Jacob Niles.

In 1956, House produced an album with the prosaic title *Sounds of Spoken English: English Speech Instruction*, reflecting his main academic pursuits. The recording is itself a kind of mini-drama, with House addressing his audience in a formal manner as "ladies and gentlemen." One of House's colleagues was a local teacher named Morris Schreiber. House and Schreiber created several mini-plays to teach literary appreciation, recording them with the "University Players," made up, one supposes, of their classroom students. (Eventually Schreiber worked on his own.) The idea of presenting subjects such as "Understanding the Essay" or "Creative Writing Skills" in the form of playlets was probably influenced by the popular radio dramas of the 1930s, 1940s, and 1950s. But certainly no one had thought previously of issuing a series of albums on these topics, in which the listener would be presented with a string of pedagogic characters.

Marketing the Catalog

The Folkways catalog grew to around twenty-two hundred releases by the time of Moses Asch's death in 1986. That's about fifty-five records a year, or more than one release per week. And—according to Asch's oft-repeated assurance—all of these albums remained in print (except when there were legal or personal objections from the artists).

Just managing such an enormous output and keeping track of inventory—not to mention promoting these albums— was an enormous enterprise. And, as in all things related to Folkways, Asch came up with some unique—and occasionally eccentric— ways of dealing with it.

The simplest way to catalog record releases is to number them sequentially, and this is what Asch did initially when he began Folkways. However, it soon became evident that this system makes for a chaotic listing that veers from American folk ballads to Haitian drumming to spoken word discs. The first division made in the Folkways listings came by 1950, when the Ethnic Folkways Library releases were separated from the regular Folkways ones.

In 1957, when there were around 750 Folkways releases, Asch hired Irwin Silber to help promote the list. It may have been Silber's idea to redo the numbering system, now combining a letter designation and a number. For example, FA stood for the Americana series, FE the Ethnic

Catalog spread from Asch Records, 1944.

Folkways Library, FC the children's recordings, and so on, followed by a number. A thousand slots were assigned for each category, with 2000 being the first number in the Americana series, 8000 in Ethnic, and 7000 in children's. Although the various letter designations were explained in the 1957 catalog—the most complete, descriptive listing that Folkways had issued to that time—these designations were somewhat loose and changed over the years. This system pretty much remained in place through 1986. (When Smithsonian Folkways introduced its label, it also simply numbered releases sequentially. However, within two years separate series were created for children's, spoken word, and world music, following the original Folkways model.)

One of the most interesting aspects of Asch's original numbering system was that periodically gaps were left in the numbers. The catalog might jump from 3020 to 3030 with no explanation. These represented albums that Asch might someday produce. As he told Izzy Young in 1970, he viewed the catalog as a "mosaic" and was always looking for the missing pieces:

I have 7 major categories and 17 subcategories.
And every issue, at least one of the categories is

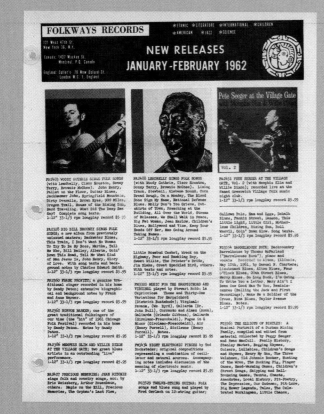

New-release sheet from January–February 1962. This was as close to PR as Folkways got.

Asch's attitude toward advertising was equally unusual. Although he did hire a PR firm from time to time to promote Folkways, he rarely if ever featured an individual album, usually refusing to send out promo copies to DJs, as most record companies did. Print advertising was even scantier, although for a period from about 1957 to 1967, Asch advertised regularly in the pages of *Sing Out!* magazine, the leading publication of the folk revival. (This was probably because he was an investor in the magazine during this decade, providing it with office space and support.)

While in the early 1950s some stores carried Asch's product for its sheer novelty value, it quickly became clear that he needed a better way to reach his audience than through record stores. His market was simply too diffuse to be serviced by a handful of big-city shops. In about 1958, Asch established RBF (Record, Book, and Film) as a Folkways subsidiary to sell records directly through the mail. At the same time, he hired Irwin Silber, the longtime editor of *Sing Out!*, to run his mail order business. Silber was an experienced PR writer and knew how to work a mailing list, and quickly saw opportunities to reach beyond record stores. Silber told Gary Kenton in 1983:

released. So I'm always looking . . . it's like a giant mosaic, that you find a piece that fits into a hole. A mosaic of the contemporary expression.

These "holes" were sometimes filled, although many remained open waiting for the right tape to arrive at the Folkways office.

Although sometimes series brochures or lists for better-selling artists—such as Woody Guthrie, Pete Seeger, or the New Lost City Ramblers—were developed, most of Folkways' promotion went into the entire catalog. Asch gave a series of different rationales for this decision, although it really boiled down to his idea that Folkways existed not as a single album or even a single type of album, but rather as a mirror and expression of all sounds that could be recorded. Thus the list was more important than any single artist or album.

He had accumulated a huge mailing list from everybody who had written in for booklets. Because every goddamn record, half of them showed up without booklets, because he didn't have the money to keep the booklets in stock until the records ran out. So he said, "OK, I'll send you your booklet later." So he had a huge mailing list, probably 10, 15, 20,000 names. And postage rates weren't very high at that time. So I started in September [1958], and the first thing we did was get out a piece for Christmas. And it was a huge success . . . we must have moved 1000s and 1000s of records, from every aspect of the catalog, it wasn't just the folk music thing.

The success of the mail order business allowed Folkways to grow exponentially; along with the folk music revival of the late 1950s and early 1960s, it led to the most financially successful years for the label.

Despite its growing commercial success, it's clear that Asch held Folkways releases to a high standard, existing somewhere outside of the crass world of the rest of the music business. Sometimes Asch would speak of his albums almost as if they were children; spending more money on one child, he reasoned, would deny the others the attention they deserved. Sam Goody, the record retailer who supported Folkways from its earliest days, commented on this in his appraisal of Asch's working methods:

> You have to know how Moe thinks about his records. It reminds me years and years ago I was walking down the street and a friend of mine . . . was wheeling a baby carriage. I took a look at his baby, which was as cross-eyed as could be, and I said to the guy, trying to console him, "Look you don't have to worry, today there's an operation where they just do a little cut and the eye just comes back where it should focus." He said, "What are you talking about?!" I said, "The baby, you know, his eyes." He said, "You dirty bastard, there's nothing wrong with this *baby*." He just thought that this baby was the most beautiful thing that had ever been brought into the world. It's the same with Moe and his records. Whether it was the first record or the last, it's still his baby. Whether it sold or not, it's still his baby. . . .
>
> Moe is not a businessman, you got to understand. He is an entrepreneur in the discovery of the kind of music he wants to put on records. . . .

In the mid-1960s, Scholastic Publications made an arrangement to market Folkways recordings to the school market. This brochure was created by Scholastic to emphasize the educational recordings on the list.

Moe doesn't really evaluate the world, he's solely interested in creating more babies!

Although occasionally the label would produce detailed catalogs, with full artist and producer information given for each album, more often the Folkways list looked like a telephone directory, with each entry varying from being somewhat cryptic to nearly indecipherable. Even major artists might not have their names appear with each of their albums, let alone multiartist collections. In most cases, a one-line title (not always the same as the name of the record) would appear in the listing, such as "Ballads—American 2" or "Concertina—Folk Music," or "Guthrie Folksongs." For those who enjoyed cryptic puzzles or deciphering foreign codes, the catalog provided hours of diversion.

The Folkways catalog also helped establish markets that were previously not known to exist. By naming a section of the catalog "Literature," Asch showed that there was a market for spoken word recordings, thus inspiring other labels to crop up, including Caedmon (founded to record the dynamic Welsh poet Dylan Thomas) and Spoken Arts. While others may have discovered these niche markets on their own, Folkways helped map them out, which made them more obvious. The many independent labels that arose in Folkways' wake shows how different parts of the catalog could be exploited. Many of these labels even copied the unique Folkways packaging: the first Arhoolie, Folk Legacy, and OJL (Origin Jazz Library) releases all had plain black covers with wraparound cover art pasted on them, with a booklet of notes inserted in the record pocket. It's as if the only way one could imagine a specialized release was in the Folkways format.

LISTEN UP!

AFRICAN AMERICAN POETRY AND SPOKEN WORD

An Anthology of African American Poetry for Young People • Arna Bontemps • SFW45044 • 1990

Langston Hughes' Jericho-Jim Crow • Hugh Porter • FW09671 • 1964

The Dream Keeper and Other Poems of Langston Hughes • Langston Hughes • FW07774 • 1955

The Voice of Langston Hughes • Langston Hughes • SFW47001 • 1995

Margaret Walker Alexander Reads Langston Hughes, P. L. Dunbar, J. W. Johnson • Margaret Walker • FW09796 • 1975

Margaret Walker Reads Margaret Walker and Langston Hughes • Margaret Walker • FW09797 • 1975

Langston Hughes' the Best of Simple • Melvin Stewart • FW09789 • 1961

Tambourines to Glory • Second Canaan Baptist Church Porter Singers • FW03538 • 1958

Sterling Brown and Langston Hughes • FW09790 • 1952

Anthology of Negro Poetry • FW09791 • 1954

Autobiography of Frederick Douglass, Vol. 1 • Ossie Davis • FW05522 • 1966

Autobiography of Frederick Douglass, Vol. 2 • Ossie Davis • FW05526 • 1966

Frederick Douglass' Speeches inc. the Dred Scott Decision • Ossie Davis • FW05528 • 1977

Frederick Douglass' The Meaning of July 4 for the Negro • Ossie Davis • FW05527 • 1975

From the Cold Jaws of Prison • FW05403 • 1971

STUDS TERKEL

Studs Terkel's Weekly Almanac: Radio Programme, No. 4: Folk Music and Blues • FW03864 • 1956

Blues with Big Bill Broonzy, Sonny Terry and Brownie McGhee • FW03817 • 1959

EMILE DE ANTONIO

Millhouse (Original Soundtrack of Film on Richard Nixon) • FW05852 • 1979

Underground • FW05752 • 1976

Senator Joseph R. McCarthy • FW05450 • 1968

GUY CARAWAN/CIVIL RIGHTS MOVEMENT

Something Old, New, Borrowed and Blue • Guy Carawan • FW03548 • 1959

Songs with Guy Carawan • Guy Carawan • FW03544 • 1958

This Little Light of Mine • Guy Carawan • FW03552 • 1959

Lest We Forget, Vol. 1: Movement Soul, Sounds of the Freedom Movement in the South, 1963–64 • Various Artists • FW05486 • 1980

Lest We Forget, Vol. 2: Birmingham, Alabama, 1963—Mass Meeting • Various Artists • FW05487 • 1980

Lest We Forget, Vol. 3: Sing for Freedom • Various Artists • FW05488 • 1980

Sing for Freedom: The Story of the Civil Rights Movement Through Its Songs • Various Artists • SFW40032 • 1990

The Nashville Sit-in Story • Various Artists • FW05590 • 1960

Voices of the Civil Rights Movement: Black American Freedom Songs 1960–1966 • Various Artists • SFW40084 • 1997

WNEW's Story of Selma • Various Artists • FW05595 • 1965

We Shall Overcome: Songs of the Freedom Riders and the Sit-Ins • Various Artists • FW05591 • 1961

The Sit-in Story: The Story of the Lunch Room Sit-ins • Edwin Randall • FW05502 • 1961

BERNICE JOHNSON REAGON

Folk Songs: The South • FW02457 • 1965

VIETNAM

Berkeley Teach-in: Vietnam • FW05765 • 1965

Good Morning Vietnam • FW05445 • 1972

The Original Read-in for Peace in Vietnam • FW09752 • 1967

WOMEN'S AND GAY RIGHTS

But the Women Rose, Vol. 1: Voices of Women in American History • FW05535 • 1971

But the Women Rose, Vol. 2: Voices of Women in American History • FW05536 • 1971

What if I Am a Woman?, Vol. 1: Black Women's Speeches • Ruby Dee • FW05537 • 1977

What if I am a Woman?, Vol. 2: Black Women's Speeches • Ruby Dee • FW05538 • 1977

Walls to Roses: Songs of Changing Men • FW37587 • 1978

Gay and Straight Together • FW08580 • 1980

INSTRUCTIONAL MUSIC

The Appalachian Dulcimer • Jean Ritchie • FW08352 • 1964

Folksinger's Guitar Guide, Vol. 1 • Pete Seeger • FW08354 • 1955

Folksinger's Guitar Guide, Vol. 2 • Jerry Silverman • FW08356 • 1964

The Flat-Picker's Guitar Guide • Jerry Silverman • FW08360 • 1966

Mandolin Instruction: Old Time, Country and Fiddle Tunes • Michael Holmes • FW08372 • 1977

Bongo Drum Instruction • William Loughborough • FW08320 • 1958

OTHER (SELECTED RECORDINGS)

Changing Regional Speech Patterns • Ruth Golden • FW09323 • 1964

Understanding and Self-Examination of Breast Cancer • George E. Caraker • FW06429 • 1974

End the Cigarette Habit Through Self Hypnosis • Leslie M. LeCron • FW06231 • 1964

Relaxation Record • Milton Feher • FW06191 • 1962

How to Write an Effective Composition • Morris Schreiber • FW09106 • 1962

The Anatomy of Language • Morris Schreiber • FW09108 • 1959

Understanding and Appreciation of Poetry • Morris Schreiber • FW09120 • 1960

Understanding and Appreciation of Shakespeare • Morris Schreiber • FW09124 • 1966

Understanding and Appreciation of the Essay • Wallace House • FW09110 • 1970

Sounds of Spoken English: English Speech Instruction • Wallace House • FW08110 • 1956

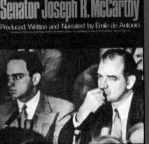

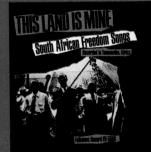

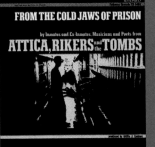

THE SOUNDS OF THE OFFICE
BY MICHAEL SIEGEL

FOLKWAYS RECORDS FX 6142

SOUNDS OF INSECTS / Recorded and Annotated by A. T. Gaul / SCHOLASTIC RECORDS SX 6178

SOUNDS OF FREQUENCY

FOLKWAYS RECORDS FX 6100

Chapter 11

THE SCIENCE OF SOUND

Moses Asch began his career as an audio engineer, and throughout his life he maintained strong ideas about how recordings should be made. He also remained fascinated with sound in and of itself; one of the first areas he built in the Folkways catalog was the Science Series, which included a large number of documentary sound recordings. As in other areas, Asch was fortunate to discover collaborators—fellow enthusiasts—to carry forward the mission. Even his other producers got into the act; when the seventeen-year locusts visited his home near Princeton, New Jersey, Fred Ramsey wrote an excited letter to Asch in which he describes how he woke early to make sure he could get a good recording. But perhaps the most important contributor was future media guru Tony Schwartz, who lugged a large tape machine around New York City, recording everything from children's games to street musicians to traffic horns, assembling this raw material into wonderful records that remain—over fifty years later—compelling listening.

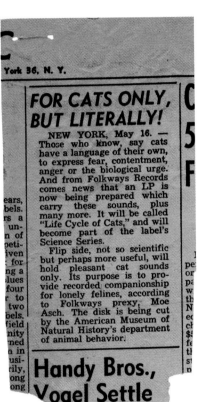

FOR CATS ONLY, BUT LITERALLY!

NEW YORK, May 16. — Those who know, say cats have a language of their own, to express fear, contentment, anger or the biological urge. And from Folkways Records comes news that an LP is now being prepared which carry these sounds, plus many more. It will be called "Life Cycle of Cats," and will become part of the label's Science Series.

Flip side, not so scientific but perhaps more useful, will hold pleasant cat sounds only. Its purpose is to provide recorded companionship for lonely felines, according to Folkways prexy, Moe Asch. The disk is being cut by the American Museum of Natural History's department of animal behavior.

Handy Bros., Vogel Settle

This 1950 news release in *Billboard* was partially tongue-in-cheek, although Asch—already working with the American Museum of Natural History—could have been working on such a project. No record appeared in the Folkways catalog, however, although over a decade later Asch released *Snoopycat*, narrated by Marian Anderson, which celebrates her favorite kitten.

SOUNDS OF A (NEW YORK CITY) RAIN FOREST

In many years of working as an installer of audio equipment, Asch was given different assignments to capture sound as it occurred. He carried forward this work in the early years of Folkways. One of his first and most interesting assignments was to produce a sonic landscape for an American Museum of Natural History exhibit that re-created a tropical rain forest. Its creation in 1951–52 by Asch, Ramsey, and the staff of the museum has become one of the enduring legends of Folkways' unique approach to making recordings. Although Asch prided himself on recording and producing albums that were documents of specific times and events, this does not mean that he wasn't willing to use studio technology to simulate reality. In fact, the record was not a real documentary at all, but an artful assemblage of sounds gathered from sources at hand—a kind of John Cage–like composition meant to simulate the sounds one might hear in a tropical rain forest.

In early 1951, Asch was approached by Dr. Harry Tschopik, then assistant curator of anthropology at the American Museum of Natural History, to create an "audio backdrop" for an exhibit of artifacts of the Montaña, eight tribes who lived in the Upper Amazon valley. Although today we are accustomed to exhibits being accompanied by various sounds, this was a novel idea at the time, and a real challenge to Asch, who lived in Brooklyn and had neither the time nor the budget to travel to the Amazon to record the real sounds. However, the new technology of recording tape and the availability of local sound sources made it possible to create a day in the Amazon without ever getting near a jungle.

Asch first met with Tschopik along with John Tee-Van, who was executive secretary of New York's Bronx Zoo. They provided a list of animals that might be heard in a tropical rain forest: "Parrots, Cicadas, Black Howler Monkeys, Toucan, Macaw were the predominant animals heard. Jaguars were hunted but these animals seldom make noise." Along with folklorist Frederic Ramsey Jr. and recording engineer Peter Bartók, Asch arranged with Tee-Van to record some of these creatures at the zoo "very early in the morning—before the people came." Asch was also able to obtain actual field recordings of some animals made by a professor from Cornell in the rain forest, the only real recordings on the record.

But what about the environmental sounds, particularly the sound of rainfall? As the zoo's director described it, "Rains are sudden and come racing across the top of the forest leaves and can be heard from a distance and sounds like a drum beating from afar." There is no mention of the sound source that Asch used to create this effect in the (otherwise detailed) description he gives in the album's liner notes, and one suspects he may have resorted to creating heavy showers in his bathroom. This is exactly how an article titled "Custom Made Noise," which appeared in June 1953 in the *New York Times*, tells the story:

> The jungle rain came about in an interesting fashion. Originally, these jungle sounds were recorded by an expedition in Africa. However, the rain did not sound sufficiently realistic. So before the disk was put out by Folkways, some experiments were conducted to find more soothing rain.
>
> In charge of this project was Moses Asch. . . . First he turned on the shower in his home and directed it against the curtain. Sounded too much like a machine gun engagement. He finally settled for the shower spray against towels. The drip of water drops from towel to tub was the finished product.

SOUNDS OF A TROPICAL RAIN FOREST IN AMERICA

PRODUCED FOR THE AMERICAN MUSEUM OF NATURAL HISTORY

DRY SEASON—Violaceous Jay, Black Howler Monkeys, Toucan, Rufus Motmot, Macaw, Barbetes, Guans, Parrots, Cicadas, Crickets, Tinamou, Chachalaca, Curassow.

RAINY SEASON—Parakeet, Tree Toads, Bufo Marinus, Three Wattled Bell Bird, Rain Sequence.

SCIENCE SERIES · FOLKWAYS RECORDS & SERVICE CORP. · NEW YORK   FX 6120

Sounds of a Tropical Rain Forest in America cover, 1952.

Peter Bartók, in an interview with me, corroborated this story, although he claims the shower recording was made by Robert Blake, another audio engineer, who volunteered to help with the project.

There remained the problem of how these sounds should be assembled. Asch had been asked to create a sixteen-minute sound collage that would be played continuously through the exhibit. He hit upon the idea of editing the sounds together to create a typical "day in the life" of the Amazon rain forest. To find out how the material should be structured, he met with the museum's head of animal behavior, who gave him a blow-by-blow account of a day's sounds. Figuring on a sixteen-minute finished recording, Asch gave two minutes to each hour to create an eight-hour day. The sound montage was broken down into bands on the record, so those teaching could quickly locate individual animal sounds, from "black howler monkeys" to "crested iguana in thunderstorm" to "big toad."

In an "About New York" feature in the *New York Times* written at the time of the exhibit, the creation of the background sound is humorously described, along with one problem that could not be corrected:

> The crickets . . . were [recorded] on an 18-hour field trip in Connecticut. Mr. Asch was careful to get day and night sounds. He had been warned that crickets' stridulation picks up after sundown.
>
> Mr. Asch thought no one would ever guess he had anything but a Peruvian jungle cricket on the record, but he was wrong. First time the thing was played, a museum visitor told a man beside him, "That's a Yankee cricket they've got in there." Turned out he'd made a life study of crickets everywhere and could spot an accent. Mr. Asch was days getting over the shock, but the Yankee cricket's still in the recording.

Peter Bartók takes credit for recording these crickets, which also make a cameo appearance on the 1953 Folkways LP *Sound Patterns*.

Sound montages such as this were made possible by the flexibility of recorded tape. Sounds could be collected from a variety of sources to create a library of material; these tape snippets could be cut, spliced, and assembled in various orders, with new materials interspersed. Overtracking allowed two sounds recorded independently—say, a tree frog and the sound of rainfall (re-created in a shower stall)—to be combined as if they were occurring simultaneously. And editing of the final product could provide exactly what was needed. Asch's first try was rejected by the museum because "the sounds were too bunched up and there were too many of them"; more silence was added, and the results were finally approved for the exhibit. Not missing an opportunity to repurpose this material, Asch created an expanded version for a 10-inch LP to be sold at the museum as well as directly to schools.

Although some might criticize this record because it was not a "real" recording made in the Amazon, the exhibit itself was an assemblage of different materials, artfully arranged, to simulate a trip to the rain forest. And, for its time, it was quite innovative to create an audio montage (what would today be called a "sound environment"). As John O'Reilly wrote in his review of the exhibit in the *New York Herald Tribune* in November 1951:

> The exhibit hall is dark. Pervading all is a series of recordings . . . which cast a jungle spell over the modern display magic of the museum. One recording is of the drumming of a tropical rain on the jungle leaves: the rain starts, increases until it seems to seep into the shoe soles, and then slowly stops.

THE SOUNDS OF A STEAM LOCOMOTIVE

Between 1955 and 1977, Folkways Records issued five albums of steam locomotive sounds—so-called stack music, because it is the steam escaping through the giant stack of the locomotive that makes the distinctive whistling sounds. All but one of these albums was recorded by a radio engineer and amateur train enthusiast named Vinton H. Wight (1908–1995), who worked for several small Nebraska radio stations throughout his professional life.

Wight's love of the various sounds made by the steam locomotives—which were quickly being replaced in the 1950s by more modern diesel and electrified trains—led him to spend many cold Nebraska nights waiting to capture the thundering of the wheels and the sighing of the great steam engines as they raced by. He rigged up recording equipment in the trunk of his car, powered off the car's battery, that enabled him to capture these fleeting moments.

> "Stack Music is that delightful sound caused by super-heated steam, exhausted from the cylinder, through the stack of a locomotive. . . . To those who love railroading, this is . . . a symphony—yes, this is stack music."
>
> —Vinton Wight

While train spotting is itself a popular rural activity that dates back to the days of the great locomotives, the sound of the train whistle calling across the night was a powerful one for many country dwellers who longed to escape rural life for the bright lights—and big sounds—of the city. The train was a symbol of both mobility and the ultimate loneliness of country life. It offered the opportunity for new life beyond the limits of the small town, but it could also be a strong lure, breaking up families and destroying once-unified communities. Early country singer Frank Hutchison expressed his dismay at the "train that carried my girl from town," with the cry of the locomotive expressing his own broken heart. Trains are culprits in breaking up many love affairs, but also offer the opportunity to escape; Bill Monroe's "I'm Blue, I'm Lonesome" expresses this sentiment perfectly, with the song's narrator moved to "pack my suitcase and go" when he hears the lonesome call of the freight train.

Recording Steam Locomotives

Vinton Wight

The following short biography written in the third person by Vinton Wight appeared along with his first Folkways album.

Vinton Wight has been interested in trains and railroads all of his life. He has been doing recording professionally for over 20 years. So, it seems only natural that these two interests should be combined in a dramatic collection of railroad recordings.

The idea [for recording locomotives] came about when he was vacationing in the Canadian Rockies. As he watched three locomotives struggle up Kicking Horse Pass with a freight train he longed for a recorder, that he might preserve the dynamic action that he witnessed.

He suddenly realized that soon the steam locomotive would be no more, so in 1952 he started recording all the material that he could find concerning them. He felt that the steam engine had individuality, personality, as well as its steam and smoke. It was a living breathing thing that made delightful sounds when it came to life and went into action.

Vinton Wight is shown next to a train track with his portable recording equipment, mounted in the trunk of his car.

This collection naturally centered around the railroad equipment prevalent in his locality and that of his greatest interest. Hence, most of these recordings were made in Nebraska and the high country of Colorado and Wyoming. It was amazing the drama that he found right in his own backyard, when he thought that all the exciting railroading was elsewhere. This type of recording was not without its problems and troubles. Number one was wind. The wind blows constantly in Nebraska, and the wind causes a noise in the microphone. The number two problem was unwanted noise such as automobile traffic, airplanes, live stock, and even bees buzzing near the microphone. It was not always possible to avoid these interfering sounds, but a technique for editing the tape was developed that made it possible to remove them. One 30 minute tape recording had to be edited in 44 places. This is tedious work but the results are worth it.

He was aided on recording sprees by his tolerant, understanding wife Dorothy, who counted the cars, noted the engine numbers, and did her knitting while waiting for the next train to come.

"STEREO IS A LIE": MOSES ASCH

As a young record producer for Moe Asch, I brought him a tape recorded in two-track stereo, admittedly primitively made in the basement of an Irish musician's home. I wrote on the tape box "STEREO" in large letters, because Moe had previously issued an album of mine in mono despite it being a stereo source. He took one look and said contemptuously to me, "Stereo is a lie."

"But all recording is a lie," I replied to Moe. "I mean, any recording that you make is a 'translation' onto tape of the real performance."

At which point he reached behind his desk, where there were several shelves of small African figures, grabbed one, and threw it in my direction.

Because he believed recordings were documents, Moses Asch had strong feelings about how recording sessions should be conducted. He had begun his career as an audio engineer and was a believer in using a single microphone, and ideally making a single take. Barring a major mistake, the "real performance" would be captured best in this way. In the early days, the recording was cut directly to a disc coated with wax or acetate, so there was no opportunity to manipulate or change the sound. In the 1950s, when hi-fi was introduced, Asch vehemently opposed it because the original recordings were being manipulated (the highs—or higher frequencies—were being boosted and the lows compressed) so that the finished records would sound better on the playback equipment of the day. Asch became known as the advocate of "flat" recordings.

Peter Bartók, a recording engineer and close associate of Moe's from his early days, commented in a lengthy interview in 2006 that an absolutely "flat" recording would be impossible to make. All equipment has built-in parameters to compensate for the mechanics of sound reproduction. Bartók noted that in the 78 era, for instance, bass frequencies had to be compensated for, otherwise the grooves on the record would have been so wide that the needle wouldn't track. When LPs were first introduced, it took a while for engineers to work out the new parameters that would make recordings sound "natural." Bartók—who did a great deal of mastering work and recording for Asch in the 1950s and 1960s—freely admitted that he used equalization and other techniques to improve the raw tapes that Asch supplied.

We have to dig deeper to truly understand what Asch meant by "flat" recording. Asch was not a Luddite when it came to audio experimentation. He admired efforts such as the early multitracked recordings of Les Paul. (Asch had helped design amplifiers to Paul's specifications in the mid-1930s.) And many Folkways records were created through the "magic" of editing and manipulating sounds.

I believe that Asch's notion of "flat" recording was integral to his belief

Peter Bartók working his mastering lathe, which is resting on the stove in the kitchen of his New York apartment. (Courtesy of Peter Bartók)

that a recording engineer and studio should be as "transparent" as possible in serving the artist's vision. The major commercial labels used the studio to create a product based on the idea of selling as many records as possible; the artist's intentions came second or third to the main purpose, which was making a profit. Asch believed that the studio should be a place where creativity was allowed to blossom. "Flatness" to him meant removing any barriers between the artist and the listener.

Just as 1950s-era color films have a glossy, surreal quality, early hi-fi stereo recordings can sound artificial to today's ears. As a member of the Recording Industry Association of America (RIAA) in the 1950s, Asch vigorously opposed hi-fi's introduction. Peter Bartók said that Moe was always particular when he was mastering a tape that Bartók take care to represent all the frequencies equally, without favoring one over the others:

He did like a certain kind of style that . . . —whether I happened to agree with it—all of the frequencies had to be represented. It shouldn't be predominantly highs at the expense of the lows, but they all had to be there in their proper relationship.

Amusingly, Asch printed on the back sleeve of some Folkways releases in the later 1950s this tongue-in-cheek tag line: "Folkways Hi Fi Records Play 2X (Twice) as Good on Stereo Equipment." He meant, of course, that if you play a mono record on a stereo set, you hear the music out of both speakers—presumably making the record sound "twice as good." Few probably realized that he was taking a jab at hi-fi's claim for superior sound quality.

Mel Kaiser, the head engineer at Cue Recording Studios, which Moe used for many of his sessions in the 1950s and 1960s, recalls that Moe wasn't against stereo, just the glitzy effects that many added to their stereo recordings. Moe would allow Kaiser to use two microphones, but he wanted him to emulate the way humans hear music in performance, rather than create an artificial sound environment. Kaiser recalls:

He was not too enamored with stereo, especially if they would start doing gimmicks. Moe, if he recorded stereo, he'd say, "Just set up two mikes in the center and record it that way. Just like you have two ears." Don't pingpong; he couldn't stand effects. Don't change or augment the stereo in any way.

Many listeners criticized Folkways recordings for their poor quality. Asch himself did little to counter this claim, gruffly answering an NPR interviewer who asked whether listeners were becoming more demanding about quality, "I tell them to go to hell! OK? Do you want the guts or do you want the quality." However, this is somewhat misleading; Asch didn't mean he would issue *any* recording; rather, the quality of the recording itself was secondary to the importance of the particular performance. He strongly objected when Izzy Young suggested that Folkways included "mistakes" in their recordings:

No, no, no. . . . I don't think I have ever issued a record with a mistake on it as such. If a singer like Lead Belly or Woody says to me don't issue those things, I made a mistake, that's something else. I would never issue those, but if an artist says after he hears the thing "We didn't do this to make a million bucks, to be a commercial record. We did this because I remembered the song and this is the way I sang it." Then I am proud to issue it.

Many artists were surprised when they first worked with Asch; he rarely interfered with a session, and sometimes even left the room while the machines ran and the musicians played. He consistently stated, "I do not edit or control my artists." This kind of freedom was absolutely unheard of in the commercial recording world. It is why so many performers and collectors remained committed to Folkways, despite Asch's sometimes unpredictable behavior and always irregular payment.

Asch realized that recording techniques had changed from when he first began work in the 1940s. He was particularly sensitive to identifying what the artist felt was important so that the recording could be more accurate, rather than just taking a shotgun approach to sound collecting:

> It used to be that sounds that we recorded were unique; we never did it before, we never did it at the locale before, so every recording is a new technique and a new discovery. Today, we're looking for sounds in context, in other words, the children sing and we record them, we want to know what time of day, what circumstances, why they're doing it. We want to give more meaning to the sound, the content, than before. . . .
>
> So the sound of the recording is a little different than it was then. The content of the sound is different. Before we set an open wild microphone and we just point it toward [where] the crowd was, or whatever was going on. . . . Today, we know more, we ask more: "Who is the leader? Who creates the thing?" There we want to set the sound, where the thing is created, and not just an overall sound. . . . We [are] thinking of it: what is it what we're recording? What is the content? Why are we standing here? . . . And we ask all of our contributors today to be much more accurate in what we are doing.

Again, the point of the documenter—as Moe liked to call himself—was to accurately reproduce what the artist intended in the performance.

TONY SCHWARTZ'S CITY OF SOUND

In 1953, the *New York Times* reviewed Tony Schwartz's first album for Folkways Records:

> Folkways Records has had the interesting idea of sending a representative named Tony Schwartz about the city to make on-the-spot recordings of kids singing at their play.
>
> The result is an unusual and diverting record, *One, Two, Three, and a Zing Zing Zing*. . . .
>
> The recording, as may be imagined, is informal in the extreme. In the

Moses Asch and Tony Schwartz hold a meeting at Sam Goody's store, c. 1958. (© David Gahr)

background can sometimes be heard the honking of auto horns, voices of other children, and in one instance a Boy Scout bugle. . . .

The recordings were made during the summer and fall of 1952 in a 20-block area of west midtown Manhattan. Most were recorded in tenements and play areas of housing projects. They are a quaint and fascinating cross-section of the unsophisticated songs heard daily in the streets of New York.

Like the live jazz recordings made by Norman Granz, this record left critics bemused—and some befuddled. The idea of issuing an album of children at play—something that you might hear on the city streets almost any day, but rarely actually listen to attentively—was both radical and to some nonsensical. But for Schwartz it was part of an endless quest to document New York City in all of its many dimensions. And Asch was happy to issue a stream of these recordings throughout the 1950s and 1960s.

Like Asch, Schwartz was an inveterate tinkerer with radio and audio equipment. He was first exposed to radio in high school, and he became fascinated with the idea of transmitting sound and the fraternity of amateur radio bugs who would become his collaborators and friends. Always a loner—Schwartz long suffered from agoraphobia—he built his own radio shed behind the family house so he could indulge his hobby; as he recalled in a 1999 interview: "I slept there, at times, and put a potbelly stove in the middle of the room. I built a phone line too, so my mother could call me up for dinner."

Promotional brochure for Tony Schwartz's Folkways recordings.

Schwartz may have come to Asch's attention through his weekly show on WNYC, *Sounds of New York*. Beginning in 1945 and continuing for thirty-one years, he presented the sounds of the city on this morning radio show, assembled into collages that told a story from a particular point of view. Many of these shows served as raw material or tryouts for his Folkways recordings. Living in New York gave Schwartz great opportunities to encounter all kinds of sound, literally within blocks of his home. He also called on his fellow recording friends to send him their own materials, so his mailbox became a kind of portal to a world of sound. For this reason, he called one of his first Folkways projects *New York 19*, after his postal zone. As he recalled in 1999 for National Public Radio:

> "New York 19" was the non-commercial musical life of my postal zone. And the postal zone was New York 19 at that time. It's 10019 now. That was the area I could travel in. I'm not able to travel far. I have agoraphobia and in walking I could just go around my postal zone in the midst of Manhattan.

Beginning with a wire recorder, Schwartz moved to the new technology of audiotape, using equipment that was generally found only in recording studios. The idea of portable tape recording was not yet developed, although Schwartz pointed the way for this nascent market:

> I made the first portable recorder. I brought the VU meter from inside the case to the top so I could look down at it and see how loud things were and I put a strap on it so I could hang it over my shoulder, that was in 1945. I could go record children in the park doing jump rope rhymes. And I recorded the street festivals. I made fourteen records for Folkways records [this way]. . . . I was interested in the sound around us.

Among Schwartz's many projects were documentaries of New York's growing Puerto Rican and African American communities, street musicians, and hawkers. Perhaps most famous was a documentary called *A Dog's Life*, which told the audio story of a young wire-haired terrier named Tina and her daily encounters with the world. As Schwartz tells it in the record's notes:

> I obtained my dog Tina on March 3, 1955. From that day on, I started recording the sounds of the dog and the people with whom she and I came in contact. I recorded the sounds of all the situations Tina led me into.
>
> After a year of tape recording Tina's life, I went to CBS with the idea . . . "Tina" was broadcast on January 26, 1956. . . .
>
> I found the most important factor in training Tina was for me to learn *how* a dog learns. Once I learned that, I did not waste time in training her in a way in which she could not learn.

The simple notion of learning how the subject thinks and feels, rather than imposing one's own ideas, sums up Schwartz's recording philosophy. He used sound as a means of learning about others.

In the late 1950s, Schwartz's vast library of sound became the basis for his entrée into producing commercials. At first he specialized in using real children's voices to promote products. He moved into political advertising, producing what was perhaps the most famous political ad of the twentieth century, the "Daisy Girl" spot for Lyndon Johnson. Although it aired only once, it managed to portray Barry Goldwater as a dangerous proponent of nuclear war, endangering the life of children everywhere.

Folkways became so famous for having a large library of natural sounds that one day a letter appeared from Senator Barry Goldwater; it read in its entirety:

> June 11, 1962
>
> Gentlemen:
>
> I am interested in securing some recordings of a waterfall or rain on the roof. Can you tell me if you have them?

Asch replied that sadly he had nothing appropriate, but he leaped on the opportunity, suggesting to Goldwater that he make a recording of his own to "expose something of your philosophy and the background to it. I believe that it would be a valuable document." Goldwater expressed interest, if the project wouldn't take too much time; Asch replied saying he would need only "about 1 and ½ hours at most" to complete the recording, and could bring portable equipment to Washington to make the record. However, despite this exchange of letters, the recording was apparently never made.

Your Annual Sound Subscription

One of the many unusual records released by Moe Asch in the early years of Folkways was *Sound Patterns* from 1953. The idea was to collect together fragments of recordings that appeared on the Folkways doorstep and release them as an annual "gallery" of sound. The anonymous author of the liner notes—probably Asch himself—explains how this record differed from others:

FOLKWAYS RECORDS . . . presents what it believes to be a departure from material generally issued on phonograph records. Like the photography and art "annuals," each issue will include the most unusual—and the most common—sounds that exist, and through aural interplay, FOLKWAYS hopes to be able to establish a mood not unlike that of seeing photographs and pictures. Taken out of context these sounds "stand" by themselves in their uniqueness, and create new auditory dimensions.

These sounds came to FOLKWAYS RECORDS from varied sources and were sent by many people . . . many were recorded on scientific expeditions. Their compilation according to their character tends to make exotic and exciting listening.

Many recording techniques were used. Motion picture sound recordings were taken "on location." Peter Paul Kellogg had recording equipment mounted in the rear compartment of his passenger car and the parabolic reflector that he used was fastened to a spare tire rig. . . . Some of the sounds were recorded on primitive disc recorders in the wilds of the Arctic and Africa, others were "taped" (30 inches) with the latest Ampex, Telefunken or RCA studio microphones; many were recorded with the new "high-fidelity" Magnamite hand-operated battery recorder that weighs less than 20 pounds

complete and which explorers frequently take now to inaccessible areas.

Peter Bartók taped the crickets in this album thus: He had a recording session in a barn in Connecticut with a string quartet; this was the only place where they felt they could get a quality of reproduction that would "sound real." That night he heard the cricket chorus (with toads in the background). He set up his Ampex, rolled out a 30-foot cable with his microphone and got to work.

Dr. Peter Kellogg was "on location" in Florida recording animal sounds. Just as he was "getting" the toad heard in this record, a storm broke. He rushed to his car with the microphone to protect it. Then he proceeded to record the storm. After it was over, he "opened up" his equipment and caught the bird (aurally). It seemed a nice sequence to include.

The individual notes for each track tell the story of where each "found" sound came from:

Monkey (happy); Monkey (same monkey—angry)
The Monkey (happy and angry) came to FOLK-WAYS with an audition tape of Sansa Music from French Equatorial Africa.
Heartbeat
Heart of a secretary. Made by Peter Bartók in 1952, using modified Altec microphone, 15" Ampex. Subject was a 23-year-old female.
Taxi Trip, through Traffic to Airport
Recorded in 1952 in Boston in a cab picked up at dusk on Boylston Street near Charles. From Boylston to Washington Street through the theatre district, where bird peeps are heard in heavy traffic sounds. As the traffic cop stops the car on a red light,

Using his portable Magnemite recording machine, Moses Asch records Elba Pineda in Chicago. (Courtesy of the Frank Driggs Archives)

people can be heard talking as they walk by: then the motor of a nearby car and a car's horn. Down Washington Street to Adams Square and through the Sumner Tunnel (the rumble of the tunnel sounds) then to the straightway and from there a short smooth trip to Logan International Airport.

N.Y.C. gardenias and Hot Dogs in Times Square
The Gardenia Caller and Hot Dog cries were recorded between 46th and 47th streets on Broadway (Times Square), N.Y. on a Magnamite by Moses Asch in 1951. It is of interest to note the jukebox recording of "Cry" by Johnny Ray in background.

Apparently, this album was not successful enough to merit a second recording in the series, and Asch's dream of a "sound annual" was forgotten.

FROGGY WENT A-RECORDIN'

The American Museum of Natural History in New York is as much a center of research as it is a museum. And it was just a short subway ride from the Folkways offices to the museum, where Asch was able to draw on a talented staff to provide him with some of his most unusual recordings. One of the most justly famed recordings was *Sounds of North American Frogs*, compiled by the chairman of the museum's Department of Amphibians and Reptiles, Charles M. Bogert (1908–1992). Bogert made several trips to the American Southwest, produc-

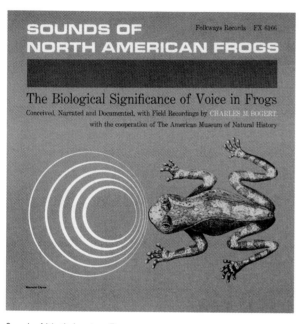

Sounds of North American Frogs cover.

ing an album of natural sounds he recorded there for Folkways in 1954, followed four years later by his masterpiece, the two-record set of frogs.

The set was accompanied by a lengthy essay by Bogert on the material, including how frogs produce their sounds and the functions of these sounds. He gives meticulous notes of where, when, and how the sounds were recorded. Here are some typical entries:

38. Warning croak of the Florida Gopher Frog, *Rana capito*, recorded on July 7, 1954, in the laboratory at the Archbold Biological Station, with a specimen taken one-fourth mile south of the station. This frog was held in the human hand. Under natural conditions, the sound would not be repeated so many times before the male would be released by another male that had seized it. . . .

73. Mating call of Couch's Spadefoot, *Scaphiopus couchi*, recorded 9 miles north of Rodeo, New Mexico, at 9:40 PM on July 17, 1955. It is unusual to hear an isolated Couch's Spadefoot calling; this one was hidden under tumbleweeds in a depression at the side of the road. . . .

84. Winter mating chorus of the Pátzcuaro Frog, *Rana dunni*, recorded in Lake Pátzcuaro, Michoacán, Mexico, on the evening of January 27, 1956. The recording was made near 11:00 PM from a dugout canoe, with air temperature at 9.5°C. And water temperature at the surface of the lake approximately 14°C.

The remarkable range of places, times, and circumstances under which Bogert was able to work is a testimony to the power of the new technology of tape recording. Just as the portable tape machine revolutionized the recording of traditional music, so the new equipment was a boon to scientific researchers such as Bogert, who could carry his machine to the most remote locations.

If I Could Talk to the Animals

As late as 1982, Asch continued to issue unusual experiments in sound and communication. Perhaps none were more unusual than Jim Nollman's record *Playing Music with Animals*. The recording opens with the traditional American folk song "Froggy Went a-Courtin'," sung by Nollman, accompanied by three hundred turkeys. On other tracks, he is joined by twelve wolves or twenty orcas. True to the Folkways aesthetic, these recordings are real collaborations, not studio creations, as Nollman explains in his liner notes:

> These pieces differ from other touted interspecies pieces in that these were mostly recorded in real time. Unless otherwise noted, there are no overdubs conveniently layered on in a studio. What you hear is what happened in the sea or in the bush. The big question for me is always whether or not the animal would be playing the same sound without my own musical stimulus. After 10 years, I've become convinced that there are many animals, especially wolves and orcas, who possess many musical "rules" concerning modulation and resolution. Many of the rules offer valuable advice for human musicians. For example, wolves will stop howling if someone is out of tune.

Nollman doesn't say what happens when you play Howlin' Wolf for howling wolves.

Here's how he got the turkeys to gobble along to the old folk song:

> I recorded this one sitting in a farmyard surrounded by 300 Tom turkeys. The Toms respond to pitch and to volume. When a certain relative intensity is reached, each turkey emits a single gobble. A large flock can be manipulated to respond in unison. . . . The trick to the process is riding the shared musical energy without aggravating the turkeys. I was once attacked by a flock for getting too frenetic.

Jim Nollman's record.

The Face of Folk Music: David Gahr

The covers of Folkways records benefited from the contributions of many great artists and photographers. Among the most influential was David Gahr, a former economics major whom Moses Asch recognized as a talented photographer. Through Asch's patronage, Gahr came to be among the leading photographers of folk, blues, and rock performers of the second half of the twentieth century.

Gahr was born in Wisconsin to a radical-left Jewish family. He joined the army in World War II and then returned to attend the University of Wisconsin on the GI Bill. There he studied economics, and he did so well that he was recommended for a prestigious scholarship at Columbia University to continue his studies at the master's level. Unhappy with the conservative faculty at Columbia, Gahr dropped out and began taking photographs as a hobby. Meanwhile, he found a job as a stock boy at Sam Goody's record store in midtown.

Goody recognized his talent and introduced the young photographer to Moses Asch. At the time, Goody was warehousing Asch's records as well as selling them, and he gave Gahr the responsibility of balancing the books. Gahr recalls that Goody would send him to Asch to get copies of records when he ran out of specific titles and that Asch in turn would ask Goody to return records when he needed to fill a more lucrative individual order. Gahr admired both men as individuals of integrity and vision. Asch took Gahr under his wing, recognizing a kindred spirit. He also admired Gahr's early attempts at photography. Encouraging him to take more pictures, Asch began using Gahr's photos for Folkways covers, paying him a flat fee of $25 per shot.

"Moe was really worth while, to learn from, although you didn't learn—it was osmosis."
—David Gahr

The Fugs at the time of recording their first album for Broadside (Folkways). The album was so successful that Asch sold it immediately to ESP Records. (© David Gahr)

As he did with many others over the years, Asch gave Gahr the opportunity to have his work seen, establishing him as an important photographer through his association with Folkways. The quality of Gahr's work was apparent from the beginning, and Gahr told me that he learned from Asch the ability to pick out the best image from among the dozens that he would typically take for an album cover:

What Moe did . . . [he] selected, he looked at my stuff every week, and picked out this or that for a cover. I did more covers for Moe than anyone else. And it was a joy, because he had an unerring good taste, and important taste. Moe was a good teacher. Not that I learned how to photograph [from him], I knew how, or I couldn't have done it.

The Memphis Jug Band onstage, 1963. From left, Furry Lewis, Gus Cannon, and Will Shade. (© David Gahr)

Some of Gahr's best-loved photos show specific details, such as close-ups of a musician's hands or the surface of the guitar that a musician played, to capture something deeper about each personality.

His selection was always . . . if he didn't like it, it didn't go in. It had to be honest, above all, it had to be honest stuff.

This emphasis on honesty in one's craft was central to all of Asch's recording work, so it's not surprising that he emphasized it with the young photographer. Furthermore, he encouraged Gahr to record not only the person but also the entire world where that person lived, to capture the cultural context as well as the individual visage:

David Gahr, 2007. (Photo by Perry Werner)

He said, "When you go in someone's house, photograph what's on the walls. . . . Sometimes in a very proper setting, you'll find a wrestler as a part of the family, and you'll find a wrestler on the wall." And I did that with the Rev. Gary Davis, people like that.

LISTEN UP!

RAIN FOREST

Sounds of American Tropical Rain Forest
• FW06120 • 1952

STEAM LOCOMOTIVES

Sounds of Steam Locomotives, No. 1: Stack Music Sampler; or Steam, Steel and Action • FW06152 • 1956

Sounds of Steam Locomotives, No. 2: Stack Music Sampler; or Make Up of a Train • FW06153 • 1957

Sounds of Steam Locomotives, No. 3: Colorado Narrow Gauge Stack Music • FW06154 • 1958

Sounds of Steam Locomotives, No. 4: The Great New York Central—Hudson, Mohawk, Niagara • FW06155 • 1958

Sounds of Steam Locomotives, No. 5: The Stack Music Spectacular • FW06156 • 1976

TONY SCHWARTZ (SELECTED RECORDINGS)

1, 2, 3 and a Zing Zing Zing • FW07003 • 1953

An Actual Story in Sound of a Dog's Life • FW05580 • 1958

New York 19 • FW05558 • 1954

Nueva York: A Tape Documentary of Puerto Rican New Yorkers • FW05559 • 1955

The World in My Mail Box • FW05562 • 1958

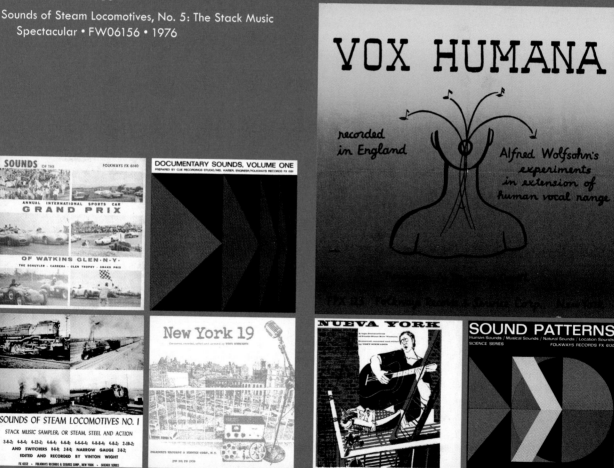

SOUND PATTERNS

Sound Patterns • FW06130 • 1953

TREE FROGS

Sounds of North American Frogs • SFW45060 • 1998

JIM NOLLMAN

Playing Music with Animals: Interspecies Communication with 300 Turkeys, 12 Wolves and 20 Orcas • FW06118 • 1982

SELECT OTHER RECORDINGS OF SOUNDS

Sounds of Animals • FW06124 • 1954

The Lyrebird: A Documentary Study of Its Song • FW06116 • 1966

Cable Car Soundscapes • FW06129 • 1982

Learning to Talk: A Study in Sound of Infant Speech Development • FW06271 • 1963

Man in Space: The Story of the Journey—A Documentary • FW06201 • 1964

Music Used in Many Popular Television Commercials and Their Sponsors • FW06109 • 1974

Science Fiction Sound Effects Record • FW06250 • 1958

Science of Sound • SFW45038 • 1990

Sounds of Frequency • FW06100 • 1954

Sounds and Ultra-Sounds of the Bottle-Nose Dolphin • FW06132 • 1973

Sounds of a South African Homestead • FW06151 • 1956

Sounds of Camp: A Documentary Study of a Children's Camp • FW06105 • 1959

Sounds of Insects • FW06178 • 1960

Sounds of Medicine • FW06127 • 1955

Sounds of the American Southwest • FW06122 • 1954

Sounds of the Annual International Sports Car Grand Prix of Watkins Glen, N.Y. • FW06140 • 1956

Sounds of the Junk Yard • FW06143 • 1964

Sounds of the Office • FW06142 • 1964

Speech After the Removal of the Larynx • FW06134 • 1964

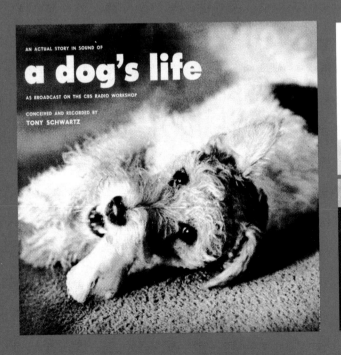

Smithsonian Folkways

WOODY GUTHRIE

BUFFALO SKINNERS
THE ASCH RECORDINGS, VOL. 4

Smithsonian Folkways

Smithsonian/Folkways

Vocal
Music
from
Central
and West
Flores

9 MUSIC OF INDONESIA

Smithsonian Folkways

Kalimantan
Strings

MUSIC OF INDONESIA 13

Chapter 12

SMITHSONIAN FOLKWAYS

A Museum of Sound

When the Smithsonian Institution purchased Folkways Records in 1987, part of the agreement with founder Moses Asch was to keep all of the recordings available—just as he had done through the years. However, it wasn't clear whether the Smithsonian would start a record label to release new material in addition to being a custodian of the original Folkways recordings. A year later, the decision was made to launch a record label—Smithsonian Folkways Recordings—to reissue older material but also release new recordings in the spirit of the original Folkways label.

A REVOLUTION FOR TWO INSTITUTIONS

Smithsonian Folkways Recordings would have to be a different type of company than the original Folkways Records and Service Corporation. Folkways was the product of the vision and determination of Moses Asch; he vetted the recordings, prepared them for release, oversaw their printing, manufacturing, warehousing, and distribution, approved their promotion, and maintained them, sometimes over several decades, often in the face of very limited interest from the consumer. Everything was subsumed to keeping the collection alive; even Asch's own health and livelihood came second. He answered to no one but himself.

The Smithsonian Institution is a vast, public trust that has over the years developed into a complex of major museums. It is governed by a secretary (head officer) who reports to a Board of Regents, which includes the Vice President of the United States, the Chief Justice of the Supreme Court, three senators and three members of the House of Representatives, and currently nine citizen-members. The board is a fairly conservative body. The Smithsonian has rules of operation that have to be followed uniformly by its many individual operating entities. These rules couldn't be changed to suit the needs of a maverick operation such as Folkways.

Ralph Rinzler recording Cortelia Clark, mid-1960s. (Photo by Bob Yellin)

Folkways was brought to the Smithsonian through the sheer determination of Ralph Rinzler. Rinzler was originally hired in 1967 as artistic director of the Smithsonian's annual Folklife Festival, and had risen to the post of assistant secretary for public service. When Asch approached him in 1984 with the possibility of the Smithsonian preserving Folkways, Rinzler mobilized a group of lawyers, accountants, and policy specialists within the Smithsonian to bring this to reality. He also had to assuage Asch's concerns about any interference with Folkways or its mission once it became part of this large, quasi-governmental organization. This delicate tightrope act pitted Rinzler against the more conservative voices within and outside the Smithsonian as well as Asch's own justifiable concerns about the future of his beloved collection.

Those opposing the acquisition voiced concerns about it from the start. An important advisor on music for the Smithsonian Institution Press was well-known critic and conductor Gunther Schuller. Although initially positive, Schuller came to strongly oppose the acquisition of Folkways. In a remarkably negative letter, he first attacked the Folkways catalog, which "looks 'impressive' at first glance" but suffers from "uneven" quality and "balance of repertory." But then Schuller lashed out at Asch's mode of operation:

Everyone in the record business knows that Moe Asch put together a catalogue—these are harsh words but they're the only accurate ones—by stealing and ripping off from various sources . . . . He is a nefarious wheeler and dealer . . . and it seems to me that the Smithsonian ought to think long and hard whether it wants to be associated with this man and be perceived as perpetuating his ethics.

It is important to note—as Asch did on many occasions—that sound recordings made before February 15, 1972, were not protected by federal copyright law, and that many labels reissued older material that they didn't "own" (see Chapter 4). Although Schuller gave Asch credit for discovering "Lead Belly and Janice [*sic*] Joplin" (of course, Moe wasn't the one who discovered Lead Belly, and he never recorded Janis Joplin), in the end he recommended that the Smithsonian accept the collection only if Asch would give it as a gift—and not as a means for him to "retire in luxury and splendor."

Schuller represented the establishment with a capital *E*. Moe's business philosophy was a political one, based on his idea that all sounds should be available to the American people and not controlled by major corporations. This undermined the very basis of American capitalism, the idea that companies can own *and* control their product. Moe saw his record company as a custodian of its recordings, not as an owner; whenever artists complained about their treatment, Moe always gave them the option of taking their material and going elsewhere. This would be a difficult attitude for a national institution such as the Smithsonian to support.

Rinzler fought against these conservative critics by rallying a group of archivists and ethnomusicologists to mount a letter-writing campaign in defense of the purchase, and most rose to the cause (although a few raised again the issue of unevenness of quality and repertory). Then Rinzler faced a new challenge; Moses Asch was expressing second thoughts about the deal. His past experiences with government agencies—to put it mildly—had been fairly negative. He had lived through the McCarthy era, when freedom of speech was severely threatened by big government. Could he trust a governmental organization to maintain his vision of Folkways?

Rinzler could have easily given up—as when he faced the earlier doubts and criticisms—but instead wrote an impassioned letter to Moe, using Asch's own long-stated beliefs to form a compelling argument for the sale:

> In a sense, Folkways is—or should be—a public trust. Your contributions were absolutely decisive, but those of many others who gave you their work for a fraction of the value of the time and money they invested in that work, must also be considered. The limited royalty or, in some cases, royalty-free basis on which many artists have continued a relationship with Folkways over the years is another subvention which has supported Folkways. . . . Can you betray the values and friends of a life's accomplishment now? . . .

Moses Asch sitting at his desk at the Folkways offices on lower Broadway in the mid-1980s. (Photo by Doug Curran, courtesy of Michael and Margaret Asch)

Legally, of course, you can sell off the assets . . . as if the company were just another retail business. That approach would seem, to many who have long admired your extraordinary work, a reversal of your commitment to higher values and a betrayal of your trusted friends who have given freely to Folkways because their values, like yours, transcend the mercenary. . . . Your lives have stood for these values; others, who have learned from your example, will carry them on if you will make it possible.

Rinzler recognized that without the Smithsonian's backing, Folkways would probably be sold to a private business (and its assets scattered to the winds) or cloistered in a private collection, with its many voices effectively silenced by their lack of accessibility. Rinzler believed that it took a conservative institution such as the Smithsonian to validate the many voices that made up Asch's worlds of sound. Folkways had done this by creating a commercial label that would give voice to those who otherwise would go unrecorded; the Smithsonian could extend that mission in the context of a national museum. As Rinzler told Asch biographer Peter Goldsmith in 1992:

The people who dealt with blue collar culture were inevitably aristocrats. The Lomaxes, although they wouldn't call themselves that, were definitely part of the literati. I mean John went to Harvard in 1907; [they] certainly [were] not blue collar people out of the meat-packing district of Chicago. . . . You couldn't come from the *lumpenproletariat* and stand up and say this is important stuff. Who, if anyone, was going to hear you and make it possible for you to be heard? John Lomax had access to the President of the United States [Theodore Roosevelt] to say that his cowboy ballads were important stuff. He knew exactly what he was doing, because you couldn't come out of nowhere and do that.

The Smithsonian had the cultural clout; Folkways had the resources. It made sense to bring them together.

Moses Asch passed away before the deal with the Smithsonian was completed, so it is impossible to say whether he would have finally agreed to entrust his legacy to it. However, it is clear that had this deal not been completed, much of his life's work would have been lost, a sad ending to such a long career.

Once the deal was made, Rinzler knew he had to find a spotless individual to serve as the director of the new archive and record label. Anthony Seeger, who at the time was director of the Archives of Traditional Music at Indiana University, appeared to be the ideal candidate. Seeger, a nephew of Pete Seeger and well connected in the folk world, was also a respected academic. As Seeger recalled to me:

> [Ralph] began to recruit me to be the first curator and director, partly— [this is what he told me]—because I was both a scholar and knew the folk music community well. And he needed someone who could stand up to the scrutiny of the Smithsonian, and wouldn't be dismissed as a "folkie." . . . What didn't seem to bother him was I had no credibility at all in terms of running a record company.

Although Rinzler had convinced the Smithsonian that owning Folkways would be an important addition to the collection, the purchase price was structured as a loan, to be paid back from income from the sale of records. Only two staff positions were initially funded: one for the director, Seeger, and the other for a full-time archivist, Jeff Place. The label would have to be run, as it was for many decades, with a tiny staff. Seeger and Place had to learn the business, sort out a large collection, and initiate a new label all at once.

The Asch Family

Moses Asch chose to make many sacrifices to keep Folkways afloat. His family had little choice but to go along for the ride, and even in his declining years they had to bow to his long-held beliefs about how Folkways should be preserved once he was gone.

Most deeply affected were his wife and son's family. They were never directly involved with the business until the final years, when Asch was increasingly so debilitated by strokes and physical ailments that it became impossible for him to run the label on his own. After his death, the burden of keeping the company intact until the Smithsonian deal could be completed—anything but a foregone conclusion—was shouldered by his widow Frances, who was not a young woman at the time. With little background or assistance, she kept the office going for over six months so that the negotiations could be completed, and she signed the deal.

Michael Asch had worked with his father briefly in the mid-1960s while he was pursuing graduate studies in anthropology at Columbia. His father introduced him to the business by presenting him with the handwritten ledger in which he kept all of the release numbers. "This is the heart of Folkways," Asch told Michael, requiring him to study it for a week before starting to work for the firm. Working part-time, Michael eventually was involved on a variety

Michael and Moe Asch at Sam Goody's store, late 1950s. (© David Gahr)

of projects: from listening to audition tapes and greeting people who came in off the street with hopes of recording for Folkways to preparing albums for release and defending them from critics.

One of Michael's more interesting projects was titled *Roots: Al White and the Hi-Liters*. Like many Folkways projects, the tapes arrived unsolicited and probably would have just sat in the offices if Michael hadn't auditioned them. Self-produced by the group at the famous Cosimo's Studios in New Orleans, the record and its notes have a charming naiveté, much like dozens of other local bands that existed on the edges of the rock era. Michael saw the possibility of using this record as the beginnings of a series on the roots of rock. (A second album, also featuring the Hi-Liters and related acts, appeared a year later.)

The record received an unkind review in *Sing Out!* magazine, prompting Michael to defend it—not for its performance quality but for its "honesty":

> The record is honest. We at Folkways took material which was given to us by the people, the creators, themselves and merely put it together on an LP. . . . The record is a reflection of a group of people as seen through their own eyes. . . . This it is an honest

expression of those people's present day concept of their music.

Michael's words are remarkably close to his father's oft-stated principles.

Michael's involvement in Folkways ended in the later 1960s, when he completed his graduate work. In the early 1970s, he settled in Edmonton, Alberta, Canada, where he taught anthropology at the University of Alberta for many years. Michael became very involved in social justice issues concerning the relationship between the First Nations and Canada. In his life's work, he, like his father, believes that it is important to serve as a conduit for the real expression of the people, without distorting their message to suit his own opinions or needs.

Michael's wife, Margaret, became involved once more in the Folkways legacy. She had worked closely with Frances during the final years of Moses' life to see that the legacy of Folkways was preserved. In recent years she has worked with a new initiative called folkwaysAlive! at the University of Alberta (Edmonton), established in 2003 in a formal association with Smithsonian Folkways. FolkwaysAlive! has assumed as its mission the preservation and study of Canadian music traditions, using the complete Folkways record collection given to the university by Moses Asch as its springboard. Margaret's special area of interest is in the visual materials—the cover art and photographs—that gave Folkways' releases their distinctive look. In 2005 she co-curated the first exhibition featuring the cover art of Folkways records in Edmonton, and currently is working

Ed O'Reilly (center) was a folklorist who was hired to work with Moses Asch to help prepare the transfer of Folkways' files from New York to Washington. Here he is shown with intern Heidi Talbot and fellow folklorist Sallie Bodie just after the material arrived at the Smithsonian in 1987. (Photo by Eric Long)

with both folkwaysAlive! and the Smithsonian Folkways archives to preserve the historically significant contributions of designers, artists, and photographers (see her essay at the end of Chapter 4).

The Asch family continues its involvement with Smithsonian Folkways in another important way: the bylaws of the Smithsonian Folkways Advisory Board require that a member of the family serve on the label's board in perpetuity. This will ensure that the Folkways mission will carry forward the seed of the Asch philosophy into the coming generations.

A Vision Shared

One of the most innovative ways to raise money—and awareness—for the Folkways acquisition that Rinzler developed was a benefit album called *Folkways: A Vision Shared*. The genesis of the album came about through a chance meeting that Rinzler had with Bob Dylan, who agreed to enlist the help of other artists. Artists ranging from Bruce Springsteen to Emmylou Harris, Little Richard, and U2 donated a performance of either a Woody Guthrie song or a Lead Belly song for the album, which was produced by Columbia, with all profits going to the purchase of Folkways. A TV special, produced for Showtime cable network, followed, and helped raise awareness of the importance of the Folkways collection to American culture.

As a companion to the *Vision Shared* album, Smithsonian Folkways issued *Original Vision*, culling the original recordings by Guthrie and Lead Belly that were "covered" on the benefit album. Archivist Jeff Place had to do some detective work to try to find originals for some of the tracks. As far as anyone knew, Guthrie had never recorded "Hobo's Lullaby," one of his signature songs. However, digging through the acetates that came with the collection, Place found one with a note, scrawled in pencil by Asch on the upper corner of its brown sleeve, that read "Weary Hobo." This turned out to be a recording of the song, which was first released on the *Original Vision* CD.

Jeff Place examines a reel of tape in the Folkways archives, 2008.

From the start, Seeger tried to bridge the gap between the work of an academic archive—preservation and documentation—and the needs of a commercial label. In some ways, he would operate the label like a scholarly press, calling on experts in the field to evaluate both the existing catalog and new materials as to their value. In other ways, he would continue to operate the label as Asch had done, by cultivating talented individuals—both on staff and from the larger community—to develop new recordings and to determine which of the legacy recordings should be reissued and how they should be presented to a new audience.

> "Moe could do things that we could *never* do. But we could do things that *he* could never do."
>
> —Tony Seeger

Seeger knew that the back catalog's prime assets for producing income were the children's recordings—particularly Ella Jenkins' records—and the recordings by Pete Seeger, Woody Guthrie, and Lead Belly that formed the backbone of the Folkways list. Seeger, who had performed at children's camps for decades, carefully courted Jenkins and made sure that she would continue to record for the new label. Meanwhile, although his distributor requested that he quickly convert all of the most popular LPs to CD, Seeger reasoned that in the long run it would be better to spread this income over a number of years, rationing the best sellers on an annual basis. This would allow him some wiggle room to take risks on other material, and to issue new material that he knew might not break even. Unlike Moses Asch, who could live on sales in the dozens on any given release, the break-even point for the new label was around 2,500–3,000 copies, a daunting task for most special-interest labels.

Tony Seeger holding his honorary trophy, given to him when he retired from his work for Smithsonian Folkways in 2000.

Seeger approached the business on a year-by-year basis, balancing the need for moneymakers with other projects that were important, if not as financially attractive:

> The way I looked at each year was that, I had to have some albums that I knew were going to sell well, and I had to have some albums that I hadn't the vaguest idea [if they'd sell], and then I had to have some that were public service albums. . . . Finally, I kept about two albums for myself that I thought would be neat to do. Some of those were artistic successes and financial failures, and some were surprising successes, one of them being the *Sounds of North American Frogs* [see Chapter 11].

The richness of materials in the archive itself inspired new record projects. Asch had made more than five thousand acetates in the 1940s, most of which survived. Asch recorded not only studio sessions but also snippets of radio broadcasts, speech, and other audio odds and ends as his imagination led him. Master tapes for all the original albums—as well as outtakes, demos, and other material—could be used to enhance the original albums or create entirely new projects. Jeff Place recalls how Ralph Rinzler listened to his thirty-year-old field tapes to totally remake the original *Old Time Music at Clarence Ashley*'s and *Watson Family* LPs. With the benefit of hindsight,

Moses Asch and Sam Charters outside of the Folkways offices, 1962. (Photo by Ann Charters)

recordings that didn't originally appear interesting were found to be valuable and worth publishing. CDs could accommodate almost twice as much music as an LP, giving collectors the ability to dig deeper into their original tapes.

As Moses Asch did, Seeger and his staff drew on outside contributors to both renew older product and create new discs. Many Folkways producers from the past were brought back into the fold to help. Mike Seeger prepared for release new versions of his first Folkways albums, notably *Mountain Music Bluegrass Style* and *American Banjo, Three Finger and Scruggs Style*, adding additional tracks from the original session tapes. He also created a new CD retrospective of his years of field work, titled *Close to Home: Old Time Music from Mike Seeger's Collection, 1952–1967*, most of which was inspired by his association with Folkways. John Cohen produced the remarkable disc *There Is No Eye: Music for Photographs*. These recordings were selected to accompany and comment on a book of his classic photographs. Sam Charters oversaw the rerelease of his Lightnin' Hopkins recordings. Ken Bilby revisited his recordings of the Jamaican Maroon community. Guy and Candie Carawan edited their landmark documentaries of the civil rights movement for a new CD titled *Sing for Freedom*, to bring together in one place a wide range of freedom songs and performers.

Smithsonian Folkways also drew on new contributors and creators. Not only did Jeff Place serve as the head archivist for the Folkways collection, but he was a walking repository of the sonic riches within it. Working with marketing director Richard James Burgess, he began a series of classic recordings from the collection that served as samplers for those new to its scope and depth, and also as a means of making available outtakes and additional material that would otherwise be inaccessible. In 2007, Place began co-hosting a radio program produced in association with Washington's public radio station WAMU that also serves as an introduction to the archives' resources. With social historian Ronald Cohen, Place produced *The Best of Broadside*, a boxed set collecting recordings made for the influential newsletter/magazine (see Chapter 9) with extensive documentary notes.

The Complete Woody Guthrie

One of the first major initiatives undertaken by archivist Jeff Place was to catalog Asch's collection of acetates made in the 1940s. Asch had lovingly preserved this material, and aside from a few discs that broke during his various office moves, they were in relatively good shape. However, there was no complete log of all of the original sessions, although in the early 1940s Asch kept a list by matrix number in the back of the corporate checkbook. Later "logs" consist of lists on company stationery, often simply giving a date and time of the session and number of discs made.

To take an overall inventory, Place and two interns performed a "needle drop" on all of the acetates, sorting them by artist (when known) or genre. This produced a rough list of matrix numbers and artists. Then all of the released Asch discs were cataloged by matrix number and compared with this list to identify specific jazz performers and others who were not immediately known. Finally, the unreleased discs could be identified by determining their place in the sequence by using the fragmentary logs and the complete list of releases.

The pile of discs identified as containing Woody Guthrie, either alone, with Cisco Houston, or in small groups, was then examined, resulting in the discovery of previously unknown performances of some of Guthrie's songs. The most exciting discovery was of a more complete version of "This Land Is Your Land." The version released by Folkways in 1950—which became the standard for almost all performances—featured only three verses. It was known, however, from Guthrie's self-published songbooks that the song originally had as many as six verses, with the three "missing" from the recording being more political in content. For years it was believed that Guthrie had never recorded a fuller version, but Place found among the acetates a version that included one of the missing verses.

The result of Place's work was the four-CD set of all of Guthrie's recordings made for Asch, with documentation by Guy Logsdon.

Undated letter from Woody Guthrie to Moses Asch (c. 1946–47). Guthrie wrote regularly to Asch in the mid- and late 1940s. This letter suggests that Asch sponsor a concert with him, Lead Belly, Cisco Houston, and Hally Wood. Like many of Guthrie's letters to Asch, it is illustrated with a watercolor sketch. (© Woody Guthrie Publications, Inc. Used by permission)

Bernice Johnson Reagon (center) singing at Newport, c. 1965. (Photo by Diana Davies, courtesy of the Ralph Rinzler Folklife Archives and Collections, Smithsonian Institution)

Josh White's biographer Elijah Wald was enlisted to document a reissue of Asch's recordings of White from the 1940s, based on Jeff Place's digitization of the original acetates and selection of the key recordings. Wald also participated in the creation of *The Mississippi: River of Song* series on PBS, documenting the rich musical traditions that developed along the path of the Mississippi River, which led to an audio documentary of the same name released by Smithsonian Folkways. Bernice Johnson Reagon assembled and annotated a four-CD set entitled *Wade in the Water: African American Sacred Music Traditions*, based on an NPR series that drew on a wide variety of recordings to document this important vocal tradition.

The Folkways tradition of providing liner notes was also carried forward by Smithsonian Folkways. For reissues, the original documentation could be included plus new material putting the older research into perspective. This enabled scholars to revisit their work—or that of others—and comment on the changes in the field. Harry Smith's *Anthology* is a prime example: the reissue included the original booklet and then an equally large, separate set of notes on the recording, its impact, Smith's life and work, and enhanced information on the selections (see Chapter 4).

With his background as an archivist as well as an anthropologist, Seeger was well connected with others around the world who managed important sound collections, most of which were unavailable to the ordinary listener unless they trekked to the far corners of the world. While in the past Folkways had primarily presented material made by Western visitors to "foreign" cultures, he reasoned that it would be valuable to partner with peoples in the actual regions themselves, to give a more complete picture of their music. Opening up the Folkways catalog to world contributors seemed a natural step forward from Asch's original mission. Partnerships resulted in many major initiatives, including Philip Yampolsky's groundbreaking twenty-CD set *Music of Indonesia* (see Chapter 5) and *Traditional Music of Peru*, which was produced in collaboration with the Archives of Traditional Andean Music in Lima, Peru. Seeger also recognized the value of video, especially for teaching. To achieve this goal, he forged a partnership with the Victor Corporation of Japan (JVC) to produce four major series of videos of music and dance with extensive documentation.

Another change was right around the corner that would transform Folkways yet again: the digital music revolution. In 1989, Seeger made a key decision to catalog the Folkways collection by individual tracks, in addition to albums. He had already begun exploring, along with electronics giant Panasonic, the possibility of a service where individuals could call in and "download" individual Folkways tracks to their answering machines. This plan fizzled as the Internet emerged as a better way to handle downloading audio. Folkways eventually digitized the entire catalog by track, giving a new revenue stream to performers and to the archive. In keeping with the Folkways spirit, the albums were digitized by a crew of bluegrass musicians, mostly members of the Johnson Mountain Boys, who appreciated the daytime work. Jeff Place notes with amusement that Folkways songs started to creep into the Johnson Mountain Boys' repertory as they were exposed to this material.

Although it was not apparent at the time, the fact that all of the original LPs were digitized early on made the transition to producing CDs on demand—and thus keeping the promise to maintain all of Folkways' records in print no matter how few copies are sold—very easy. Smithsonian Folkways today uses a robotic system that enables them to run as few copies of a disc as needed—fifty, ten, even one—with the entire process automated.

The marriage of streaming and eventually downloadable audio, the Web, and cooperative agreements with other archives led Seeger to envision a new way of distributing important recordings that could not pay their way on a commercial CD release. For decades, Alan Lomax had dreamed of creating a "global jukebox" that would make music available equally to all listeners. Seeger built on this concept in proposing a new Web resource, Smithsonian Global Sound. The idea was to build on the Folkways library by partnering with others and then making the music available in affordable downloads. This would eliminate the need to produce a physical CD for those recordings that were by their very nature unable to sell the minimum number to break even. Smithsonian Global Sound was officially launched in 2005.

Adding to the Collection

Besides reissuing old material and seeking out new recordings, Seeger reasoned that the best way to build on the Folkways acquisition was to pursue other labels that specialized in particular niche markets whose recordings would otherwise be unavailable or lost. As Seeger told me, "It seemed to me that if Smithsonian was a repository for some of the great independent, important music of the world, then we ought to be looking for other labels like Folkways." In many cases, the original founders had died, retired, or become unable to continue running their companies or find a buyer for their backlist. The first label added to the collection was Cook Records, an eccentric catalog built by audio engineer Emory Cook as much as a way of pursuing his own interests in sound recording as a commercial venture.

Here, alphabetically, is a list of the labels that have since been added to the Smithsonian Folkways holdings.

Collector Records. Founded in 1970 by labor songster Joe Glazer, initially to issue his own recordings, the label grew to feature various labor and politically active singers. The label's catalog was donated in 2005 to the Smithsonian.

Cook Records. Emory Cook shared with Moses Asch a love of sound recording and the many possibilities that it offered. Unlike Asch, Cook founded his self-named label in 1956 with the idea of presenting high-quality recordings, ranging from stereo demonstration records to recordings of calypso and other specialized musics. Cook was interested primarily in illustrating the capabilities of sound reproduction equipment, so even the music recordings were presented to highlight the sound reproduction. The label folded in 1966 and its master tapes came to the Smithsonian in 1990.

Dyer-Bennet Records. Richard Dyer-Bennet was an early folk revivalist whose cultured style of singing and playing was influential in his day and helped revive interest in traditional English and American balladry. Dyer-Bennet was among the first artists to form his own label to ensure the quality of his recordings; in 1955 he began issuing recordings under his self-named label. He issued fifteen albums on his own, which came to the Smithsonian in 1995.

Fast Folk Records/Magazine. Founded in 1982, Fast Folk was designed as an "audio magazine," issuing on a regular basis compilation albums of new singer-songwriters primarily based in New York's Greenwich Village. Some of its more notable alumni include Richard Meyer, Jack Hardy, Suzanne Vega, Shawn Colvin, Tracy Chapman, Richard Shindell, and Lucy Kaplansky. Seeger pursued obtaining its files and master tapes, feeling that this type of contemporary singer-songwriter material was not well documented on Folkways' recordings.

Minority Owned Recording Enterprises (M.O.R.E.). Also known as Más, M.O.R.E. is a small label created in the 1960s by Roberto Martínez of Albuquerque, New Mexico. Martínez was inspired by awareness of the civil rights movement, burgeoning pride in—and defense of—New Mexican Hispanic cultural heritage, and a personal response to discrimination. The approximately two dozen M.O.R.E. releases focused on traditional music of Hispanic New Mexico; Martinez, his group Los Reyes de Albuquerque, and several of his children were the primary artists. Two early recordings of his violinist son Lorenzo had particularly wide impact throughout the interior West.

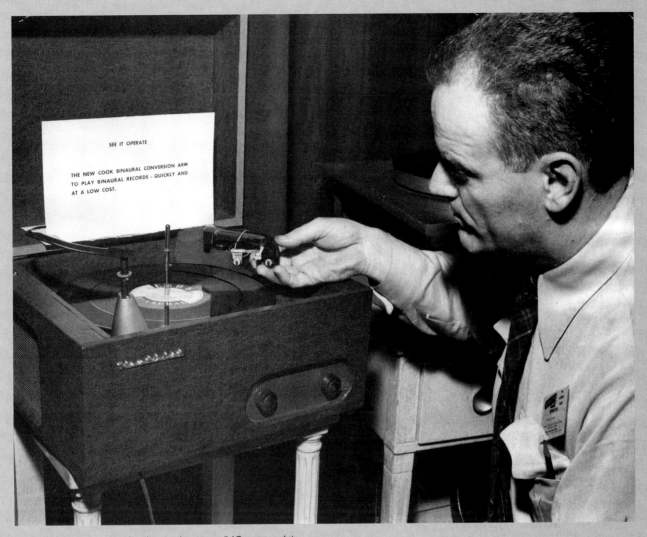

Emory Cook demonstrates his "binaural tone arm." (Courtesy of the
Ralph Rinzler Folklife Archives and Collections, Smithsonian Institution)

Monitor Records. Michael Stillman and Rose Rubin
founded Monitor in 1956 as an outlet for Eastern
European and Soviet recordings of Western classical music at the height of the McCarthy era. Eventually, the label broadened into national folkloric
ensembles, as well as making its own albums of
American folk and other world musics.

Paredon Records. Irwin Silber had served as a
marketing director and right-hand man to Moses

Asch from 1958 to about 1967. Two years later, he
founded the Paredon label with his wife, activist
and singer Barbara Dane, as an outlet for political
and social-activist music from around the world.
Paredon's covers and presentation were very much
in the Folkways mold, although its message was
consistently more politically radical. The label
issued recordings through the 1980s and came to
the Smithsonian in 1991.

THE CONTINUING MISSION

Tony Seeger left Smithsonian Folkways in 2000 to return to academia. What began as a two-person operation in 1987 had expanded greatly over the years of his stewardship. Many of the functions of producing and promoting the label's recordings, previously farmed out to third parties, have been brought in-house. Today, Smithsonian Folkways has grown into a complex operation, and an integral part of the Center for Folklife and Cultural Heritage. Everyone has given all they've got to the mission—not just the directors, archivists, and iconic stars, but also the interns and volunteers; the production, financial and marketing, and mail order and sales staff; the manufacturing coordinator, audio supervisor, assistant engineers, and Web production manager; and the financial assistants. Perhaps several hundred folks have contributed a great deal over the past two decades.

Seeger's replacement was another respected ethnomusicologist, Daniel Sheehy, who also had a long record in public service as director of folk and traditional arts at the National Endowment for the Arts. Sheehy's area of specialization is Mexican regional music specifically and Latin American music more generally. Like many of his peers, his experience of hearing a Folkways record helped galvanize his career choice:

> I can remember a recording of Aymara Indian music from Lake Titicaca on Folkways that I heard at UCLA as a beginning graduate student that had all these long flutes, troupes of Aymara Indians playing flutes and drums, that I never heard or heard about before, and that really almost knocked me off my axis. It certainly expanded my horizons at the time. I came *this* close to spending the next two years and who knows the next 20–30 years of my life in Lake Titicaca and following this music and these artists wherever [it] would take me.

Sheehy believes that the initial decision to make Smithsonian Folkways a self-supporting entity within the larger Smithsonian Institution was a sound one, because it kept the archive and its work focused on its mission: to reach as many new listeners as possible:

> I think there was not only a "keep it clean and outside the government support" realm, but also a concern for accountability to the public. . . . In our situation, selling a recording almost always equates to public impact. Because if you don't sell a recording, it means somebody didn't get it or didn't hear it and it didn't have any role in their lives. Whereas if somebody did buy it, you could almost be certain that they *did* get it and they *did* hear it and it *did* have some sort of impact on their lives.

As part of this mission, Sheehy has built on and expanded the label's partnerships with other branches of the Smithsonian. Working with the National Museum of African American History and Culture, the label has begun issuing a series of both archival and new recordings documenting not only the music but the entire cultural history of African Americans. Moses Asch was a strong believer in the importance of African American history; he went out of his way to issue (marginally commercial) recordings from Folkways' very earliest years, including those by poets such as Langston Hughes and statesmen such as W. E. B. Du Bois (see Chapter 10). A new partnership with the Smithsonian Latino Center has enabled Smithsonian Folkways to greatly expand its releases of Latino roots music and to send recording and video technicians to parts of the world that they could never have reached without this support.

Dan Sheehy (center, with trumpet) with Mariachi Los Amigos, an ensemble that he directs in the Washington, D.C., area.

As Sheehy notes, the impact of a series of recordings can be far greater than just an individual CD here and there: "This is part of the Folkways message: The magnificent panorama of cultural expression that exists in the world. And if you can have a series of twenty or thirty recordings, as opposed to a single album, you're able to send that message in a much more powerful way."

Finally, the world of online digital transmission has made it possible to spread the world of sound much farther than anyone could have imagined even a decade ago. As ethnomusicologist Atesh Sonneborn, the associate director of Smithsonian Folkways, put it to me:

> The idea that someone in Kazakhstan can hear *Mountain Music of Kentucky*, or someone in Australia can experience the initiation rites of the Bosavi people of the Eastern Highlands Province in Papua New Guinea or a Navajo rite, it's extraordinary in terms of what the culturally significant affect on identity is at a world-wide level, what this fabric seeded by Folkways, becomes—and how we play a part in that.

Like any new technology, digital distribution offers enormous opportunity but also challenges. The once utopian idea that every voice would have equal access to the world's ears has been tempered somewhat by the reality of the expense, time, and effort needed to put large digital collections online. Plus, once the music is available, that's no guarantee that the world will listen. As Sheehy lamented:

> In the world of Internet distribution . . . there was lots of promise at the beginning: "Everybody's stuff is going to be available; the 'long tail' is true!" . . . But then a few years later stories started coming out that, "Well, there's all this Chinese music that's available digitally, but nobody seems to be downloading it. They don't know anything about, it doesn't speak to them." Even though it's 10 percent of what's available, it doesn't come near to reflecting the much lower percentage of downloading that's happening.

But this apparently disappointing news has opened up a new opportunity for the Smithsonian. It is more important than ever that the music be placed in context so that listeners around the world can not only hear but also understand it. This contextualization was a role that Moses Asch held dear—he never issued a recording without "proper documentation," and the booklets of notes that came with every Folkways release were much prized by listeners for giving some background to the recorded sounds. Now digital text, sound, teaching tools, and moving images can all be bundled together to give a total experience of a musical culture far beyond what Asch was able to do. As the cost of this technology comes down, it becomes possible to put it into the hands of the individuals everywhere who create cultural materials. This revolution has the potential to put cultural power back in the hands of the creators—the ultimate goal of the original vision of Moses Asch and Folkways Records.

LISTEN UP!

Folkways: The Original Vision: Woody Guthrie and Lead Belly, 2nd ed. • SFW40000 • 2005

Roots: The Rock and Roll Sound of Louisiana and Mississippi • FW02865 • 1965

Roots: Rhythm and Blues • FWRBF20 • 1966

Woody Guthrie: The Asch Recordings, Vols. 1–4 • SFW40112 • 1999

American Banjo: Three-Finger and Scruggs Style • SFW40037 • 1990

Mountain Music Bluegrass Style • SFW40038 • 1991

Close to Home: Old Time Music from Mike Seeger's Collection, 1952–1967 • SFW40097 • 1997

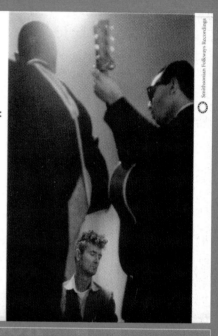

there is no eye:
music for
photographs

recordings
of musicians
photographed
by john cohen

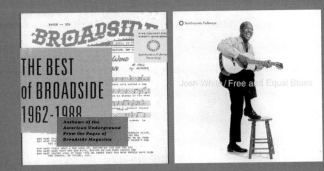

There Is No Eye: Music for Photographs
• SFW40091 • 2001

Wade in the Water: African American Sacred Music
Traditions, Vol. I–IV • SFW40076 • 1996

Music of Indonesia • SFW40055- 057; SFW40420–29;
SFW0441–47

Traditional Music of Peru • SFW40466–69, 40448–51

Sing for Freedom: The Story of the Civil Rights Movement
Through Its Songs • SFW40032 • 1990

The Best of Broadside 1962–1988 • SFW40130 • 2000

Josh White: Free and Equal Blues • SFW40081 • 1998

The Mississippi River of Song: A Musical Journey Down the
Mississippi • SFW40086 • 1998

INDEX

House, Wallace, 222

Houston, Cisco, 44, 46, 47, 158, 183, 198, 261

Hughes, Langston, 1, 209, 210, 267; children's records of, 135, 145; *Weary Blues, The*, 210

Hurt, Mississippi John, 62, 69, 114

Huston, John, 97

Hutton, Bruce, 170

I

"I Ain't Got No Home," 48

"I Will Overcome," 216

"I'm Blue, I'm Lonesome," 232

"Independent, The" (Asch), 8

Indian Music of Mexico, 106

Indonesia, music of, 104–05

Instructional recordings on Folkways, 221–22

Iron Mountain String Band, 171

Ives, Burl, 152, 212

Iwo Jima, 198

J

Jackson, Aunt Molly, 204

Jackson, Jim, 124

Jamaica, music of, 99–101

James, Skip, 114

Jarrell, Tommy, 170

Jasen, David A., 32–33

Jazz (record series), 26

Jazz at the Philharmonic (concert), 25

Jazz Men (book), 21

Jazz Music (magazine), 41

Jazz, recordings on, 5, 6, 7, 19, 21–31, 32–33, 72, 75, 76, 89, 113, 122, 145, 261

Jefferson, Blind Lemon, 111

Jenkins, Ella, 15, 142–44, 151, 259

Jenkins, Gordon, 185

"John Henry," 124

"John the Revelator," 69

John's Island, South Carolina, music of, 97

Johnson family (bluegrass band), 179

Johnson Mountain Boys, The, 263

Johnson, Blind Willie, 69, 122

Johnson, Bunk, 21

Johnson, David, 179

Johnson, James P., 5, 20, 23, 24, 25, 32

Johnson, Lonnie, 117

Johnson, Lyndon, 241

Joplin, Janis, 253

Josephson, Barney, 24

Joyner, Claude, 219, 220

Juilliard School, The, 144

JVC. *See* Victor Corporation of Japan, The

K

Kahn, Ed, 166

Kaiser, Mel, 13, 237

Kanuteh, Alhaji Fabala, 102–03

Kaplan, Paul, 196

Kaplansky, Lucy, 264

Keating, Kenneth B., 152

Kellogg, Peter Paul, 242

Kenton, Gary, 13, 16, 62, 64, 70, 87, 136, 224

Kentuckians, The, 179

King (record label), 117

"King Kong Kitchie Kitchie Kit-Me-O," 68

King, Nora Lee, 24

Kingston Trio, The, 158, 174, 175, 190, 201

Kiowa, 72

Kirk, Andy, 23, 24

Klatzko, Bernard, 32

Koester, Bob, 119

Kora, 102

Korean War, 198

"Kum Ba Yah," 191, 222

Kunstadt, Leonard, 117

Kuykendall, Pete, 173, 176, 177

L

La Farge, Peter, 197–98

Laibman, Dave, 190–91

Lamb, Joseph F., 30–1

Landau, Ernie, 50

Landeck, Beatrice, 137, 140

"Last Payday at Coal Creek," 166

Latin Grammy award, 107

Latino and Latin American recordings on, 106–07, 267–68

Lead Belly, xvii, 5, 11, 19, 37–43, 44, 49, 51, 92, 111, 112, 115, 130, 136, 137, 183, 197, 237, 253, 258, 259, 261; and